THE GOLDEN BAND

The Golden Land

The Golden Band

African American Spirituals and the Hermeneutics of World

Asante U. Todd

William B. Eerdmans Publishing Company
Grand Rapids, Michigan

Wm. B. Eerdmans Publishing Co.
2006 44th Street SE, Grand Rapids, MI 49508
www.eerdmans.com

© 2025 Asante U. Todd
All rights reserved
Published 2025
Printed in the United States of America

30 30 29 28 27 26 25   1 2 3 4 5 6 7

ISBN 978-0-8028-8514-2

Library of Congress Cataloging-in-Publication Data

A catalog record for this book is available from the Library of Congress.

Contents

Introduction: On the Spirituals, Prophecy, and Theomusicology vii

PART ONE: THE CULTURAL LOGIC OF SOVEREIGNTY AND THE THEOLOGICAL HERMENEUTICS OF WORLD

1. African American Religious and Cultural Criticism 3
2. The Global Leviathan Appears 27
3. The Sense of Another World 48

PART TWO: AFRICAN AMERICAN RELIGIOUS THOUGHT

4. Mind, Body, and Spirit 69
5. Covenant, Law, and the Sound of Jazz 90

PART THREE: THE SPIRITUALS

6. Ring Shout to Heaven, Call and Response 113
7. Nature, Spirit, and Song 132

Contents

8. De Lord Is Per-Wide, Rock O' My Soul,
   and Holy-Ghost the Pilot   154

9. Roll, Jordan, Roll   173

Index of Names and Subjects   189

Index of Spirituals   204

Introduction

On the Spirituals, Prophecy, and Theomusicology

THERE ARE CURRENTLY MANY FINE BOOKS ON the Spirituals, several of which are aimed at transforming or renewing Christian theology and practice. Examples include Luke Powery's *Dem Dry Bones* (2012), which offers insights from the Spirituals as musical sermons for preaching and worship; Yolanda Y. Smith's *Reclaiming the Spirituals: New Possibilities for African American Christian Education* (2004); and Cheryl Kirk-Duggan's *Exorcising Evil: A Womanist Interpretation of the Spirituals* (1997), which asks about how the Spirituals participate in African American responses to suffering and evil. These theologians are situated within a discursive legacy of legendary African American thinkers like W. E. B. Du Bois, Alain Locke, James H. Cone, Cornel West, and others who also believed that the Spirituals offer religious and cultural resources for African American empowerment, for the improvement of African American life chances and quality of life, and by extension, for the renewal of American democracy and international society. As I discuss in further detail below, my own work is marked by three features. First, I am interested in approaching the Spirituals from the perspective of African American public theology, where I ask about how the Spirituals may influence our perspective on current public debates, opinions, and policies. Second, my analysis of the Spirituals attends to the specific problem of the cultural logic of sovereignty, a problem that I bring into this project from previous research. Finally, as indicated by the previous two points, I am interested in how the Spirituals are related to culture and to politics. My work is perhaps best understood by situating it in relation to Kirk-Duggan's as well as other contemporary conversations on African American

Introduction

religion and culture like Donald Matthews's *Honoring the Ancestors* (1998) and George Shulman's *American Prophecy* (2008).

For Matthews, the centrality of the Spirituals should be emphasized more in discussions on African American religion and culture. He argues that a retrieval of the Spirituals even gives voice to an Afrocentric theology that has also successfully incorporated Western Christianity, thus giving shape to a particularly African American cultural form. The Spirituals offer us a synthesis of "structure and meaning" that has implications for African American religion and culture. Yet Matthews's approach remains limited to the extent that he focuses on narration to the exclusion of description. Thus, Matthews arrives at the "off-key" conclusion that African American religious and cultural narratives may be rightly framed with the Spirituals' metaphors of family, freedom, and the ancestors. "The African concept of extended family was combined with a Christian sense of the family of God in a social situation plagued with family dissolution. . . . [In] the African American Spirituals . . . persons of religious maturity became spiritual fathers and mothers to those who need the nurture and guidance that only family can provide."[1] While Matthews's narrative approach retrieves a romanticized harmonious African ancestral family and narrates a decline into the evil of Anglo-Saxon society, my own approach makes use of the cultural hermeneutics of Clifford Geertz to combine a phenomenological-hermeneutical approach with pragmatist empirical methods. I thus take up the Spirituals not only hermeneutically but also historically and descriptively, with attention to cultural theory and also to social science, ethnomusicology, composition theory, and content analysis. I also take up the Spirituals as musical practices, rather than solely as narratives, which connects me to conversations on music composition, musical form, and modes of social exchange. A content analysis of the antebellum Spirituals fails to disclose any mention of the word "family."

Cheryl Kirk-Duggan's *Exorcising Evil*, which offers a womanist perspective on the Spirituals, gives attention to the Spirituals' theological and musicological aspects in relation to culture. Her work thus offers the closest approximation to my own project, and in many ways has made mine possible. Kirk-Duggan offers insight not only as an accomplished scholar of religion but also as an organist and vocal performer in the Christian Methodist Episcopal Church, and with an MA in applied voice from the University of Texas. "When we explore the musical style of the Spirituals by asking questions specifically related to the divine, we move into the realm of theomusicology. Theomusicology is a

---

1. Donald Matthews, *Honoring the Ancestors: An African Cultural Interpretation of Black Religion and Literature* (Oxford: Oxford University Press, 1998), 139.

On the Spirituals, Prophecy, and Theomusicology

discipline, a way of using music to talk about the sacred ... the secular ... and the profane."[2] For Kirk-Duggan, the very constitution of the Spirituals blurs the lines between what one considers sacred and what one considers profane, and in the process offers critical and democratically constructive insight on North American society, which continues to be plagued with the evils of racism and sexism. In her analysis, the Spirituals tell of a personal, powerful, and liberating God "who encompasses masculine and feminine qualities and cares about individuals and communities."[3] This compassionate God calls for inclusiveness, for a concern for the least of these, and for respect for all of life. She argues that the integrative function of music can be seen in the mass meetings prevalent during the 1960s' civil rights movement; the solidarity and community were replicated especially during the summers of 1963 and 1964. I believe that Kirk-Duggan's theomusicological approach is correct for studying the Spirituals, and this approach informs my own book, especially part 3. One key difference between Kirk-Duggan's approach and my own is that I study the nineteenth-century antebellum Spirituals, and from a compositional view.

George Shulman's *American Prophecy* also explores the relationship of African American religion to culture, and with particular attention to Anglo-American democratic culture. His basic conclusion is that African American religious voices have institutionalized the African American jeremiad within American culture as a cultural-critical countervoice. "Prophecy does not found a law of laws or seek obedience to one ... instead, prophecy bears an ever-renewing uncontainable 'word' in a visionary practice of reimaging the world ... prophecy is a rhetorical practice and political office that recasts how people judge the past and their choices ... an office that involves making certain kinds of claims in certain registers of voice."[4] For Shulman, prophecy is the divine law of love incarnated. The logic of the incarnation appears as the democratization of prophetic voice, and prophetic voice as vernacular language. Thus, a range of prophets like Martin Luther King Jr., James Baldwin, and Toni Morrison register as authoritative religious critics, even in relation to American liberal democratic society. "Each embodies an ethos to foster democratic contestation; each confronts existential resentment to resist demonizing their adversaries." Shulman's work represents not only an attempt to place Black religious studies in conversation with modern political thought but also a growing

---

2. Cheryl Kirk-Duggan, *Exorcising Evil: A Womanist Perspective on the Spirituals* (Maryknoll, NY: Orbis Books, 1997), 97.
3. Kirk-Duggan, *Exorcising Evil*, 140.
4. Kirk-Duggan, *Exorcising Evil*, 231.

Introduction

appreciation of African American thought by Anglo-American thinkers that desire to overthrow white supremacy. Yet Shulman's interpretation of African American cultural form as "prophetic voice" seems to ultimately be a strong liberal interpretation of African American religion and culture, one that remains somewhat individualized and quite disembodied, and to the exclusion of (possibly African) social and communal forms, especially musical ones. Shulman also fails to address any of his interpretive fore-understandings as an Anglo-American man and Western political theorist.

One way that the Spirituals should be understood is as prophecy, as Howard Thurman acknowledged in *Deep River*. "The fundamental significance of all these interpretations of life and death ... [is] the profound conviction that God was not done with them, that God was not done with life ... that God had not exhausted His resources.... This is the secret of their ascendancy over circumstances."[5] I discuss Thurman in greater detail in this book, but here I note that although Thurman acknowledges the prophetic dimensions of the Spirituals, he does not discuss their musicological or hermeneutical significance. In the antebellum period, the Spirituals were not simply songs but sacred dances, emerging from the ring-shout dances of slaves during secret prayer meetings. Prophecy among African American slaves during the antebellum period was thus not simply or even primarily a matter of voice, as Shulman argues, but was a holistic endeavor that engaged body, mind, and soul, and according to its own logic, *rhythmically*. In many ways, the Spirituals share less in common with diatribe and more in common with the prophetic dance rituals that began to be practiced among many Native American tribes during the mid to late nineteenth century, as Native Americans, European Americans, and African Americans came into more frequent cultural contact and conflict. Black Elk of the Oglala Sioux's recounting of the birth of the Sun Dance sounds similar to the accounts of the Spirituals discussed in this book: "The old men were sitting and having a council, when they noticed that one of our men, Kablaya (Spread), had dropped his robe around his waist, and was dancing there all alone with his hand raised toward heaven. The old men thought that perhaps he was crazy.... Kablaya then explained them ... I have just been shown, in a vision, a new way of prayer.... This is to be the sun dance."[6] As with the Sun Dance among Native Americans, many slaves took the Spirituals as religious oracles, guideposts, and prophecies.

---

5. Howard Thurman, *Deep River: Reflections on the Religious Insight of Certain of the Negro Spirituals* (New York: Harper, 1955), 41.

6. Black Elk, *The Sacred Pipe: Black Elk's Account of the Seven Rites of the Oglala Sioux*, ed. Joseph Epes Brown (Norman: University of Oklahoma Press, 1989), 67–68.

On the Spirituals, Prophecy, and Theomusicology

On the Logic of Sovereignty and the Logic of Our Spiritual(s) Strivings

My study of the Spirituals is conducted with special attention to the problem of the cultural logic of sovereignty. The cultural logic of sovereignty refers to the phenomenon where culturally constructed social divisions, orders, and exclusions are rendered categorical rather than accidental, and where the absolute powers of life and death—the power to ensure, maintain, develop, or deny life—are isolated into one particular social order over against another. In my dissertation research, I found that the cultural logic of sovereignty was present in several key texts in Western canonical political theory, including those produced by John Locke, Jean-Jacques Rousseau, Immanuel Kant, and Carl Schmitt, and with disastrous results for African Americans and the world's poor. The cultural logic of sovereignty is usually communicated through a thinker's "state of nature" doctrine, a metaphor and primordial myth that is taken as a true account of the history of the natural world. Across the various academic disciplines such as theology, political theory, and social theory, the state of nature doctrine is given different labels, such as the doctrine of creation, natural theology, philosophy of nature, and cosmology. Yet, in the most general sense, the cultural logic of sovereignty divides the state of nature into the categories of mere "bare life" (*zen*) and good life (*eu zen*), and bare life is only included by way of an exclusion. In turn, the excluded are rendered possible subjects of sovereign violence. For all the good that African American thinkers on the Spirituals like Powery, Kirk-Duggan, and Thurman have produced, none have taken them up in relation to the cultural logic of sovereignty. Thus, a study was needed to investigate this question. My understanding of the cultural logic of sovereignty is drawn from philosopher Giorgio Agamben, who sees this logic as pervasive throughout much of Western politics: "Western politics first constitutes itself through an exclusion (which is simultaneously an inclusion) of bare life . . . life presents itself as what is included by means of an exclusion. . . . In Western politics, bare life has the peculiar privilege of being that whose exclusion founds the city of men. . . . The living [human] has *logos* by taking away and conserving its own voice in [the *polis*], even as it dwells in the polis by letting its own bare life be excluded, as an exception, within it."[7]

Although Agamben uses Aristotle as the prime example of the phenomenon of the cultural logic of sovereignty, he also discusses how sovereignty still circulates as a cultural logic throughout modern societies (e.g., in the form

---

7. Giorgio Agamben, *Homo Sacer: Sovereign Power and Bare Life*, trans. Daniel Heller-Roazen (Stanford, CA: Stanford University Press, 1998), 7–8.

Introduction

of the ban), in events where populations are abandoned by both human and divine law and treated as persons with savage, semihuman, semi-inhuman status.[8] Agamben's account offers one way to interpret and consider the predicament of African Americans in the modern West, where African American peoples continue to struggle against various attempts at social and political exclusion and enslavement in a society that has never possessed a political sovereign and whose constitution is rooted in the idea of inalienable rights and republican government. I go into a deeper discussion on the significance of the cultural logic of sovereignty throughout the book. I keep this problem in play as my primary object of criticism not only in Anglo thought but also in African American religious thought. Thus, my ultimate criterion for evaluating each thinker is his or her ability to transcend or effectively deal with the problem of the cultural logic of sovereignty. It was the inability of most thinkers to solve this problem that ultimately led me to the Spirituals, which I did not initially plan to study as a source for African American theology. Yet upon studying thinkers like religious historian Albert Raboteau, mystic Howard Thurman, and theologian Barbara Holmes, it became apparent that the Spirituals were one of the primary sources of African American religious and cultural composition in the antebellum period and might hold an answer to the problem of the cultural logic of sovereignty, being the key form of religio-cultural expression just before the US struggle for emancipation from slavery. Yet, I had no sound evidence to justify my hunch, and I had no idea of the intellectual challenges and rewards that lay ahead.

Perhaps the most eminent thinker on the Spirituals remains W. E. B. Du Bois, who in many ways initiated academic conversation on the significance of the Spirituals and relationship between the Spirituals, African American culture, and American culture in the early twentieth century. Du Bois believed that the Spirituals in particular served as paradigms for the spiritual life of America. Du Bois suggested that the Spirituals were significant not only for African American religion and culture but also for Anglo-American culture and the larger US society. He expressed this conviction in *Souls*: "And so by fateful chance the Negro folk song . . . stands to-day not simply as the sole American music, but as the most beautiful expression of human experience born this side of seas. It has been neglected . . . but notwithstanding, it still remains as the singular spiritual heritage of the nation and the greatest gift of the Negro people."[9] In the final analysis, Du Bois was unsure exactly what the contribu-

---

8. Agamben, *Homo Sacer*, 28.
9. W. E. B. Du Bois, *Souls of Black Folk* (Chicago: A. C. McClurg & Co., 1903), 286.

tion of African American religion would be to American culture by way of the Negro church, but he held fast to faith that the Spirituals played a key role.[10] In Du Bois's view, the pressing task was to pick back up the spiritual strivings to which the antebellum slaves were committed. This included a range of social endeavors, including equal opportunity for development, instilling in Black men a strong work ethic, liberal arts education, and also the *conservation* of the races. Yet Du Bois's strong emphasis on self-help and individual freedom left untouched questions about the logic of identity and difference and cultural aesthetics. Du Bois hoped for a root metaphor, but in this way, *Souls* remains unfinished, and while Du Bois inquired extensively into the "other world" of Black post-Reconstruction society, he asked only marginal questions about the world constructed by the antebellum slaves.

The Golden Band: African American Spirituals and the Hermeneutics of World is a constructive African American public theology that uses the Spirituals to struggle with the problem of the cultural logic of sovereignty. This means that in addition to attention to literatures on music, I also had to attend to the discourse on African American political theology. In an odd way, I am attempting to bridge two literatures, one focused on African American music and another on African American political thought, in an attempt to construct an aesthetic horizon of meaning for the conditions of possibility of democratic-republican political norms. This approach makes the study unique not only among scholars on the Spirituals but also among other political theologians who are writing on the problem of sovereignty like J. Kameron Carter, Willie Jennings, and John Milbank. *The Golden Band* analyzes and critiques the discourse on African American political theology before offering its own constructive world-horizon, rooted in the hermeneutics of world discerned in the nineteenth-century antebellum Spirituals. In turning to the Spirituals, I conduct an ethnographic, musicological, and theological analysis to invite readers into the musical play and hermeneutical outlooks of the antebellum Spirituals. From these I discern a constructive musical theology, or, as Kirk-Duggan would say, theomusicology of the band, including discussions of social exchange and musical form. This book was written for specialists in religion and philosophy who are interested in conversations on cosmology, metaphysics, symbolic interactionism, and world hermeneutics. However, the breadth of its subject matter also offers much for the generalist and even the novice.

---

10. See Roger Baumann, "Race, Religion and Global Solidarities: W. E. B. DuBois and 'The Black Church' as a Contested Category," *Journal for the Scientific Study of Religion* 62, no. 51 (December 2023): 48–67.

Introduction

As such, it may serve to introduce readers to a range of topics including the Spirituals, African American theology, ecology, cosmology, African American music composition, and the hermeneutics of world.

My approach to the Spirituals takes account of African American religious experience hermeneutically. Following Hans-Georg Gadamer, hermeneutics is about understanding those other worlds presented in works of art and texts that pose challenging questions for our own world.[11] The key point of the method of the "hermeneutics of dialogue," as Gadamer calls it, is to understand the alternative world presented in art. The hermeneutics of dialogue thus pushes us beyond historical-critical biblical hermeneutics and textual interpretation to consider the implications of "the Bible as art" and also opens the field of hermeneutics to art in general and to questions of ontology. Hermeneutics is an open dialogue of question and answer with a work of art that allows us to experience and understand the world imagined within the work of art, even as the art questions our own taken-for granted assumptions about the world. Gadamer says that "in linguistic communication, 'world' is disclosed. Reaching an understanding in language places a subject matter before those communicating like a disputed object set between them. Thus the world is the common ground, trodden by none and recognized by all, uniting all who talk to one another."[12] This book places the subject matter of the "state of nature" doctrine before interested readers as interpreted in the African American Spirituals, songs that were themselves constituted at the intersection of American English, rooted in West Germanic languages and with connection to Romance languages, and African American vernacular English, rooted in the tonal languages of West and Central Africa. Moreover, while I hold hermeneutics to be a vital aspect of method, I also use African American critical social thought, as hermeneutics alone—whether Gadamer's hermeneutics of dialogue, Heidegger's hermeneutics of facticity, or Ricoeur's narrative hermeneutics—tends to have unclear social and political implications.

My use of the phrase the "hermeneutics of world" emphasizes that my particular use of hermeneutics is concerned with the ontological, metaphysical, and cosmological aspects of the Spirituals. I also use it to emphasize other aspects of "world" like literary studies, symbol systems, and ecological studies. In fine, the concept of "world" is a polyvalent symbol, capable of reflecting a myriad of temporal and spatial imaginings of the human mind. The German *Welt* can mean a range of things, such as reality, history, society, or future

---

11. Hans-Georg Gadamer, *Truth and Method*, 2nd rev. ed. (New York: Continuum, 2004).
12. Gadamer, *Truth and Method*, 443.

hopes. This polyvalence reflects the openness of the concept and the awareness that one may use the word "world" at various times to indicate one or more of these meanings. For Gadamer, one key implication of the use of the concept of "world" was transcendence beyond the (natural-scientific) field of "environment," and this was joined to moving beyond the natural-scientific understanding of language as exhibited in the fields of philology and comparative linguistics. For Gadamer, this meant a move into language as literary studies and rhetoric. "Unlike all other living creatures, man's relationship to the world is characterized by *freedom from environment*. This freedom implies the linguistic constitution of the world. . . . To rise above the pressure of what impinges on us from the world means to have language and to have 'world.' . . . Man's freedom in relation to the environment is the reason for his free capacity for speech and also for the historical multiplicity of speech in relation to one world."[13] Thus hermeneutics takes natural-scientific accounts of material entities seriously yet also understands these entities in light of the human capacity for rhetorical language, and thus for the possibility of a limited freedom from environment and freedom to rise to world.

For all that appears in the research, consciousness of an original justice or original truth of nature does not. I hoped to discover in the discourse a natural law, spiritual principle, or the imprint of divine will built into the moral structure of the cosmos, perhaps detectable only to African American slaves because they lived on the margins of society. Yet, these romantic intimations were quickly dashed to pieces, as African American slaves left no hint of such a cosmological key. I was met only with an archaic silence, much like that described by philosopher Charles Long in his *Significations*: "God as a structure of intimacy has disappeared . . . [and] the eternal silence of these infinite spaces terrifies me."[14] In the contemporary discourse on the cultural logic of sovereignty, most discussions about a "theology of nature," "natural theology," or "theological naturalism" are treated as social and theological risk. Theological discourse tends to discipline and punish the state of nature into silence rather than discuss it explicitly. Yet even as there is an archaic silence on questions of the state of nature in contemporary discourse, the Spirituals may still function as musicological sketches toward the outlines of a world marked by the music of divine providence, one hermeneutically discerned, as it reflects through the collective mimetic consciousness of the "invisible institution."

13. Gadamer, *Truth and Method*, 441.
14. Charles H. Long, *Significations: Signs, Symbols, and Images in the Interpretation of Religion* (Minneapolis: Fortress, 1995), 61–62.

Introduction

Chapter Breakdown

In chapter 1, I explain the method that I used for this study. I define African American religious and cultural criticism, with special attention to the balancing of both empirical and phenomenological aspects of African American religious experience. This means in part that the method also involves unpacking the author's own fore-understandings. I also clarify my conception of African American religious experience. Key words in this chapter are "African American religious experience," "social theory," "cultural criticism," "signification," the "hermeneutics of dialogue," and "thick description." Chapter 2 defines the problem and significance of the project in further detail. I rehearse my definition of sovereignty as a cultural logic and distinguish it from other forms of sovereignty by way of historical and political analysis. Here I draw from some of my previous research to discuss sovereignty as conceived in the thinking of canonical figures in Western political theory, such as Jean Bodin, John Locke, Carl Schmitt, and Friedrich Hayek. Key words in this chapter are "sovereignty," "neoliberal rationality," "technological rationality," and "political theology." The third chapter takes up the question of naturalism, which poses challenges for the prospects of an African American public theology. I argue for a pragmatic naturalism, which opens the possibility for a phenomenological hermeneutics of world, and thus for an African American public theology. Key words include "naturalism," "logical positivism," "scientific naturalism," "pragmatic naturalism," "hermeneutics of world," "process metaphysics," "public theology," and the "theology of creation." These first three chapters constitute the first part of the project, which focuses on theory and method.

If the first three chapters constitute part 1 of the book, the next two make up the second part. Chapters 4 and 5 are given to discourse analysis of canonical figures in African American religious thought, with specific attention to the question of the doctrine of the state of nature. Chapter 4 asks about the state of nature doctrine as it is conceived in the discourse on African American spirituality. I argue that on the one hand, much of the discourse on African American spirituality evades an explicit account of the state of nature, implying that nature is impure or totally depraved. Key words in this chapter include "mysticism," "contemplative spirituality," "rhythmic spirituality," "consciousness," "theology of spirituality," "ecowomanism," "Sacred Earth," and "African ancestral spirituality." Chapter 5 discusses the state of nature doctrine in the discourse on African American theology. I argue that African American theology either disciplines and punishes or sublimates nature, thus reproducing the cultural logic of sovereignty. Yet I also use the thinking of one contemporary

On the Spirituals, Prophecy, and Theomusicology

theologian to point me in the direction of musicology and aesthetics. Key words include "natural law," "grace," "supersessionism," "covenant theology," "theology and economy," "Christology," "genealogy," "narrative hermeneutics," "historical materialism," and "Black theology of liberation." In part 2, I find that while topics like racism and white supremacy, the nature of God, the self, and the Black church are prevalent in African American religious thought, relatively little attention is given to the question of the state of nature in a systematic manner. The discourse on African American theology is in the practice of downplaying the meaning and significance of the state of nature.

In part 3 of the book, I begin my own theomusicological reading of the antebellum Spirituals. I carry out this effort for the remainder of the book, thus giving chapters 6 through 9 over to analyzing the Spirituals. Chapter 6 introduces the antebellum Spirituals as a theological source for a hermeneutics of world. I discuss the epistemological sources of the Spirituals and use cultural hermeneutics and musicology to describe the practice of the Spirituals as the ring-shout dance. Key words include "Spirituals," "mimesis," "signifyin'," "ring shout," "the erotic," "tonal languages," and the "invisible institution." In chapter 7 I discuss the logical and compositional features of the Spirituals. I argue that the practice and pattern of the "call and response" is a musical as well as cultural logic, and one that avoids the trap of the cultural logic of sovereignty. I also construct a musical aesthetic predicated on both the logic of call and response and the compositional features of the Spirituals, giving rise to a musical formalism that is rooted in the practices of the Spirituals. Key words include "theory of practice," "call and response," "atonement theory," "scapegoat mechanism," "musical form," "ostinato," "blues scale," "pentatonic scale," and "musical progression." Chapter 8 discusses the Trinitarian God of the antebellum Spirituals, with attention not only to pneumatology, Christology, and theology proper, but also to the topic of heaven, a place that plays a pivotal role in the songs. I argue that in the Spirituals, each person of the Trinity is expanded descriptively into its own threefold form. Key words include "crossing over," "providence," and "possible futures." Chapter 9 discusses in detail the geographic aspects of the hermeneutical world of the Spirituals. I argue that the antebellum Spirituals offer us at least four distinct landscapes and sketch out the general contours of each terrain. I also discuss the cosmological implications of the aesthetic features of the Spirituals, with attention to the questions of the state of nature and meaning in history.

While this book engages in an extensive analysis of African American religious thought, it also has its limits. One important limit is that this book focuses on the questions of the state of nature and the cultural logic of sover-

Introduction

eignty but leaves untouched two additional thematic centers in the discourse on sovereignty. In my dissertation research, I found that the discourse on sovereignty in Western canonical political theory is constituted not only by the question of the state of nature but also by questions of the body and the political body. Ideally, I would have been able to discuss all three themes in this book, but the more pressing task was to gain clarity on questions of theory and method and to ask thorough questions about the state of nature doctrine in the discourse on African American religion. This meant that before I could discuss either the theme of the body or the political body, I had to take some more basic steps to gain clarity on the state of nature doctrine as it is discussed by each thinker. These basic steps included background reading in a wide range of areas of study, including philosophy, cosmology, ethnomusicology, antiquities studies, music theory, ecological and environmental studies, and African religion and culture. Basic steps also included actual steps in walking to gain access to a wide range of texts at a wide range of libraries, some of which are rare and hard to find, or located at a faraway distance that require hikes into hilltops of library stacks. Basic steps also included walking through key texts written by each thinker, taking extensive notes, and reading other excellent thinkers that have also studied these figures and questions. In the future, I plan to return to questions concerned with the two additional thematic centers, as the three really form a constellation in the discourse of sovereignty in political theory and public theology.

Part One

THE CULTURAL LOGIC OF SOVEREIGNTY AND THE THEOLOGICAL HERMENEUTICS OF WORLD

1

African American Religious and Cultural Criticism

On Approach and Arrangement

I GREW UP IN THE WEST TEXAS REGION known as the Permian Basin, an area south of the Texas Panhandle where southward meets westward, and a place equally distant from all major cities in Texas. Some have affectionately called it the "dust bowl," and travelers foreign to the region are likely to comment on its Texas-sized tornadoes and tumbleweeds, as well as its long stretches of fields of cotton, wheat, grain sorghum, and in the right season, bluebonnets. The bluebonnets and cotton are a sight to behold, but strong gusts of West Texas wind have been known to flip even eighteen-wheelers. Travelers also frequently remark on the pungent smell that hovers on the outskirts of the smaller satellite towns in the region. The livestock, petroleum, and natural gas industries have left a lingering stank in particular locales, an odious offense that frequently descends on passers-by unawares. I was born in a town called Big Spring and grew up in Midland, Texas. I was baptized as a young teen at a small, simple, nondenominational church no bigger than a large assembly room. It was located on the outskirts of town, and as we didn't have a car at home, I caught a ride to church with some of the members. After accepting my call to the ministry at age fifteen, I practically lived at that church. I was there for worship, and for its antecedent Sunday school, and for its antecedent Sunday morning ministers' meeting. I was there Sunday night, Wednesday night, Saturday morning for the men's prayer breakfast, and also for fasts, Bible studies, and so forth. I labored alongside the men, women, and children of the poor and working-class congregation to add on to the room-church, beam by beam, nail by nail, board by board.

The Cultural Logic of Sovereignty and the Theological Hermeneutics of World

My faith was nurtured to maturity by the Black church in Midland, Texas. C. Eric Lincoln and Lawrence H. Mamiya define the Black church as "the pluralism of black Christian churches in the United States."[1] In general usage, all Black Christian persons are included in "the Black church" if they are members of a predominantly Black congregation. Lincoln and Mamiya list the three features of the Black church isolated by W. E. B. Du Bois at the beginning of the twentieth century: the preacher, the music, and the frenzy, a.k.a. "shouting." Most of my training and ministry occurred in nondenominational or Baptist congregations, and these tended to be less consciously tied to the historic legacy of protest of the Free African Society in the North as they were to what Christian ethicist Jonathan Walton calls "rural Southern Black Evangelicalism." In his *Watch This*, Walton describes this orientation of the Black church as one that places an emphasis on personal conversion, holiness, and humility, which in West Texas entailed a strong emphasis not only on the authority of the Bible but also on the incorporation of West Texas white cultural and social values. "It was the charge of all black Christians," says Walton, "to live up to Victorian standards of decorum and morality."[2] In West Texas, this meant Sunday morning church, hard work during the week, and Friday or Saturday night football at the local high school stadium. Black preachers preached that Black and brown Christians should get along with their white neighbors, and many white Christians in West Texas preached the same. But structural and systemic racism changed little, and preachers also seldom preached about either wealth or poverty. Relations remain amicable among the various peoples of West Texas, but the quiet tradition observed by all is that most white kids graduate and either go to college or get a decent job, while most Black and brown kids graduate and either get a dead-end job or end up in jail.

In West Texas, we always said in everyday conversation that one would either get out or end up in jail. We didn't know how accurate we were. In 2010 Robert Perkinson published *Texas Tough*, arguing that "just as New York dominates finance and California the film industry, Texas reigns supreme in the punishment business."[3] Texas houses 173,000 inmates, which is two times the number of employees at Google, and three times the number of prisoners

---

1. C. Eric Lincoln and Lawrence H. Mamiya, *The Black Church in African American Religious Experience* (Durham, NC: Duke University Press, 1990), 1.

2. Jonathan M. Walton, *Watch This: The Ethics and Aesthetics of Black Televangelism* (New York: New York University Press, 2009), 54–55.

3. Robert Perkinson, *Texas Tough: The Rise of America's Prison Empire* (London: Picador, 2010), 49–53.

in the Islamic Republic of Iran. At the date of the publication of *Texas Tough*, Texas led the nation in prison growth, in for-profit imprisonment, in total number of adults under correctional justice supervision, and in executions. The overwhelming majority of these inmates are Black or brown. The roots of Texas's racialized punishment go deep. In 1836 Texas fought wars of secession against both Mexico *and* the United States for its freedom to keep its slaves. Both the United States and Texas exterminated slavery, but Stephen F. Austin issued generous allotments of land to settlers, and additional acreage for every imported slave. Key areas of Texas lands—from the Sabine River to the western hill country and the Nueces River in the south—are known as the "cotton-slavery belt." These lands were initially acquired and cleared for slave-based agriculture. White planters replaced corn crops with their own cotton, and these plantations would later become home to the largest penal plantations in the nation. The Texas constitution of 1876—the "Redeemer Constitution"—is still the supreme law of the land. In the original constitution basic rights were allotted by race, and not even masters could emancipate their slaves without the express written consent of the Texas legislature. It has been amended nearly seven hundred times. Fewer than five of those amendments have concerned matters of racial equality; none have attended to matters of land; and traces of the racial penal code of the Old South remain within it.

Although Lincoln and Mamiya are correct to note that symbolic weight is given to the word "freedom" in the Black church, my experience also presented to me the concept of *sovereignty* as central to vernacular discourse on African American faith. God is a God who can "make a way out of no way." God is "able." God is an "on-time God." These and other sayings prevalent in the Black church refer to a confidence in the sovereignty of God, thus enfolding a strong Reformed Christian element within my Black church experience, which primarily means an emphasis on an all-powerful God, articulated as God's *sovereignty*, wherein God acts according to God's will and God's will alone, "so as to leave nothing to be done by humanity with regard to cosmic governance."[4] The sovereignty of God implied a divine covenant with the converted and required personal piety from the converted. In a cosmological sense, divine sovereignty means that God's will and providence is the leading principle of history, and that history itself is the playing out of God's redemp-

---

4. John Calvin, as quoted by Vincent Bacote, "John Calvin on Sovereignty," in *The Sovereignty of God Debate*, ed. D. Stephen Long and George Kalantzis (Eugene, OR: Cascade, 2009), 65.

tion and reconciliation of creation. I was reading A. W. Tozer, Pastor Tony Evans, Myles Munroe, and J. I. Packer. Looking back, I see that much of the leadership in our congregation had drawn connections between this providential covenant and late twentieth-century American market society. Added to this general perspective was a heighted apocalyptic sensibility brought on by neo-dispensationalists like Tim LaHaye and Jerry B. Jenkins. Many of us lived in perpetually imminent end times. We debated about the forthcoming "mark of the beast"—would it be a tattoo, or an implanted simple microchip? We guessed about the forthcoming rapture event, whether it would be before we graduated college, or right at the year 2000, or if it had already happened. Some of us would finally take comfort in noticing that certain revered saints of the congregation were still among us.

Upon leaving West Texas, I moved to Austin in central Texas, and spent some time there attaining both my bachelor and master of divinity degrees while serving in church ministry.

The University of Texas at Austin was a different place than Midland, Texas, as was the mainline progressive Austin Presbyterian Theological Seminary that I subsequently attended. During this time, three key traditions impacted my intellectual development. The first was American literature, the second was Black church music, and the third, Black liberation theology. My interest in American literature came as a surprise to me. I was a premedical student when I encountered a range of authors and their works that captured my imagination, including F. Scott Fitzgerald's *The Great Gatsby*, Emily Brontë's *Wuthering Heights*, and Charles Dickens's *Great Expectations* and *Oliver Twist*. A common theme among them that I didn't notice then is a generally critical view of the American Dream, as well as a tip of the hat to the orphan, Pip, the sparrow that somehow still flies his way home. In one of my courses on American religious literature, I encountered *The Autobiography of Malcolm X* for the first time. What most captivated me about this book was his journey of spiritual and moral development. He had started out as Malcolm Little in Omaha, Nebraska, and then Lansing, Michigan, where he lost his Garveyite father and mother to the destructive forces of white racism. When Little left Michigan, he also eventually left behind his old identity, picking up the "Detroit Red" during his time in Boston and New York before becoming Minister X in Nation of Islam. Near the end of his life, Minister X would experience a final transformation, this time to the Muslim name Malik el-Shabazz, which may be translated "Shabazz the sovereign," after his conversion to Sunni Islam. X's final agenda took the form of fighting for both Black cultural integrity and human rights.

In the Black church, ministers are not only involved in local congregational life but are also often involved in other forms of public leadership. These various forms of leadership beyond the church reflect the view that many African American minsters understand church and society as distinct yet interconnected publics. My own sense of public Christianity was shaped by cultural critic Cornel West, who calls for a prophetic Christianity in the face of American empire. "The values engendered by Christian belief were crucial in fueling first the democratic energy . . . [of] the American revolution."[5] West calls for care for the poor and public service. During my time in Austin, I was able to gain some experience in public service. For example, I volunteered for the Honorable Representative Dawnna Dukes of the Texas State Legislature as policy analyst and networking staff. I also held a small position as project director at a local branch of the Urban League, a national social services organization that seeks to build communities through family, career, medical, and advocacy support. In these publics, everyday and not-so-everyday people are working hard to increase the quality of life for Black folks and for folks in general. However, I also learned that many of these institutions and organizations are under great strain, primarily due to the society-wide shift away from participation in civic affairs and public service toward a more market-based, social-entrepreneurship model where businesses provide community services at cost to clients. This phenomenon is indicative of the larger social shift away from the spirit of volunteerism. My time of service in these organizations ultimately directed me to pursue graduate study in the then-emerging area of "public theology."

Austin was a world apart from West Texas, but one area of overlap between the flat West Texas plains and the central Texas hill country was in Black church music. In West Texas, I participated in the local church choir, and in Austin, I participated in the Innervisions Gospel Choir at the University of Texas at Austin, coming to serve as choir president during my junior year. In Midland, the church choir was composed of the entire range of working-class Black folk, including schoolteachers, air-conditioning repair men, correctional officers, high school students, and cooks. They would stay late after hours for Wednesday night rehearsal preparing for the upcoming Sunday morning. It always took me to another world when I heard Ms. Bridgette, one of the best singers at the church, sing "Silver and Gold" by Kirk Franklin. The church didn't have full-time musicians, so the choir would sing along to an audiotape,

---

5. Cornel West, *Democracy Matters: Winning the Fight against Imperialism* (New York: Penguin Books, 2004), 152.

but one soon forgot these when they heard the choir. Ms. Bridgette would always sound best during the vamp of the song, as she belted out improvisational leads—"Late in the midnight hour!" or "Don't give me the world! You can have the world!"—against the repetitive, rhythmic background to the choral repetition of "I'd rather have Jesus!" This same back-and-forth play of the musical call of the soloist and the response of the congregation was also present in the university choir, this one composed of the entire range of university students, including artists, athletes, aspiring doctors, lawyers, and entrepreneurs, and from all over Texas, including cities like Dallas, Houston, Tyler, and Fort Worth. We rehearsed every Thursday night at a Presbyterian church near the university. We would gather in a circle, and one of us would start by singing an opening line, to which the group responded. When one closed one's eyes in these musical spaces, it seemed like the very chorus of creation itself and God's heavenly band had joined in on the singing.

Austin Seminary was another formative institution in my intellectual development. This was my first encounter with formal religious denominationalism. It was here that I was introduced to academic theology beyond the limits of American evangelicalism, and theologians James Cone and Karl Barth captured my attention. Cone argued that the biblical story of God's deliverance of the Israelites from Egyptian captivity shows us that God's desire is for the liberation of the poor and oppressed. Cone reflected the sentiments of Blacks who rioted across the nation upon the deaths of Malcolm X and Martin Luther King Jr., among others, during the late 1960s. Cone's argument made sense to me. Why had I not heard it before? Karl Barth's theology was a response to the atrocity of the Nazi Holocaust and the Third Reich. Here was another theologian writing indirectly about politics. Barth criticized early twentieth-century German Christianity and called into question the doctrine of God's *exclusive* covenant with only certain peoples. Based on his understanding of God as revealed in the person and work of Jesus Christ, he could not come to terms with the idea of double predestination, that is, that God would issue a sovereign decree of eternal salvation for the elect and eternal condemnation for the nonelect. To those who ask the question "to whom does election apply?" Barth would reply "Who is the God who elects and what does a knowledge of this God tell us about the nature of election?" For Barth, God is God *for us* as the multiplicity of creation, as the heavenly entourage of God.[6] In earthly terms, Barthian redemption appears as the kingdom of heaven on earth, but

---

6. Karl Barth, *Church Dogmatics* III/3, *The Doctrine of Creation*, ed. G. W. Bromiley and T. F. Torrance (New York: T&T Clark, 2009), 159–60.

the kingdom "is not at a single stroke, on a single note, or in a single shade or form, but in a concentrated multiplicity of revelations and declarations, of events and relationships, of individuals and societies, which have their constitutive centre in God Himself."[7]

My research on the topic of sovereignty began to take shape at Vanderbilt University in Nashville, Tennessee. Although West shaped much of my thinking before Vanderbilt, it was the writings of French social theorist Michel Foucault (1926–1984) and Italian political theorist Giorgio Agamben (1942–) that convinced me to write on sovereignty. I came to critical political consciousness by reading Cornel West. However, I also found that his sole focus on questions of culture left larger social forces unattended, especially political and economic ones. I was introduced to Foucault in my "Theories of Practice Seminar," specifically his *Discipline and Punish: The Birth of the Prison* (1986).[8] Foucault argues that sovereign power now works primarily through various subtle forms of social discipline (exams, normalizing judgments, hierarchical observations, classifications, confinement) rather than through its older, more spectacular methods of punishment (town scaffold). The operations of sovereign power are mobilized to protect the sovereign social body. Foucault's text put sovereignty on my radar, but Agamben's *Homo Sacer: Sovereign Power and Bare Life* (1998) compelled me to take sovereignty seriously as a research topic. I was introduced to Agamben in my biopolitics and biopower course. Agamben discusses how the logic of sovereignty still circulates throughout modern societies in the form of the ban, an event where one is abandoned by both human and divine law.[9] Caught in this double exclusion, the abandoned is rendered "bare life," that is, "life that is able to be killed but not sacrificed"[10] and life that is always already under the threat of the law-suspending violence of sovereign power. Between Foucault's and Agamben's writings, I began to see how the concept of sovereignty was linked to my concern for the "least of these."

---

7. Barth, *Church Dogmatics* III/3, 160.

8. Cornel West rejected Foucault's analysis of power in *The American Evasion of Philosophy: A Genealogy of Pragmatism* (Madison: University of Wisconsin Press, 1989), 223–26. West's humanist conception of human agency would not allow him to acknowledge Foucault's description of modern power, that is, biopolitics. See Howard McGary Jr., "The Political Philosophy and Humanism of Cornel West," in *Cornel West: A Critical Reader*, ed. George Yancy (Malden, MA: Blackwell, 2001).

9. Giorgio Agamben, *Homo Sacer: Sovereign Power and Bare Life*, trans. Daniel Heller-Roazen (Stanford, CA: Stanford University Press, 1998), 28.

10. Agamben, *Homo Sacer*, 99.

The Cultural Logic of Sovereignty and the Theological Hermeneutics of World Manifold under Signification: On African American Experience

According to philosophical theologian Victor Anderson, African American religious and cultural criticism makes use of both religious and social scientific languages toward the successful cultural fulfillment of African American religious experience.[11] It analyzes the conditions by which it is either satisfied or frustrated and then makes interpretive and critical judgments about formations of religion in the lives of Black people. These moves of analysis and criticism give rise to the critic's utopian move, which discloses vistas of transcendence and emancipation. Anderson reminds us that this approach is empirical, beginning with the particularity of African American (religious) experience. Religious experience is linguistically structured and is thus not beyond the scope of ordinary human knowledge. Formally, experience is the content of consciousness or statements, or both. As we receive impressions from objects, we cognitively intuit the object through apperception. That is, we bring our languages, symbols, paradigms, and other ideal constructive artifacts to bear on objects in an attempt to comprehend them. Thus, alongside the empirical element there is also a phenomenological element present in religious experience, and the chapter seeks to acknowledge both the empirical and the phenomenological as aspects of my use of African American religious and cultural criticism. Theologian Tyron Inbody notes that "experience is never 'pure experience' [but] always . . . shaped, and interpreted in a social context, including both a natural environment of interrelationships and interdependence (nature) and a cultural environment of language, symbol, and myth (tradition)."[12] For Inbody, language arises as an organism encounters a complex environment in experience, and tradition shapes and reshapes the experience of an organism in its natural, social, and cosmic environment through language, symbol, and myth. Consciousness is thus not an object but a cooperative, creative, psychical, and reflexive process, knowledge being only one of its functions. Objects and states of affairs such as the external world, the past and the future, and other bodies exist independently of our own minds with possibility for both foreclosure and transcendence.

11. See Victor Anderson, "Theorizing African American Religion," in *African American Studies*, ed. Jeanette Davidson (Edinburgh: University of Edinburgh Press, 2010), 270–75. Also see Anderson's *Creative Exchange: A Constructive Theology of African American Experience* (Minneapolis: Fortress, 2008).
12. Tyron Inbody, *The Constructive Theology of Bernard Meland: Postliberal Empirical Realism* (Atlanta: Scholars Press, 1995), 232, as quoted by Anderson, *Creative Exchange*, 3.

Empirical research thus takes priority for the empirical theologian, but phenomenological hermeneutics reminds us that scientific views of the world are themselves constructed. Humans construct all views of the world on the basis of phenomena, that is, facts or events observed through one of the senses.[13] We observe facts and events through a grid of intelligibility that gives us a way to interpret and understand these facts and events. Thus, even valid scientific theories must make room for the notion of a phenomenon. For example, optical scientists and engineers will say that light and color are not objective, but a specific sense-energy. Optic nerves react together with phenomena of light and color in the same way that they react to a puff of air in the eye when visiting the optometrist. The visual apparatus of the nervous system has a specific energy that is seen in response not only to light and color but also to electric stimulation or mechanical jolts. Light stimuli don't actually possess the "nature" of the light or color and might actually be called illusions or delusions as they deceive us regarding the true nature of the stimulation. Many qualities that we ascribe to physiological objects are often those of the perceiving organism or even the *phenomenological subjectivity* of the object. Phenomenological hermeneutics acknowledges the possibility of a subject or consciousness behind phenomenal consciousness that is as ontically real and independent as the world. With respect to method, this first means that I must take account of my own taken-for-granted assumptions about the world to the extent that I am able to do so. This also means that I must be open to the possibility that objects in the material world might also present to me or the world a phenomenological subjectivity. For example, in the early years of slavery, African American musicians often spoke of their drums as "talking drums," whose calls resounded as far as twenty miles for all to hear.

This study may be located within the tradition of American empirical theology as explicated by thinkers like D. C. McIntosh, Henry Nelson Wieman, Schubert Ogden, and others who had practical questions about how religion functions in relationship to society and culture. They remained open to reflecting on the insights of the human and social sciences. They took a pragmatic-naturalist approach to the study of religion, prioritizing human experience as both epistemological source and an outcome or goal of their research. One primary distinction between this study and many empirical approaches is my adoption of a phenomenological-hermeneutical approach alongside my

---

13. Susann M. Laverty, "Hermeneutic Phenomenology and Phenomenology: A Comparison of Historical and Methodological Considerations," *International Journal of Qualitative Methods* 2, no. 3 (2003): 21–25, https://tinyurl.com/59hy4d3n.

empirical approach. I do this because I understand there to be a difference between an object, for example, the practice of the Spirituals as observed by researchers, and a person's or group's *perception* and *consciousness* of that object, for example, the researcher's perception versus the slaves' perception of the practice of the Spirituals. Perception and consciousness of an object require mental, tactile, spiritual, and sonic participation; such participation and experience change my consciousness about the object, opening the pathway to novelty and creativity. Consciousness is thus a transcendental act that goes beyond the object to something independent of it, to something that can't be registered in natural-scientific terms. In this way, my study may also be located in the ontological-hermeneutical tradition explicated by thinkers like Martin Heidegger, Maurice Merlau-Ponty, Hans-Georg Gadamer, and others.

The centrality of experience in an African American public theology raises questions about the nature of experience. Here I discuss the tension that arises in the nature of experience from the fact that African American experience is simultaneously constituted by variety as well as by linguistic significations that give rise to a sense of unity. Black experiences are constituted on one hand by the permanency of race as an effective category in identity formation, and on the other hand by existential and social variety. Postmodern Black thought emphasizes the varieties of African American religious and cultural experiences. These extend beyond experiences framed primarily by race to those framed by gender, sexuality, class, disability, or other vantage points. African American experiences also extend beyond Christianity, to include Islam, Santeria, and the Nation of Islam, among other religions. In America, Black experiences have historically been talked about and studied as if they were a monolith. Yet, two decades into the twenty-first century, postmodern African American thinkers like Cornel West, bell hooks, Tommie Shelby, and Victor Anderson argue that Black experience must account for its own internal differences and variegation.[14] These postmodern voices are themselves in contention regarding which forms of difference are primary. For Shelby, black solidarity should be primarily *political* and provisional rather than rooted in a sense of shared racial identity.[15] For hooks, class matters are primary over those of race and possibly even gender.[16] Some of the most difficult experi-

---

14. For an example of African American cultural theorists of difference, see Cornel West's "The New Cultural Politics of Difference," *Humanities as Social Technology* 53 (1990): 93–109, https://tinyurl.com/48f2j49n.

15. See Tommie Shelby, *We Who Are Dark: The Philosophical Foundations of Black Solidarity* (Cambridge, MA: Belknap Press of Harvard University Press, 2005), 1–2.

16. See bell hooks, *Where We Stand: Class Matters* (New York: Routledge, 2000).

ences in her life have been around questions of crossing class boundaries. Yet all advocate for the new cultural politics of difference, which reminds us that African American religion and culture is manifold and pluriform. It reminds us that our religio-ethical projects must somehow account for difference and otherness that will always be.

Cultural critic and theologian Victor Anderson's critique of conceptions of Black experience as a monolithic unity remains exemplary. He argues against what he calls "ontological blackness," that is, the practice of reifying race rhetorically, treating it "as if it objectively exists, independent of historically contingent factors and subjective intentions."[17] In so doing, we collapse metaphysics onto ontology, thus essentializing blackness into an unyielding, unchanging mass. For Anderson, it is important to remember that blackness is socially constructed rather than ontological. We commit the error of ontological blackness when our language about Black experience depicts blackness in essentialist, categorical, and representational ways. Sourcing bell hooks, Anderson charts his own understanding of Black experience in *Beyond Ontological Blackness* (1995):

> Postmodern blackness recognizes the permanency of race as an effective category in identity formation. However, it also recognizes that black identities are continually being reconstituted as African Americans inhabit widely differentiated social spaces and communities of moral discourse. African American life and experience occur in differentiated socio-economic spaces along divisions of education, income, and occupation. And the varieties of communities of moral discourse that influence black life and experience may include churches, temples, mosques, and many non-religious voluntary organizations. In these multiple sites, African Americans are continuously negotiating the various languages of race, class, gender, and sexuality. Explicating these languages requires historical research and analysis of the ways that African Americans constitute and negotiate their identities under changing social conditions.[18]

For Anderson, Black religious and cultural studies must take account of Black experience in ways that resist monolithic and one-dimensional readings. Postmodern blackness recognizes that all Black folk do not experience the

---

17. Victor Anderson, *Beyond Ontological Blackness: An Essay on African American Religious and Cultural Criticism* (New York: Continuum, 1998), 11.
18. Anderson, *Beyond Ontological Blackness*, 11–12.

world in the same way. For example, contemporary culture studies discern a conflict within African American culture. According to Black feminist pioneer Patricia Hills Collins, Black cultural life in the United States exhibits a conflict between the "civil rights and Black power" generation on one hand, and on the other hand, the "hip-hop" generation. The civil rights generation tends to emphasize the egalitarian status of African Americans in relation to whites in US society. The civil rights generation's vision of the country is framed largely by the grit, gains, and glory of the Black-led US Freedom Movement (1955–1970), one that battled the antidemocratic, white supremacist aspects of the nation to achieve civil rights and create a new US society.[19] The civil rights movement achieved goals of historic proportions. The enactment of the Civil Rights Act of 1964 and the Voting Rights Act of 1965 reinforced the guarantees of full citizenship for African Americans and others and marked the end of the Jim Crow system of segregation. Legally, racial desegregation erased the color line recognized by W. E. B. Du Bois.[20] Today, the civil rights generation holds in esteem a cultural politics of respectability, whereby politics is rooted in a categorical distinction between those with distinctive personalities able to practice autonomy and general humans more inclined to disobey the law and do evil. Respect is reserved for those given to respectability politics.[21] This cultural politics of respectability casts the civil rights generation in a conservative light for the hip-hop generation, which understands the civil rights and Black power generation as part of a US establishment oriented toward the inhibition of social freedoms.

The hip-hop generation was born over a period of two decades, from around 1965 to 1984. It was born in a post–civil rights, free-trade, free-market era, one marked not by the social equality envisioned by the civil rights generation but by a hostile US government intent on ordering the economy of Black

---

19. Vincent Harding, *Hope and History: Why We Must Share the Story of the Movement* (Maryknoll, NY: Orbis Books, 2009), 4–7. See also Kwame Anthony Appiah and Henry Louis Gates Jr., eds., *Africana: The Encyclopedia of African and African American Experience—the Concise Desk Reference* (Philadelphia: Running Press, 2003), 135.

20. Historian, sociologist, and philosopher W. E. B. Du Bois set the tone for public conceptions of African American experience with his notion of the "color line" in the seminal work *The Souls of Black Folk* (1903). Du Bois's central claim was that the definitive problem and experience for Black folk was the problem of the color line—that is, the relation of the darker to the lighter races of men in Asia and Africa, in America and the islands of the sea. Postmodern theorists of blackness have called this theory into question. (See W. E. B. DuBois, *The Souls of Black Folk* [n.p.: G&D Media, 2019], 9.)

21. See Paul Ricoeur, *Oneself as Another*, trans. Kathleen Blamey (Chicago: University of Chicago Press, 1992), 204.

life through various modes of governance including prison, juvenile detention centers, police, assistance bureaucracies (Medicare, EBT), and housing projects designed to warehouse lives. Poor Black folk are governed from birth to death. Most live in government-funded housing and work government jobs. Many have family spending time in the ultimate public housing, prison. The result has been social confinement, poverty, and vulnerability to disasters like Hurricane Katrina and the Flint water crisis. The story of hip-hop is thus the story of the hustler, the hustler with his back against the wall in a "do-or-die" situation. It's the story of the struggle to survive, to go from nothing to something, and to win and to make sense of it all.[22] In our postmodern moment, hip-hop has reached beyond the ghettos of America to become itself the new common ground and collective aesthetic, especially for those rejected by the US establishment. Hip-hop fuses a range of popular music traditions like bohemian, revolutionary, and space-age southern boys. Hip-hop is often associated with gang violence, sex, and drugs. Yet beyond caricature and generalizations, hip-hop calls into question the cultural politics of respectability. In creating a space where all kinds of music can meet, without contradiction, the hip-hop aesthetic highlights the moral contradictions of a nation that preaches equality and liberty on one hand, and places poor Black and brown folk in prison on the other. The status of the hip-hop generation thus tests the nature of the neighborliness of American society.

Its variety notwithstanding, African American religion and culture exists within the context of Western symbolic orders and is signified by these orders as a unity. Philosopher Charles H. Long notes in his *Significations* (1995) that the Black community is signified by another community, namely, American culture.[23] Long uses the term "signification" to describe how names were given to realities and peoples during the modern period of conquest. This naming, or signification, is at the same time an objectification of realities that appear as novel or other to the culture of conquest. There is power in this process of naming and objectification. The hidden power of naming consists in the fact that names usually reflect, yet also conceal, larger social power dynamics and relationships. "The actual situation of cultural contact itself is never brought to the fore within the context of intellectual formulations. . . . [Instead,] descriptive and analytical categories and taxonomies form the basis for an ac-

---

22. Jay Z, *Decoded* (New York: Spiegel & Grau, 2011).

23. Charles H. Long, *Significations: Signs, Symbols, and Images in the Interpretation of Religion* (Minneapolis: Fortress, 1995), 2. Hereafter, page references from this work will be given in parentheses in the text.

cusatory or compensational order of meaning" (5). Long explains that the differences that separate cultures, and also the new orders of meaning that arise, are produced as one dominant system of values interacts with another, subjected system of values. "More often than not, the differences that bring a culture of a people to the attention of the investigator are not simply formed from the point of view of the intellectual problematic; they are . . . the nuances and latencies of that power which is part of the structure of the cultural contact itself manifesting itself as intellectual curiosity. In this manner the cultures of non-Western peoples were created as products of a complex signification" (5). The modern West's acquisition of knowledge about peoples and planet earth in Asia, Africa, and the Americas was done from the perspective of Western Renaissance and Enlightenment imperial culture. This is the signature of all things in our time.

According to Long, to be signified is to become integrated into a culture's structures of interpretation as it strives toward self-definition. In the United States, to be signified is to be "part of a cultural code whose euphemisms and stereotypes have indicated their meaning within the larger framework of American cultural languages" (4). In the movements of modern economic and military conquest, religion and cultures and peoples throughout the world were created anew as they were signified in various Western cultural productions such as art, literature and other media, and academic disciplinary orientations. "The situation of cultural contact brought about changes in the cultures of the signifiers. . . . [There is thus] the hermeneutical problem of the making of the modern Western culture and thus the formation of the modern human being in the West in relationship to the situation and confrontation of the cultures of the world" (6). The West and the cultures of the world share mutually interdependent identities within a perceived order of being. The cultural reality of Blacks in the United States has to an extent been fashioned by those with the powers of cultural signification. In this regard, Blacks are a part of the same structures of cultural categories that create the categories of colonized peoples of the contemporary world (8). Long's argument regarding signification and the signified has implications for postmodern arguments about varieties of African American religious and cultural experience. It shows that the existing variety of Black experiences highlighted by Anderson, hooks, and others is real, but nonetheless framed within symbolic structures that provide the conditions for the possibility of racial and national thinking. These significations, ambiguous in nature and shifting with context, enable us to talk about African Americans as a distinct people group even as we acknowledge the differences that make each of us who we are as individuals.

In this text, I take account of African American experiences in a manner that takes account of both Anderson's concern about difference and Long's claim about unifying signification. In a previous study, I found that dark peoples of the globe were taken up in canonical Western politico-philosophical discourse under the theme of the "state of nature." The state of nature is a metaphor and framing device symbolizing that which is outside/beyond the boundaries of civilization. It has been a prevalent theme in political theory since at least the seventeenth century, when English philosopher Thomas Hobbes (1588–1679) theorized Africa and other New World lands as the "state of nature" in his *Leviathan* (1641), a space of competition, diffidence, and "Warre... And the life of man, solitary, poore, nasty, brutish, and short."[24] For Hobbes, the state of nature is a place of chaos and lawlessness, of unchecked power and desire, and the space that provides the backdrop for the formation and self-understanding of civil society and the state. Hobbes's rhetorical interpretation of travelers' reports during colonization and competitive colonial wars reflects the darkest dimensions of frightened white Western fantasy in its encounters with darker peoples. Since the time of Hobbes, this doctrine has been read onto Black and colored bodies in an effort to order them "appropriately" in relation to Euro-American civilization. This doctrine, more than any absolutist theory of government, continues to frame Black experience and vitiate African and African American struggles for freedom. In social, political, economic, and religious thought, the state of nature doctrine continues to serve as a framing device for understanding and interacting with African Americans and other poor or colonized peoples. One definite consequence of this framing device is the legitimation of the operations of sovereign power—the powers of life and death—over African Americans.

Up to this point, my discussion of Western signification of Black experience has made these significations seem *absolutely* determinate. However, it is important to note that Western significations on Black experience were *not* so determinate that all traces of alternative forms of cultural consciousness were completely destroyed. This may seem erroneous, given that so many of the visible signs of West and Central African indigenous religion and culture have vanished. These social institutions and traditions, including art, religious practices, and rites of passage, became more torn apart and frayed with every market exchange of enslaved Black bodies. Western signification also framed Black experience to the degree that it introduced Scripture into the episte-

---

24. Thomas Hobbes, *Leviathan*, ed. Richard Tuck (Cambridge: Cambridge University Press, 1996), 88–89.

mological orbit of West and Central Africans, even as we will also see that this biblical framing of Black experience did not imply the sovereignty of the Western interpretive paradigm for Blacks. Western signification was limited in its reach over Black life. Religious historian Albert Raboteau offers another telling example in his *Slave Religion* (1978), where he documents how most white planters and slave owners were frustrated in their attempts to completely shut down religious dancing. "Methodist, Presbyterian, and Baptist revivalists condemned [religious dancing]. . . . The unusual religious behavior of slaves at camp meetings aroused the disapproval of some Christian evangelists."[25] Evangelist John Watson called religious dancing "a most exceptionable error,"[26] Bishop Daniel Alexander Payne called it the "ridiculous and heathenish way,"[27] and even those like scholar William Francis Allen who appreciated the Spirituals would condescendingly say that Black music had an "intrinsically barbaric character."[28] Yet in the Spirituals, we see an example of the limits of the reach of Western signification, and thus, the site of further excavation for an alternative perspective.

The Hermeneutics of Dialogue

My approach to African American experience takes account of experience hermeneutically. Hans-Georg Gadamer gives direction in this area, arguing for a hermeneutics of dialogue. "The classical discipline concerned with the art of understanding texts is hermeneutics. If my argument is correct, however, the real problem of hermeneutics is quite different from what one might expect. . . . Hermeneutics would then have to embrace the whole sphere of art and its complex of questions. Every work of art, not only literature, must be understood like any other text that requires understanding and this kind of understanding has to be acquired."[29] In the hermeneutics of dialogue, dialogue has primacy in the act of understanding a work of art, the dialogue itself is structured by the logic of question and answer, and the goal of the

---

25. Albert J. Raboteau, *Slave Religion: The Invisible Institution in the Antebellum South* (New York: Oxford University Press, 2004), 66–67.
26. Raboteau, *Slave Religion*, 67.
27. Raboteau, *Slave Religion*, 68.
28. William Francis Allen, Charles Pickard Ware, and Lucy McKim Garrison, compilers, *Slave Songs of the United States: 136 Songs Complete with Sheet Music and Notes on Slavery and African American History* (n.p.: Pantianos Classics, 1867), x.
29. Gadamer, *Truth and Method*, 157.

conversation is a fusion of horizons. For Gadamer, a work of art (or a text) can become an experience that changes the person who experiences it, usually as the work of art poses a question to us and as we answer in response. In this way, hermeneutics grounds aesthetic experience (*Erfahrung*) as a unique mode of knowledge in distinction from the natural sciences.[30] While art and art's truth are always already mediated by historical consciousness, artistic experience may still communicate its "own" truth. Aesthetics thus becomes a history of worldviews, and the task of aesthetics becomes both artistic understanding and creation. African American public theology foregrounds and understands dialogical play as central to this project, where the Spirituals and other works of art pose questions as art to the cultural logic of sovereignty and call us to consider another horizon of meaning, specifically with respect to the question of "the state of nature" doctrine.

Gadamer argues that hermeneutics is ultimately about the disclosure of worlds toward a fusion of horizons. In the act of understanding a work of art or text, we learn both about the world presented in the work of art and about our own world. Hermeneutics is about using the back-and-forth play of question and answer to come to a better understanding of both one's own vantage point and the vantage point of a work of art, and hermeneutics is furthermore about fusing these vantage points into a new perspective. "Coming to an understanding through human conversation is no different from the understanding that occurs between animals. But human language must be thought of as a special and unique life process since, in linguistic communication, 'world' is disclosed. Reaching an understanding in language places a subject matter before those communicating like a disputed object set between them. Thus the world is the common ground, trodden by none and recognized by all, uniting all who talk to one another."[31] The goal in hermeneutics is the fusion of horizons where we both put forth our own understanding of the world even as we open ourselves to being transformed by the art or text. While I hold hermeneutics as a vital aspect of method, I also understand that it has historically been tied to ambiguous political views. This may explain, in part, how some hermeneutical thinkers like Edmund Husserl and Hans-Georg Gadamer rejected Nazism while others like Martin Heidegger embraced it. It is vital for thinkers to also

---

30. *Erfahrung* (experience) isn't simply the cataloguing of sense-images under formal rules (as Kant argued), but is *mimetic*, identifying correspondences between different areas of social life. This idea of experience preserves the "Hegelian" idea of a "cultural unity" without the metaphysics of speculative idealism, a shared, prediscursive collective level of experience, or a historicized Kantian transcendental subject.

31. Gadamer, *Truth and Method*, 443.

embrace critical social thought alongside hermeneutics. In this respect, this book deploys the method of African American cultural criticism. Cultural criticism is commensurable with a hermeneutical approach and also with certain iconoclastic formations in theological discourse.

Even as we approach a work of art or a text for understanding, we do not do so as an objective disinterested scientist (if such a scientist exists). Hermeneutics thus also involves the crucial principle of effective history, which notes the historicity and historically mediated consciousness of all human understanding and the "social base" of all interpretations. Our intellectual ability to reason is always secondary to prelinguistic meaning and truth. I discussed my own tension-filled fore-understandings above. They include Black folk religious traditions of passionate praise and worship; a constellation of theological themes, including covenant and exodus liberation of the poor; education in the liberal arts and humanistic studies; and prophetic and democratic public activism and volunteerism in a quickly vanishing republican civil society. My horizon is also constituted by the very neoliberal market culture that I set out to criticize in this book, one intensely nationalistic, militaristic, fiercely individualistic, competitive, and capitalistic. I'm also a child of hip-hop, a critical aesthetic born in response to a hostile US government. Therefore, I must provisionally bracket and suspend my fore-understandings as I enter into a dialogue with various texts regarding the question of the "state of nature" doctrine. Thus, the forthcoming chapters analyze the discourse on African American spirituality by first listening to the text as a subjectivity, as possessing an agency to bear forth a modicum of its truth by way of back-and-forth play between itself and the reader. I must also attend to how Western significations of Black life as a monolith snuff out the manifold variety that constitutes Black life. This means that the voices of the discourse in African American religion will likely have a difference of opinion on certain matters rather than a unified voice.

Thick Description, Symbol System, and Social Critique: On Using Social and Critical Social Theory

Empirical research is a key task for the religious and cultural critic alongside the continuous work of unpacking one's fore-understandings. Like a bee, the empiricist, by means of his inductive methods, collects the cultural matter or products and then works them up into knowledge in order to produce honey, which is useful for healthy nutrition. Since the emergence of empiricism in the early modern (British) context, practitioners have emphasized that the method isn't equal to logical positivism. For example, Francis Bacon (1561–1626) argues that we should build our knowledge on sense experience because it extends our knowledge of nature in ways that practices and argumentation do not. He also emphasized that science extends beyond its limits when it pursues "the ambitious and proud desire of moral knowledge to judge good and evil."[32] Yet since the dominance of logical positivism in American academies, especially from the 1940s until the 1970s, empirical approaches to knowledge have been held hostage by criteria for truth rooted in the positivist thinking of David Hume (1711–1776). According to Hume, knowledge of the world can be justified *only* by the testimony of the senses, and interpretive or symbolic theories that cannot be verified or falsified by experience are, strictly speaking, meaningless.[33] With the hegemony of logical positivism, technological rationality reigned supreme, and technology offered itself not only as a tool but also as metaphor, value, and symbol for life. As I discuss in my chapter on naturalism, many positivist social scientists remain blind to their own use of symbols to represent social facts and data, and continue to hold that knowledge is simply about acquiring information and big data for formal or quantitative use.[34] African American cultural criticism takes account of experience empirically and interpretively, using cultural analytical tools, for example, ethnography and culture studies.

In the social sciences, the empirical method was wedded to interpretive and symbolic approaches most definitively in the work of symbolic anthropologist Clifford Geertz (1926–2006). Geertz's applied pragmatic phenomenological and hermeneutical method calls the anthropologist to move beyond methodological individualism toward an analysis of the meaning of symbols that constitute cultures.[35] A symbol includes "any object, act, event, quality, or relation which serves as a vehicle for conception—the conception is the symbol's 'meaning.'"[36] Symbols are a social event, ones whose impacts are

---

32. Francis Bacon, "The Great Instauration," in *The English Philosophers from Bacon to Mill*, ed. Edwin A. Burtt (New York: Modern Library, 1994), 13.

33. Alexander Rosenberg, *Philosophy of Social Science*, 4th ed. (Boulder, CO: Westview, 2012), 14.

34. See W. James Bradley and Kurt C. Schaefer, *The Uses and Misuses of Data and Models: The Mathematization of the Human Sciences* (Thousand Oaks, CA: Sage, 1998), 182. Also see Brian Brock, *Christian Ethics in a Technological Age* (Grand Rapids: Eerdmans, 2010), 10.

35. Arun Micheelsen, "'I Don't Do Systems': An Interview with Clifford Geertz," *Method & Theory in the Study of Religion* 14, no. 1 (2002): 2–20, https://tinyurl.com/mthm998f. Also see Clifford Geertz, *The Interpretation of Cultures: Selected Essays* (New York: Basic Books, 1973), 91.

36. Geertz, *The Interpretation of Cultures*, 91.

far more important for social purposes than biology or genetics. They create intersubjective worlds that operate as means of communication with others, as a means for comprehending the world, and as cultural patterns that deeply influence the character, outlook, moods, and motivations of people. "But meanings," says Geertz,

> can only be "stored" in symbols: a cross, a crescent, or a feathered serpent. Such religious symbols, dramatized in rituals or related in myths, are felt somehow to sum up, for those for whom they are resonant, what is known about the way the world is, the quality of the emotional life it supports, and the way one ought to behave while in it. Sacred symbols thus relate an ontology and a cosmology to an aesthetics and a morality: their peculiar power comes from their presumed ability to identify fact with value at the most fundamental level, to give to what is otherwise merely actual, a comprehensive normative import.[37]

For Geertz and those who follow his semiotic account of culture beyond structuralist sociology, (e.g., Niklas Luhmann, Roland Barthes), culture isn't a superorganic, reified monolithic reality, nor is it reducible to behavior events. Culture isn't a psychological structure, nor is it about material items. Culture is public, consisting of socially established symbolic structures of meaning about the world, self, and others.

Although Geertz did much to establish hermeneutical approaches to culture studies, his particular definition of culture has been expanded in light of postmodern criticisms. In *The Interpretation of Cultures* (1973), Geertz defined culture as "a historically transmitted pattern of meanings embodied in symbols, a system of inherited conceptions expressed in symbolic forms by means of which [people] communicate, perpetuate and develop their knowledge about and attitude towards life . . . ; a system or web of inherited conceptions expressed in symbolic forms by means of which people communicate, perpetuate, and develop their knowledge about and attitudes toward life."[38] Influenced by philosopher Hans-Georg Gadamer's "hermeneutics of dialogue," Geertz came to believe that culture gives meaning to the world, making it understandable. For Gadamer, language is most itself not in propositions but in dialogue, and a proposition can never be removed from the context of motivation. Thus philosophy's logical positivist decision to construct logic on the

---

37. Geertz, *The Interpretation of Cultures*, 127.
38. Geertz, *The Interpretation of Cultures*, 89.

basis of the proposition, where the sentence consists in a self-sufficient unity of meaning, must be rejected.[39] For Geertz, this meant that culture should be regarded as texts to be read rather than as scientific objects to be observed. His approach was to offer a "thick description" of culture. "Ethnography is thick description . . . the ethnographer is in fact faced with . . . a multiplicity of complex conceptual structures . . . which he must contrive somehow first to grasp and then to render." Geertz's thick description method has remained. Yet theologian Kathryn Tanner notes other aspects of conceptions of culture that have been criticized and reconstructed.[40] For example, cultures do form a whole beyond their individual elements (i.e., organicist "holism"); they aren't internally consistent wholes or sharply bounded, self-contained units. Cultures are discontinuous, porous.

As with the study of culture, African American religious and cultural criticism also begins with an interpretive/symbolic approach to the study of religion. Geertz's conception of religion is notable. He conceives of religion as a "system of symbols." These symbols act to establish powerful, pervasive, and long-lasting moods and motivations in people. They do so by formulating conceptions of a general order of existence and also by clothing these conceptions with an aura of factuality that makes the moods and motivations seem uniquely realistic. Yet for African American religious and cultural criticism, Geertz's conception of religion is itself symbolic of a more general empirical approach to the study of religion. Empirical theology allows religion to disclose itself as a distinctive feature of human life. Following Anderson, an empirical approach to the study of religion does not legislate in advance the nature of religion but understands religious discourse as a reflection of the "qualitative value of the self's extreme, subjective integration" as well as the "qualitative feeling of unity or integration not only with other selves but also ultimately with world processes."[41] Indeed, "religious meaning reflects a plenitude of being, a plenitude that is not reducible to human agency but one that also admits a resignation of human life and practices to larger wholes." Religious

---

39. Jean Grondin and Joel Wensheimer, *Introduction to Philosophical Hermeneutics* (New Haven: Yale University Press, 1997), 118. Also see Gadamer, *Truth and Method*, and Geertz, *The Interpretation of Cultures*, 10.

40. See Kathryn Tanner, *Theories of Culture: A New Agenda for Theology* (Minneapolis: Fortress, 1997). Also see Jere Paul Surber, *Culture and Critique: An Introduction to the Critical Discourses of Cultural Studies* (New York: Perseus, 1998), 63.

41. Victor Anderson, *Pragmatic Theology: Negotiating the Intersections of an American Philosophy of Religion and Public Theology* (Albany: State University of New York Press, 1998), 101.

experience has individual and social aspects, mystical and material, and may be accounted for in a variety of ways (narrative, testimony, text, art, language, practice). This is the case even as we acknowledge that religious claims can't be reduced to history, aesthetics, or morals. Religion may be taken up experientially, substantively (beliefs of religion), or by way of a functionalist account, where one observes what role religion plays in people's everyday lives. Religion may also be framed by way of family resemblances, looking at overlapping similarities rather than strict religious identity.

Sociologist Uta Gerhardt has shown that the tensions between Weberian-derived systems theory and Marxian-derived critical theory need not imply incompatibility.[42] Systems theory, represented by Geertz and sociologist Talcott Parsons, interprets contemporary modern society sociologically as a social system. Systems theory thus serves as the "skeleton" of science, giving systematic framework to objects of study. A key debate concerns how this system is generated. On one hand, some say that mathematics is the most effective way to systematize the real connections of our social reality. The implicit assumption is that it's possible to study all thinkable relationships abstracted from concrete situations. In this way, systems theory continues to embrace a positivist methodological individualism. On the other hand, some systems theorists such as Clifford Geertz, Stuart Hall, and Niklas Luhmann approach systems theory ethnographically and contextually. Geertz resists the algorithmization of knowledge by way of thick description within a symbolic interactionist framework. "The task of theory building here is not to codify abstract regularities but to make thick description possible, not to generalize across cases but to generalize within them . . . ways of thinking that are responsive to particularities, to individualities, oddities, discontinuities . . . [and] a sense of connectedness, a connectedness that is neither comprehensive nor uniform, primal nor changeless, but nonetheless real."[43]

If systems theory focuses on the connectedness of society's social systems and tends toward the theme of social integration, critical theory, represented by Max Horkheimer and Theodor Adorno, tends toward the theme of conflict or dialectic and interprets society psychologically as (Marxian) false, (Freudian) repressed, or (Humean) scientistic consciousness, a.k.a. ideology. Repressed consciousness both alienates us from and instrumentalizes "na-

---

42. See Uta Gerhardt, "Worlds Come Apart: Systems Theory versus Critical Theory; Drama in the History of Sociology in the Twentieth Century," *American Sociologist* 33, no. 2 (Summer 2002): 5–39, https://tinyurl.com/mr3m3mb3.

43. Geertz, *The Interpretation of Cultures*, 224.

ture" by insisting on a rigidly defined identity and an ethic of cunning that avoids suffering at all costs. Critical theory also goes beyond psychoanalytic interpretation to advance aesthetic critique and activist and revolutionary politics. A key exception to these alternatives is Jürgen Habermas, who instead opts for communicative action within a context of communicative freedom. Habermas's goal sits at the intersection of Enlightenment ideals of politics as conversation and postliberal visions of more socially oriented politics. The goal of communicative action is mutual understanding (*Verstandigung*) of the agents' situation, and communicative freedom allows one to say yes or no to various proposals. In this way, he leaves open Karl Marx's thesis that "The philosophers have only *interpreted* the world, in various ways; the point, however, is to *change* it."[44] Other key critical theorists have also been formative for my thinking, especially the "recognition v. redistribution debate" hosted by Axel Honneth and Nancy Fraser. Honneth argues for a conception of justice as a three-tiered distribution of recognition. Recognition in the spheres of love (intimate relationships), law (legal relations), and achievement (professional status) is key. Fraser embraces a "double vision" of justice, one that accounts for "*both the mutual irreducibility of maldistribution and misrecognition and their practical entwinement with each other.*"[45] In sum, interpretive and critical theory work cooperatively.

Toward Social Construction

Finally, an African American public theology not only describes and critiques vicious social formations but also theorizes, articulates, and socially constructs alternative visions of hope. In this way there is not only an acknowledgment of the social dialectic but also a move toward "integration" of sorts. Cultural criticism positions itself iconoclastically against cultural idolatries and heroisms and calls for a new politics of identity. This new politics affirms creative possibilities for human emancipation, thriving, cultural fulfillment, and transcendence. Symbols of interdependence and sameness come into balance with those of individuality and difference. I am reminded of the working-class folk of my home church in Midland, Texas, coming together to erect a new "house

---

44. Karl Marx, "Theses on Feuerbach," in *The Marx-Engels Reader*, ed. Robert C. Tucker, 2nd ed. (New York: Norton, 1978), 145.

45. Nancy Fraser and Axel Honneth, *Redistribution or Recognition? A Political-Philosophical Exchange* (New York: Verso, 2003), 48.

of hope." Construction can be composition, for example, the antebellum African American Spirituals. In the Spirituals, enslaved African Americans composed an "Ole Ship of Zion" to carry them home. "'Tis the old ship of Zion . . . O what ship is this, That will take us all home? . . . She has landed many thousand And she'll land as many more."[46]

---

46. "The Old Ship of Zion," in Allen, Ware, and Garrison, *Slave Songs of the United States*, 118.

2

The Global Leviathan Appears

On the Significance of Sovereignty

WHY IS THERE A NEED FOR YET another book on sovereignty, and why now? Indeed, there are many books on sovereignty from a range of disciplinary perspectives. Provisionally, we can say that sovereignty is "highest (i.e., supreme) in rank, authority, control, rule, and/or power."[1] In considering literature on sovereignty, three texts may serve as models for this chapter's discussion. One model might be called the *classical* approach or conception of sovereignty, represented by political theorist Wendy Brown's *Walled States: Waning Sovereignty* (2010). Here sovereignty is depicted in its monarchial or decisionist mode, as a solitary will that descends from above, bringing order to "social chaos." Alongside the classical approach there is the *enlightened* approach, exhibited by Robert Jackson's *Sovereignty: Evolution of an Idea* (2007). This model acknowledges the people as the sovereign, and this authority isn't absolute but is exercised within the limits of a representative constitutional democracy. The sovereign will of the people is checked by a constitution, as well as by human rights, elected representation, and public discussion and debate. Such a formation, Jackson argues, keeps the sovereign from becoming dictatorial or totalitarian. Finally, there is the *existential* approach to sovereignty, as exhibited by Jens Bartelson's *A Genealogy of Sovereignty* (1993). Bartelson sees sovereignty as emerging from a dialectical conflict rather than descending from a unity or from a constitution. For Bartelson, the sovereign comes into existence only as it overcomes this conflict. Here, sovereignty is not perpetual, as it is in the classical model, but must be installed in a united national will, and

---

1. *Oxford English Dictionary*, s.v. "sovereignty."

the primary aim of sovereignty here is not so much *decision* as it is *recognition*. The sovereign state is recognized as the manifestation of true "Man." These approaches have value, yet none of them takes up the topic of sovereignty from an African American religious and cultural-critical viewpoint.

Indeed, throughout US slave society, into Jim Crow segregation, and even in our present post–civil rights era, African American life has been determined by three critical categories, namely, *sovereignty*, modernist conceptions of *race*, and *American expansionism*, that is, the American empire. In disciplines such as history, sociology, and philosophy, African American scholars have contested these categories insofar as they determine African American experience. However, when compared to European reflections on dynamics of sovereignty, race, and empire operating in the culture wars of the eighteenth and nineteenth centuries and the Holocaust of the early twentieth century, surprisingly few African American religious thinkers have produced political theologies given nearly four hundred years of experience under American imperial expansionism, slavery, and oppression. This book is a contribution to the theorization of an African American public theology that critiques the categories of sovereignty, race, and the American empire from deconstructive moves derived from Cornel West's analysis of power and his account of radical democracy, especially as voiced in his *Democracy Matters* (2004). This book critiques not only the categories determinate of the American empire but also historical narratives of resistance produced, circulating, and reproduced throughout current African American religious discourse on the American empire. My fundamental thesis is that the cultural logic of sovereignty is the prerequisite political practice and theory for modern imperial expansionism.

Four scenarios have pushed this questioning. They are mass incarceration, Abu Ghraib, Guantanamo Bay, and the Texas-Mexico border. They display what West calls *antidemocratic dogmas*: the dogmas of free-market fundamentalism, aggressive militarism, and escalating authoritarianism.[2] At Abu Ghraib, a largely illegally detained Muslim population was brutally tortured. Prisoners were demeaned and degraded as they were forcefully subjected to

---

2. See Cornel West, *Democracy Matters: Winning the Fight against Imperialism* (New York: Penguin Books, 2004), 3–7. On Abu Ghraib, see Seymour M. Hersh, "Torture at Abu Ghraib," *New Yorker*, April 30, 2004, https://tinyurl.com/mr7rscbd. Drafted in 1863 and revised in 1949, the Geneva Conventions commit all participating states to humane treatment of POWs, civilians, and the sick or injured who find themselves in enemy hands. The conventions forbid various sorts of cruel treatment, including but not limited to insult upon dignity, mutilation, murder, and torture. The Department of Justice ruled that the Geneva Conventions did not apply to the US conflict with Al-Qaeda.

sexual stylizations and religious sacrilege after the Department of Justice set aside the Geneva Conventions. At Guantanamo Bay, detainees were subjected to similar conditions of religious abuse, sleep deprivation, starvation, and waterboarding. National security beat out basic rights against unlawful imprisonment and violated *habeas corpus*, a fundamental tenet of US jurisprudence, as is also the case at the Texas-Mexico border and with mass incarceration. These scenarios rightfully engender questions regarding recent US military, political, and economic practices. Moreover, these antidemocratic dogmas call into question America's rational structures of justificatory conditions, that is, its founding narratives of a "City on a Hill," of a "Christian nation," and of the "land of liberty." America imagines itself as distinct from Europe in that its models for civic virtue emerged from Bible-based Puritan churches rather than solely from Greco-Roman philosophy and art. Europe vied to recover antique glory, but the New England colonies existed for the glory of the Christian God. The treatment of prisoners at Abu Ghraib; Guantanamo Bay; Eagle Pass, Texas; and Louisiana State Penitentiary suggests that US society despairs of nihilism, meaning that *the highest values devaluate themselves*, the goal is lacking, and the answer is lacking to our *why*. We have found that our values are worthless, our ends do not give our lives any purpose, and pleasures do not give us happiness.[3]

The object of inquiry for African American public theology is the everyday life of Black folk, primarily within, but not limited to, the US context. Rather than a scientific discipline or field of study, Victor Anderson notes, "African American public theology is a genre of writing, a textuality, and a mode of discourse that seeks to effectively transform African American life through religious and cultural criticism toward the satisfaction of basic categorical needs and critically interrogated religious goals." The libations poured out for the limits of logical-empirical research, especially since Hans-Georg Gadamer's hermeneutics of "horizons" (*Truth and Method*, 1975), prompt a turn to hermeneutical-phenomenological approaches in the study of religion.[4] The work of Charles Long and Victor Anderson frames my own approach, rooting my African American public theology in the empirical givenness of the world (*Erlebnis* and *Erfahrung*), and seeking to understand a world interpreted, that

---

3. A paraphrase of philosopher Walter Kaufman's interpretation of Nietzsche. See Walter Kaufman, *Nietzsche: Philosopher, Psychologist, Antichrist* (Princeton: Princeton University Press, 2013).

4. Victor Anderson, "Theorizing African American Religion," in *African American Studies*, ed. Jeanette R. Davidson (Edinburgh: University of Edinburgh Press, 2010), 260–78. Also see Alexander Rosenberg, *Philosophy of Social Science*, 4th ed. (Boulder, CO: Westview, 2012), 14.

is, a world-making and world disclosure through worldviews (*Weltanschauungen*) and picturings (*Anschauungen*) from an African American religious perspective. In this way African American public theology listens for lifeworlds (*Lebenswelten*) or world-horizons (*Welthorizonte*) of cultures. Here, faith plays a double role, both as pragmatic understanding (*Verstehen*) of social reality by way of the commonsense practices of people, and as a work of understanding of spiritual reality by the Holy Spirit. Through the power of the Spirit, we are able to reorient our personalities to affirm self-worth and the worth of others, even in the silence of absolute contingency. Humanity can of itself accomplish much, but this tells us little of its meaning and significance. Faith cries out in angry opposition to God and simultaneously refuses to compete with God. Faith directs us away from doubt, fear, and shame and affirms the noninstrumental worth of self, of others, and of the created, choreographed world. It is still common among Black folk to cease activity to listen when there's thunder, lightning, or other signs that "the Lord is doing his work."[5]

Sovereignty: The Five Powers

This story of sovereignty doesn't begin in America or in Africa, but in western Europe, from whence America receives its cultural logic. The term "sovereignty" emerged in the thirteenth century in France, where Philippe de Beaumanoir's (ca. 1246–1296) law book *Coutumes de Beauvaisis* (ca. 1279–1283) uses the term *souverains*. Yet its meaning is ambiguous, indicating both the supremacy of a king over his realm and that of barons over their baronies. According to Robert Jackson, the term initially had a range of meanings, including the mayor or provost of a town, a husband in relation to his domicile, and the superior of a monastery.[6] In the fifteenth century, the term came to have singular reference to states—a distinct set of political institutions concerned with the organization of power and domination and a group of people occupying areas under the rule of one government.[7] This occurred first among the "Five Powers" of Renaissance Italy. In the wake of the collapse of the Holy Roman

---

5. See C. Eric Lincoln's "The Racial Factor in the Shaping of Religion in America," in *African American Religious Thought: An Anthology*, ed. Cornel West and Eddie S. Glaude Jr. (Louisville: Westminster John Knox, 2003).

6. See Robert Jackson's *Sovereignty: The Evolution of an Idea* (Malden, MA: Polity, 2007).

7. See Ian McLean and Alistair McMillan, *Oxford Concise Dictionary of Politics* (New York: Oxford University Press, 1996, 2003), and the *Shorter Oxford English Dictionary: On Historical Principles* (New York: Oxford University Press, 1973, 2007).

Empire, the Italian powers of Naples, Florence, Venice, Milan, and the Papal States became the first recognizably sovereign city-states in the early modern period. Each state was self-governed according to its own rules, customs, and forms of government. The Italian Renaissance sovereigns were prosperous for a time, but this arrangement broke down with the Wars of Italy (1494–1529), as the city-states banded together against one of their own—Milan. Yet, even as the Italian city-states crumbled, the idea of sovereignty as state sovereignty became more pervasive and would come to apply to western European nation-states. Robert Jackson explains that the meaning of sovereignty during the sixteenth century was grounded on three premises: "that the land surface of the planet is partitioned into a number of separate bordered territories, that certain determinate authority is supreme over all other authorities in each territory, and that those supreme authorities are independent of all foreign authorities."[8]

Sovereignty Reborn: Monarchial State Sovereignty

Early modern intellectual, social, and political changes made possible new discourses on sovereignty, not only about the general idea of state sovereignty but also about the *locus* of sovereignty within the state. For example, until the mid-sixteenth century, sovereignty referred not only to state sovereignty but also to the idea that the monarch was the sovereign within the state. Sovereignty referred primarily to the doctrine of the divine right of kings, placing sovereignty squarely in the person of the monarch to yield monarchial states. Thus, legal theorist Jean Bodin (1530–1596) theorized sovereignty (*summum imperium/summa rerum*) in support of the Queen Mother Catherine of Medici and the French Catholic establishment. "The first attribute of the sovereign prince," says Bodin, "is the power to make law binding on all his subjects in general and on each in particular.... He does so without the consent of any superior, equal, or inferior being necessary ... [sovereignty] lasts the lifetime of the sovereign, and subjects cannot resist or disobey the monarch, even under the 'pretext that honour and justice require it.'"[9] Bodin's theory of monarchial sovereignty remains canonical: "I see the sovereignty of the state involved in five *functions*. One, and it is the principal one, is creating the most important

---

8. Jackson, *Sovereignty*, 22, 46.
9. Jean Bodin, *Six Books of the Commonwealth*, trans. M. J. Tooley (Oxford: Blackwell, 1955), 43. For Bodin's discussion on sovereignty, see 25–36.

magistrates and defining the office of each one; the second, proclaiming and annulling laws; the third, declaring war and peace; the fourth, receiving final appeal from all magistrates; the last, the power of life and death when the law itself leaves no room for extenuation or grace."[10] Bodin's theory of monarchial state sovereignty signified the emergence of the discourse of sovereignty in political theory. Bodin's discourse was only possible given the idea of the sovereign state itself. Historian Ernst H. Kantorowicz has shown how early modern jurists played a role in this process as they developed secularized concepts of the state as "sempiternal sovereign, corporate bodies" that existed independently of both absolutist rulers and state subjects.[11] Kantorowicz's *The King's Two Bodies* argues that during this time (ca. 1600–1800), the notion of "*corpus mysticum*" (the mystical body), grafted from Christian angelology, endowed the state with a "halo" of autonomous value. In this way, the state itself became a legitimate authority alongside the monarch and, indeed, would outlive the age of kings altogether. The singular, self-progenerating, sempiternal, and even divine nature of the state was most frequently depicted with the metaphor of the Phoenix, that mythical creature who, after setting his own nest ablaze and perishing in the flames, resurrected himself from his own funeral pyre to soar once again. For all its links to angelology, state sovereignty implied conflict with and a break from the *respublica Christiana*. Jackson argues that these early modern conflicts between the Holy Roman Empire and states were between two conceptions of public life: one organized on a universal theological-political vision and another constructed on the foundations of separate kingdoms, the intimation of an international stage. Thus a Western political *imperium* beyond the jurisdiction of the *respublica Christiana* of Christendom emerged for the first time in 1,500 years. The "idea of state sovereignty sorted out the ... confusion around the question of authority and law ... in the late Middle Ages [as r]ulers escaped from the cosmopolitan authority of *respublica Christiana* by successfully enforcing royal authority over both church and state."[12]

Roughly two centuries after the Italian city-states, then, states rejected the jurisdiction of western European Catholicism and embraced their own independence. They were sovereign, that is, autonomous and mutually recognizing.

10. Jean Bodin, *Method for the Easy Comprehension of History*, trans. Beatrice Reynolds (New York: Columbia University Press, 1566, 1945), 172–73.

11. Ernst H. Kantorowicz, *The King's Two Bodies: A Study in Mediaeval Political Theology* (Princeton: Princeton University Press, 1997), 304. *Corpus mysticum* is used interchangeably with *universitas*, corporation sole, *corpus politicum*, or body politic.

12. Jackson, *Sovereignty*, 47–55.

The Global Leviathan Appears

Historically, this was symbolized by the Peace of Westphalia (1648), established at the end of the Thirty Years' War (1618-1648). Each sovereign state controlled its own affairs, and together they composed an international system of western European society.[13] Political theorist Wendy Brown articulates other key features and hallmarks of state sovereignty that emerged during this time and that remain with us even today, if in fragments: state supremacy (there is no higher power than the state), the state's perpetuity over time (the state has no term limits), state decisionism (the state is not bounded by or submitted to the law), state absoluteness and completeness (the state's sovereignty isn't probable or partial), nontransferability of sovereign authority (sovereignty cannot be conferred without canceling itself), and sovereign jurisdiction and territory (sovereignty has *both* a limited scope *and* the ability to define inside and outside).[14] From an African and African diasporic perspective, this is important because the idea of sovereignty was the most pervasive political idea as western Europe began its projects of imperial expansion and colonization, which included African colonization and the Atlantic slave trade. Even as western Europeans encountered dynamic and internally vibrant societies in Africa, the principle of sovereignty would justify colonization, Christianization, and commercialization of the continent.

Enlightened Sovereignty: Rational Proprietary Sovereignty

During the Enlightenment, the locus of political sovereignty would shift yet again from the state *qua* monarchial state to "the people." Key political documents here are the US Declaration of Independence (1776) and the French Declaration of the Rights of Man and Citizen (1789). Key theorists include Jean-Jacques Rousseau, Immanuel Kant, and John Locke. Both key documents lay out the self-evident rights of men—women were excluded on both occasions—and emphasize the *inalienability* of natural rights. The documents place the property of nontransferability on human persons rather than the state. Among the theorists, Locke's thinking has had the most formative and lasting impact on the American democratic experiment. Locke argued for proprietary sovereignty of the individual, and this sovereignty came with an underside for Africans in America, namely, Locke's doctrine of natural inequality, predicated on what Locke believed to be the rationality of man. Here, sovereignty moves

---

13. Jackson, *Sovereignty*, 55.
14. Wendy Brown, *Walled States, Waning Sovereignty* (New York: Zone Books, 2014), 22.

from a solely political concept to a proprietary and economic one, and this, combined with Locke's doctrine of natural inequality among rational, laboring men and irrational, enslaved ones, served to effectively theorize a doctrine of natural sovereignty. Sovereignty is no longer merely political, but it is also natural, extending over both men and property. This shift is difficult to perceive for many people because the thrust of Locke's argument is a defense of liberty and democracy, and directed against monarchial sovereignty (*dominium*), and because Locke also argues for constitutional rights. Yet, Locke's theory of property dictates that rational and industrious labor is what gives value to things in the world and what gives authority to acquire property for oneself, away from the commons. Land is for "the use of the Industrious and Rational . . . not to the Fancy or Covetousness of the Quarrelsom and Contentious."[15]

Locke's theories of proprietary sovereignty and natural inequality justified not only bourgeois property ownership against disenfranchised English classes but also American colonial slavery. The English landscape had been in the process of transformation for roughly a century before the capitalist social order of Locke's time emerged. Pastures once available to entire parish administrative districts for grazing cattle were enclosed and declared the private property of the lords of manors. Land enclosures were unlawful in England apart from the consent of the common will, but now they were maintained, fortified, and secured by state law. Disenfranchised farmers of the common lands became agricultural proletarians, beggars, robbers, or paupers, and English Parliament created the first modern ghettos to "remedy" the disturbances caused by the ensuing peasant riots. The newly impoverished class was confined to the ghettos, and wanderers were whipped, branded, or mutilated. Against the disenfranchised classes, then, Locke sanctified and naturalized property ownership for the emergent bourgeoisie apart from the consent of the common will. In the American colonies, Locke's natural philosophy had direct connections to developments in plantation slave labor. Locke had a personal hand in the drafting of the Fundamental Constitutions of Carolina, a document that granted every free white man "absolute power and Authority over his Negro slaves."[16] Thus, we must demythologize the extent to which the Enlightenment meant

---

15. John Locke, *Two Treatises of Government*, ed. Peter Laslett (Cambridge: Cambridge University Press, 1960, 1999), bk. 2, chap. 5, sec. 34, p. 291. Also see bk. 2, chap. 5, sec. 31, and bk. 2, chap. 5, sec. 28.

16. See "The Fundamental Constitutions of Carolina," March 1, 1669, Yale Law School, Lillian Goldman Law Library, The Avalon Project: The Fundamental Constitutions of Carolina: March 1, 1669 (yale.edu). For counterargument, see James Farr's "Locke, Natural Law and New World Slavery," *Political Theory* 36, no. 4 (August 2008): 495–522. Farr argues that

the end of sovereignty, for what Locke's theory shows us is that sovereignty migrated from the state to the white plantation and property owner. In Locke's thinking, the white property owner becomes sovereign. He has agreed to a social contract and limits his powers by way of constitutions, but the theory of proprietary *dominium* requires that the constitution maintain supreme power over African American bodies.

In Locke's natural philosophy we see not only the sovereignty of the white property owner but also the persistence of the *cultural logic* of sovereignty in his doctrine of natural inequality. The cultural logic of sovereignty refers to the phenomenon where the absolute powers of life and death—the power to ensure, maintain, develop, or deny life—are isolated into one particular order of social identity. Those in society that are seen as mere "bare life" (*zen*) rather than good life (*eu zen*) are included by way of an exclusion. My understanding of the cultural logic of sovereignty draws from philosopher Giorgio Agamben, who identifies it in Western politics: "Western politics first constitutes itself through an exclusion (which is simultaneously an inclusion) of bare life . . . life presents itself as what is included by means of an exclusion. . . . In Western politics, bare life has the peculiar privilege of being that whose exclusion founds the city of men. . . . The living [human] has *logos* by taking away and conserving its own voice in [the *polis*], even as it dwells in the polis by letting its own bare life be excluded, as an exception, within it."[17] Agamben discusses how the logic of sovereignty still circulates throughout modern societies (in the form of the ban), an event where one is abandoned by both human and divine law.[18] This can be considered an accurate description of the status of African Americans in Locke's thinking, as African Americans are socially excluded from US society by way of a cultural logic of sovereignty. This same cultural logic of sovereignty is seen in the thinking of Thomas Jefferson, who argued that whites were superior to Blacks based on natural law.[19] "It will probably be asked," says Jefferson in his 1781 *Notes on the State of Virginia*,

> Why not retain and incorporate the blacks into the state, and thus save the experience of supplying, by importation of white settlers, the vacancies they

---

Locke did *not* justify slavery. Also see Locke, *Two Treatises of Government*, bk. 2, chap. 2, secs. 8 and 10.

17. Giorgio Agamben, *Homo Sacer: Sovereign Power and Bare Life*, trans. Daniel Heller-Roazen (Stanford, CA: Stanford University Press, 1998), 7–8.

18. Agamben, *Homo Sacer*, 28.

19. See Victor Anderson, *Beyond Ontological Blackness: An Essay on African American Religious and Cultural Criticism* (New York: Continuum, 1998).

will leave? Deep rooted prejudices entertained by the whites; ten thousand recollections, by the blacks, of the injuries they have sustained . . . the real distinctions which nature has made; and many other circumstances, will divide us into parties, and produce convulsions which will probably never end but in the extermination of the one or the other race. . . . With the Romans, the regular method of taking the evidence of their slaves was under torture. . . . Yet notwithstanding these and other discouraging circumstances among the Romans, their slaves were often their rarest artists. . . . But they were of the race of whites. It is not their condition then, but nature, which has produced the distinction.[20]

Up to this point, Jefferson has been only suggesting what he finally makes explicit in a section on Virginia law, one where his state of nature doctrine and the cultural logic of sovereignty exclude blacks from the state:

I advance it therefore as a suspicion only, that the blacks, whether originally a distinct race, or made distinct by time and circumstances, are inferior to the whites in the endowments both of body and mind. . . . This unfortunate difference of colour, and perhaps of faculty, is a powerful obstacle to the emancipation of these people. Many of their advocates, while they wish to vindicate the liberty of human nature, are anxious also to preserve its dignity and beauty. Some of these, embarrassed by the question "What further is to be done with them?" join themselves in opposition with those who are actuated by sordid avarice only. Among the Romans emancipation required but one effort. The slave, when made free, might mix with, without staining the blood of his master. But with us a second is necessary, unknown to history. When freed, he is to be removed beyond the reach of mixture.[21]

Thus, the intellectual roots of America simultaneously declare that all persons are created equal and that African American slaves are to be segregated and only count as three-fifths of a person for individual states' representation in Congress. Jefferson's logic of sovereignty emerged from natural law thinking, vetted by Lockean Enlightenment reason, which argued for the universal natural rights of all. Yet Jefferson denied Blacks constitutional protections because of a perceived natural inferiority. This culturally constructed boundary

---

20. Thomas Jefferson, "Notes on the State of Virginia," electronic ed. (Philadelphia: Prichard & Hall, 1787, 2006), 147, https://tinyurl.com/bddtt37v.

21. Jefferson, "Notes on the State of Virginia," 153.

justified the exclusion of Blacks from the American body politic. Race and ethnic divisions frame the American democratic ethos and practices. This ethos and set of practices display the determinacy of sovereignty and imperialism based on a plutocracy oriented toward violence. It is a violence that operates in "the discipline(ing) and punish(ing)" of the Other, locally and globally. The logic of sovereignty is problematic not only in its significations on Black and brown bodies, but also in its justification of governmentality, that is, those practices that deliberately seek, in authoritarian fashion, to direct, guide, or control others' conduct. In turn, these operations of sovereign power as authoritarian governmentality frustrate processes of successful cultural fulfillment, not only for African American life but also for the prospects of American democratic society.

Existential Sovereignty: The Sovereign Dictator

In the thinking of early twentieth-century political theologian Carl Schmitt, the discourse on sovereignty rejects the classical and enlightened approaches for an existential one. Schmitt's theory of sovereignty was not concerned with the preservation of monarchial power as Bodin's was, nor with bourgeois property and social institutions as Locke's was, but with what he perceived to be a matter of survival against an imminent threat to both Germany and the very *cosmos* itself. This threat was embodied in early twentieth-century revolutionary European politics as accompanied by an apocalyptic ethos. Schmitt's prime case example was the 1917 Russian Bolshevik Revolution, where labor unions had not only disempowered the Russian state with the general strike but also permanently ended czarist rule in Russia after nearly five hundred years. He saw this event as a sign that both law and the state were losing their legitimacy. His writings attempted to restore a waning state authority by way of sovereignty. Yet Schmitt was no friend of the modern liberal state, either. He was an antimodernist on most accounts, primarily because he believed that Enlightenment-era thinkers denied the reality of the cosmic spiritual conflict that stood behind revolutionary politics. "Nothing is more modern than the onslaught against the political. American financiers, industrial technicians, Marxist socialists, and anarchic syndicalist revolutionaries unite in demanding that the biased rule of politics over unbiased economic management be done away with. There must no longer be political problems."[22] Schmitt thus

---

22. Carl Schmitt, *Political Theology* (Chicago: University of Chicago Press, 2005), 65–66.

denounced modern democracy, the Enlightenment, and the scientific perspective on reality altogether. Both Enlightenment-era democrats and parliamentarians failed to comprehend the absolute spiritual depravity of *everyone*, since all were caught up and implicated in the battle. They also failed to see that the cosmic battle was spilling over into politics, only making more real the threat of a decisive, bloody, destructive battle for true faith and goodness.

Schmitt argued that the political sovereign should be instituted as the office of the dictator, but this was based on an existential perspective. His own response emerged from French counterrevolutionary thinkers like Joseph de Maistre (1753–1821) and Louise de Bonald (1754–1840) and Spanish Catholic theologian Juan Donoso Cortés (1809–1853). These thinkers gave Schmitt his language about the world as the site for a cosmic spiritual-political conflict of good against evil, between the forces of Satan and those of the Christian God. Schmitt also called this "the political." "The political" doesn't refer to politics, polity, the state, or anything related to modern political theory at all. Nor does it refer to an accommodationist attitude among a secular state and a democratically oriented public theology. "The political," and thus also Schmitt's "political theology," refers to a cosmological perspective marked by the reality of a definitive, decisive, and permanent cosmic conflict, one that forces humanity to draw hard-and-fast lines between friends and enemies. Here is where the cultural logic of sovereignty appears in Schmitt's thinking. Political theology's controlling metaphor is "the political," which Schmitt defines as "the utmost degree of intensity of a union or separation, of an association or dissociation" and its accompanying "friend/enemy" distinction.[23] Political theology's controlling logic is the logic of sovereignty, as exhibited in the friend/enemy distinction. It signifies the most extreme antagonism and thus the most decisive one, surpassing aesthetic, moral, or economic differences, and serving as the key uniting factor. Schmitt's own friend/enemy distinction was constructed on an anti-Jewish, anti-Semitic, German Christian–nationalist myth. Schmitt's friend/enemy distinction incited an unprecedented wave of anti-Semitic cultural violence and cacophony that finally crashed with the Allies' interruption of the German holocaust at the end of World War II.

Thus, we see that although the language of sovereignty has been associated with Western states since the Renaissance, the discourse on sovereignty has

---

23. Carl Schmitt, *The Concept of the Political* (Chicago: University of Chicago Press, 1932), 26. Also see Heinrich Meir, *The Lesson of Carl Schmitt: Four Chapters on the Distinction between Political Theology and Political Philosophy* (Chicago: University of Chicago Press, 1998), 34.

not been uniform over time. Nor can the history of discourse on sovereignty be traced in a straight line. Philosopher Jens Bartleson follows the thinking of philosopher Michel Foucault to show how the discourse on sovereignty has shifted in tandem with changes in *episteme* and thus also with changes in cosmological and ontological frames.[24] During the Renaissance (ca. 1400–1600), discourse on state sovereignty was framed by a cosmology of resemblance (between the Renaissance period and various pasts). State sovereignty was articulated in response to the ethical negativity beyond the state (for example, piracy), a negativity that simply didn't exist in the universal cosmology of the *respublica Christiana*. During the classical age (ca. 1600–1800), state sovereignty was articulated as *interest* and *power* within a cosmology of *mathesis*, or "simple naturism," alongside other states, which are tabulated, calculated, and taxonomized. In the modern age (ca. 1800–), state sovereignty is articulated as the integrity of a pure national identity, within a cosmology of "the dialectic," that is, of conflict and war. Thus today, state sovereignty may be understood as the supremacy, autonomy, particularity, and individuality of nation-states in an international society of firm demarcations of what is inside and outside a particular territory. Yet alongside state sovereignty, the question of the cultural logic of sovereignty has appeared. In political theology, the question of sovereignty is answered according to the cultural logic of the political, where the state is an existential entity, a product of a dialectical conflict within the very nature of existence, and where states relate to one another in cosmic wars, spiritual battles, or apocalyptic "last stands."

There are at least three approaches to sovereignty. The most glaring similarity among them is sovereignty's power to designate inside/outside boundaries and spaces. This has implications for territoriality, property, land, and bodies. Yet approaches to sovereignty differ on key points. There is the renaissance approach, represented by Bodin, in which state sovereignty comes forth in its decisionistic and enduring features such as perpetuity and absoluteness. Sovereignty comes forth as a solitary eternal will from on high, set to order the world accordingly. This final authority is absolute, as in Bodin's model, and the sovereign has *summum imperium*. In the enlightened approach to the question of sovereignty, the state is constituted against the monarchial will and consists

---

24. Jens Bartleson, *A Genealogy of Sovereignty* (Cambridge: Cambridge University Press, 1995), 49–52, 189–91. Also see Michel Foucault's *The Archaeology of Knowledge and the Discourse on Language*, trans. A. M. Sherida Smith (New York: Vintage Books, 1972, 2010), 191–92, and Foucault's *The Order of Things: An Archaeology of the Human Sciences* (New York: Vintage Books, 1970, 1994).

of electoral, representative, and constitutional democracy as well as a parliamentary government. Yet sovereignty reappears as proprietary sovereignty, where one has *dominium* over property, and alongside proprietary sovereignty, the cultural logic of sovereignty appears as the doctrine of natural inequality. Locke's basic distinction between the rational property owner and slave justified conditions where white property owners had absolute dominion over land enclosures, English peasant classes, and "Negro slaves." (A similar "master/slave" cultural logic appears in the early nineteenth-century philosophy of G. W. F. Hegel.) In the existential approach to sovereignty, politics emerges from a cosmic dialectical conflict, one that the state must overcome through a sovereign dictator. In material reality, sovereignty is not perpetual but must be installed in a united (national) will, and the primary aim of sovereignty here is not so much decision as recognition, recognition of the state as manifestation of true faith and true humanity. The cultural logic of sovereignty here appears as nationalism, oriented on a friend/enemy distinction.

Sovereignty in Economy: Global Technological Rationality

Today, the sovereign state system is global but precarious, but the cultural logic of sovereignty exerts increasing force in global civil society. Political theorist Stephen D. Krasner highlights the global nature of state sovereignty, noting that postcolonial developments in the British and French successor states, as well as in most successor states to other European empires, "generally conform with the Westphalian model.... If the Third World is examined, events suggest that ... sovereignty [is] embedded."[25] Indeed, postcolonialism meant that virtually every state in Africa, Asia, and Latin America rejected modern European colonialism and acquired sovereignty. Yet this moment also signaled the decline of state sovereignty as a global system of political organization. Bartleson argues that the key feature of state sovereignty, its "parergonality," or its ability to frame things as inside and outside, is fading. "The problem of sovereignty resembles the problem of the parergon in aesthetic discourse ... a frame, a line of demarcation, an ontological divide, or a geographical ... boundary all manifest class membership of phenomena ... the discourse of sovereignty functions according to the same logic as the parergon.... [Today,] the parergonal divide between the domestic and international spheres is in-

---

25. Stephen D. Krasner, *Sovereignty: Organized Hypocrisy* (Princeton: Princeton University Press, 1999), 201.

creasingly blurred... this [is] a loss of parergonality."[26] Historian Adam Burns observes the practical loss of European autonomy after the US occupation of Axis territories in Germany (and the whole of Japan), after 1945.[27] This erosion continued with the 1947 creation of the Organization for European Economic Cooperation (OEEC), which initiated the European Union (EU), a supranational economic arrangement that compromises member state autonomy and territoriality. In these ways, the concept of sovereignty is in many ways a dead concept, an outdated concept, one ripe for the trash bin. But not so with the cultural logic of sovereignty.

The argument that states' sovereignty is waning may seem incorrect given the increased phenomena of neo-fascism in Western countries and the erection of walls between states. Political theorist Wendy Brown argues that state sovereignty is indeed waning despite increased efforts to build walls at state borders.[28] Our globalized world now harbors tensions between opening and barricading, fusion and partition, erasure and reinscription. The proliferating phenomenon of state "walling" is novel in that the walls aren't built at the command of traditional Westphalian sovereigns, but in response to transnational mobility that points to decreased state power and a post-Westphalian world. Brown argues that these walls are "performances of sovereignty" in response to the decline of state sovereignty due to both global political economy and the rise in the legitimation and conduct of religious violence. Nation-states are erecting border walls, barriers, and other modes of enclosure as a performance of a bygone era. Since the 1960s, transnational flows of capital, people, and ideas have compromised the sovereignty of the nation-state. The same may be said of emergent neo-fascism. Political theorist Jennifer Van Bergen sees fascism as a threat to state sovereignty: "The PATRIOT Act creates a structure that allows too much power in the executive branch. The Act creates an enabling structure for fascism and oligarchy. It is a structure that could consume democracy. The mere existence of such a structure in our government should alarm us."[29] She uses "Britt's list"—a widely reputed list that notes the marks of fascist government—and concludes, "it is no stretch to call the Bush government fascist."[30] Faith Agostinone-Wilson sees the same tendency in

---

26. Bartleson, *A Genealogy of Sovereignty*, 49–52, 189–91.

27. Adam Burns, *American Imperialism: The Territorial Expansion of the United States, 1783–2013* (Edinburgh: Edinburgh University Press, 2017), 146.

28. Brown, *Walled States, Waning Sovereignty*, 39, 23, 247–48.

29. Jennifer Van Bergen, *The Twilight of Democracy: The Bush Plan for America* (Monroe, ME: Common Courage, 2005), 110.

30. Van Bergen, *The Twilight of Democracy*, 76.

neo-fascism as promoted by Steve Bannon and the Proud Boys, noting "links between neoliberalism, fascism, and authoritarianism, which involve the dismantling of democracy."[31]

Yet even as state sovereignty wanes, the specter of sovereignty remains with us in the contemporary postmodern moment, as well as the cultural logic of sovereignty. State sovereignty in our times has been surrendered to the global market, but sovereignty now appears as *rationality*, that is, a way of thinking about things and a set of values. Political economist David Harvey notes how the global market has transformed the nation-state into a market state, or what he also calls the "neo-liberal state." Coordinating structures emerge across a transnational field to guarantee international agreements between states and freedom of trade. They also assume responsibilities for protecting the rule of law, yet their relationship to the United Nations and the International Court of Justice remains unclear. These market-coordinating structures include the World Bank, the International Monetary Fund (IMF), and the World Trade Organization (WTO). These institutions work to coordinate international trade, but in so doing they divest states, and the people, of their publicly owned assets, turning the assets over to private owners. Private owners and coordinating structures thus control state development policies, effectively removing the resources from the hands of the people. Land enclosures toward private, rather than state, ownership are encouraged and the primary task of government is to secure the conditions for the possibility of continued market development. This means that the state must help to establish the market as a game of competitive freedom. Practically, this means state policies that destroy public facilities such as public housing, urban development agencies, community clinics for poor people, public spaces like parks and playgrounds, labor unions. This also meant a rollback of New Deal policies during the late twentieth century in the United States, and thus fewer forms of unemployment relief, fewer public works projects, and less small business support. Policies now tend to create government-business consortia, and workfare, as opposed to welfare policies.[32]

Although international trade-coordinating structures have emerged across the globe since the 1960s, these institutions do not themselves possess sovereignty. Instead, they operate according to neoliberal rationality, also called

---

31. Faith Agostinone-Wilson, *Enough Already! A Socialist Feminist Response to the Reemergence of Right-Wing Populism and Fascism in Media* (Leiden: Brill, 2020).

32. Jason Hackworth, *The Neoliberal City: Governance, Ideology, and Development in American Urbanism* (Ithaca, NY: Cornell University Press, 2007), 11.

"risk-rationality" by, for example, social theorist Mitchell Dean, and "cost-benefit analysis" by, for example, policy theorist Deborah Stone. The commonality among them is that they point to how market rationality operates by way of the principle of "catallaxy," a term that entrepreneur and Christian ethicist Charles McDaniel defines as "the idea that the dynamics of exchange, when reinforced by certain cultural institutions, is sufficient to guide society to desired ends without need for the collective ordering of those ends."[33] Yet these dynamics operate according to the logic of sovereignty. According to Stone, the United States first began using cost-benefit analysis in 1936 in the army. Personnel were tasked with evaluating alternative means for achieving a goal by tallying the negative consequences of certain actions against the positive consequences to bring forth the true value of an action.[34] What began as a test case for problem solving in military contexts has, since the early twentieth century, come to exercise increasing authority over state policy. In everyday politics, this means that risk rationality decides various matters of "social" insurance, entitlements, health care, and even education. It also means that risk rationality creates bonds of solidarity like those in political communities, that is, a nation, with the power to unite and divide citizens of a country. Dean describes how risk rationality determines insurability among populations, deducing risk through calculating reason by way of statistical tables, probability figures, or background.[35] Risk rationality may also appear as epidemiological risk (morbidity/mortality rates) or case-management risk, where "at-risk" persons are subject to detention, incarceration, or medicalization without due process.

Discussions about the divestment of public state resources according to the sovereign dictates of technological rationality often ignore how this relates to the church and religion. While not all changes in religion are linked to the supremacy of cost-benefit rationality, there are some connections between the global shift away from state sovereignty and transformations in US religion. Religious movements like the prosperity gospel, Word of Faith, and the Christian Right were blessed by the sovereign calculus. Yet social ethicist Helene Slessarev-Jamir

---

33. Charles McDaniel, *God and Money: The Moral Challenge of Capitalism* (Lanham, MD: Rowman & Littlefield, 2006), 11.

34. Deborah Stone, *Policy Paradox: The Art of Political Decision-Making* (New York: Norton, 2012), 248–50.

35. See Mitchell Dean, *Governmentality: Power and Rule in Modern Society* (Thousand Oaks, CA: Sage, 1999, 2009); Mitchell Dean, *Governing Societies* (New York: Open University Press, 2007); and Michel Foucault, *The Birth of BioPolitics: Lectures at the College de France, 1978–1979*, ed. Michel Senellart (New York: Palgrave Macmillan, 2004).

notes how neoliberal policies have led to the decline of local congregational and social institutional membership, as well as prophetic religious activism, especially since the 1990s.[36] As neoliberal policies both displace local policies and gentrify the local population, one major effect has been unprecedented global migration. In 2011, "there [were] roughly 200 million immigrants scattered across the globe. . . . Some are refugees, but the majority are labor migrants whose traditional means of earning a livelihood have been penetrated by capital intensive production into less developed economies."[37] As public institutions are destroyed and as private institutions proliferate, civil rights organizations, unions, and activist elements in religious denominations have declined. "As the processes of neighborhood demographic transition accelerated in the 1970s, many community organizations, which had relied on what was considered a stable membership base, began to find it increasingly difficult to turn out the large numbers required to carry out actions against local business or political leaders."[38] The decline in religious and social voluntarism has led to the shrinkage of community organizing in civil society, including local networks of mutual aid and collective service, religious activism, and the family.

The sovereignty of market rationality yields a particular social ordering, exhibited in our postmodern moment by the civilized individual over against the collectivist savage. This dichotomy comes from economist Friedrich Hayek, lead scholar for neoclassical liberal, or neoliberal, economics. For Hayek, the civilized human, a.k.a. the entrepreneur, undergoes a cultural evolution by way of competitions, such that competition becomes the primary value for the individual. In so doing, the civilized human must leave behind natural instincts for collectivism, solidarity, altruism, and trust. Because civilized humans don't give in to instinctual desire but are instead guided by a Stoic disciplining of themselves according to the rules of individual responsibility, they are justified in ownership of land, of several properties, and wage labor is justified. "Continued obedience to the command to treat all men as neighbors would have prevented the growth to an extended order. For those now living within the extended order gain *not* from treating one another as neighbors, and by applying, in their interactions, rules of the extended order—such as those of several property and contract—instead of the rules of solidarity and altruism."[39] For

---

36. Helene Slessarev-Jamir, *Prophetic Activism: Progressive Religious Justice Movements in Contemporary America* (New York: New York University Press, 2011), 80–85.

37. Slessarev-Jamir, *Prophetic Activism*, 80.

38. Slessarev-Jamir, *Prophetic Activism*, 78.

39. F. A. Hayek, *The Fatal Conceit: The Errors of Socialism*, ed. W. W. Bartley III (Chicago: University of Chicago Press, 1991), 13.

Hayek, lands that were once designated for public parks, public housing, urban development agencies, community clinics for poor people, playgrounds, and meeting spaces for labor unions, religious activists, and local volunteer groups have been handed over to private competitors. According to political economist Manning Marable, capitalism has exploited and underdeveloped Black America to a genocidal degree. "America's 'democratic' government and 'free enterprise' system are structured deliberately and specifically to maximize Black oppression. Capitalist development has occurred not in spite of the exclusion of Blacks but because of the brutal exploitation of Blacks as workers and consumers."[40]

This brief analysis of sovereignty in neoliberal perspective also brings into relief certain key differences between neoliberal economics and classical political economy. One major difference between the two pertains to the locus of authority. For classical thinkers like Adam Smith, John Stuart Mill, and Thomas Malthus the locus of authority for the economy was the state. The name of Adam Smith's discourse was *political* economy, rather than economics, and he considered political economy to be "a branch of the science of a statesman or legislator . . . to supply the state of the commonwealth with a revenue sufficient for the public services."[41] Political economy understood the modern state as a foreign commercial endeavor within a world that was larger than both state and market. Neoliberal economics understands the market order as *all-encompassing*, changing the laws and character of nations and peoples according to the laws of supply and demand for the benefit of private owners. Hayek rejects both socialism and collective action and appears to see these two very different concepts as essentially the same. A second key distinction between Smith and Hayek concerns their moral philosophical orientation. Hayek has clearly rejected any form of social sympathy, but Smith's philosophy is rooted in it. Philosopher Alexander Broadie explains that sympathy, or "fellow feeling with any passion[,] . . . is the bridge across our separateness . . . allowing us to place ourselves in an agent's situation."[42] For Smith, without the virtues of justice, benevolence, and prudence, we would not be human. For Hayek, the entrepreneur must reject benevolence and sterilize prudence

---

40. Manning Marable, *How Capitalism Underdeveloped Black America: Problems in Race, Political Economy, and Society* (Chicago: Haymaker Books, 1983, 2015), 2.

41. Adam Smith, *The Wealth of Nations* (CreateSpace Independent Publishing Platform, 1776, 2013), 186.

42. See "Imagination: Morals, Science, and Arts," in *The Cambridge Companion to Adam Smith* (Cambridge: Cambridge University Press, 2006), 25. Also see the introduction by Knud Haakonssen in the same volume.

of any social sympathy. Hayek transforms all social institutions—work, family, religion, and government—into competitive sports. Ironically, Hayek's aggregate of entrepreneurs comes forth in pluralistic society as a new collectivism, that is, as exclusionary teams.

In sum, sovereignty remains with us today, consisting of the questions of state sovereignty and sovereignty as a cultural logic. With respect to state sovereignty, the status of sovereign has alternated between state sovereignty and sovereign stateless property, for example, Bodin's monarch versus Locke's industrial property owner. The state and stateless property struggle with the other for the administrative authority of earth's resources. Each has had victories and losses, but one constant factor has been the destruction of the poor. Despite shifts in discourse on sovereignty from the 1500s until today, Western powers didn't recognize indigenous African, Asian, and Latin and South American societies as sovereign, or today, as developed. Dark peoples were considered unfit for basic statehood and were subjected to colonization. In philosophico-political discourse, dark peoples were taken up as the "state of nature," a metaphor and framing device symbolizing that which is outside/beyond the boundaries of civilization. Even as Europe celebrated the Peace of Westphalia, it waged competitive colonial wars on Africa, and from the world's leading empire, England, philosopher Thomas Hobbes theorized the "state of nature" as a space of competition and war. The logic of the struggle between the sovereign state and stateless property is itself waged according to the logic of sovereignty, whereby an escalating intensity between state and property implies that one must eventually annihilate the other. Also, the path of their struggle is directed inward, from the material, physical body toward a *disembodied* rationality, beginning with Bodin's monarch, to Locke's property owner, to Schmitt's dictator, to Hayek's abstract reason. In African American aesthetic sense, this struggle sounds like a double tonic in search of a proper chord progression and harmony, or like back-and-forth rhythmic movements searching for the beat.

Prospects for an African American Public Theology

Scottish political theologian Alisdair Kee and cultural critic Victor Anderson have been especially controversial in critiques of Black liberation theologians' negligence to deal with the questions of globalization and political theology. In the foreword to Alisdair Kee's *The Rise and Demise of Black Theology* (2006), Anderson cautiously agrees with Kee that Black theology has to "move on" from its preoccupation with internal US forms of historical oppression of Blacks to enlarge itself in the arena of globalization, or as Kee frames it, the "world's poor." Although sovereignty is not necessarily a theological signifier, Christian moral philosopher H. Richard Niebuhr draws out its religious significance by signaling sovereignty as a deity. A deity is, for Niebuhr, an entity, whether person or idea, that has the power to evoke absolute loyalty and devotion as its ultimate cause and center of value.[43] In his *Radical Monotheism and Western Culture* (1943), Niebuhr depicts Western culture as constituted by three deities: "the many," which are the objects of desire (polytheism); "the one among the many" (henotheism), and "the One beyond all the many" (radical monotheism).[44] These deities are in perpetual competition for human faith, which for Niebuhr was human "dependence on a value center or loyalty to a cause."[45] The concept of sovereignty plays itself out in our contestations over faith on earth and the battle of the gods. Sovereignty here has an accidental rather than formal status; it has to do with the historical development of encounters between human communities. Public theology acknowledges the permanency of sovereignty as an effective theme in identity formation, yet it also recognizes that it is contested as African Americans and others inhabit various social spaces and communities of moral discourse. This book is concerned with the cultural logic of sovereignty and advances public languages to the fulfillment of our best spiritual strivings.

43. H. Richard Niebuhr, *Radical Monotheism and Western Culture* (Louisville: John Knox, 1943, 1960), 24.
44. Niebuhr, *Radical Monotheism*, 24.
45. Niebuhr, *Radical Monotheism*, 24.

3

The Sense of Another World

On the Hermeneutics of World

IN THE INTRODUCTION, I BRIEFLY DISCUSSED the "state of nature" doctrine, a metaphor and framing device used to symbolize that which is outside boundaries of civilization. In a previous study, I found that dark peoples of the globe were taken up in canonical Western politico-philosophical discourse under the theme of the "state of nature," and that this theme was thus critical in the production of the cultural logic of sovereignty. In this chapter, I clarify with more specificity that the state of nature metaphor is a hermeneutic, rather than a natural scientific, concept. The hermeneutical understanding of "world" and the natural scientific explanation of environment both offer us perspective on nature, but they take up opposing positions on questions regarding the character, objectivity, and meaning of nature. These debates on the state of nature pivot on the philosophical question of naturalism. The *Oxford English Dictionary* defines philosophical naturalism as "the belief that only natural (as opposed to supernatural or spiritual) laws or forces operate in the world.... Also, the belief that moral concepts can be analyzed in terms of concepts applicable to natural phenomena." "Natural" means regularly occurring and (theoretically) observable patterns, processes, or forces inherent to a thing. This chapter uses Hans-Georg Gadamer's "hermeneutics of world" to discuss the significance of naturalism for African American public theology. Gadamer's hermeneutics of world allows me to locate African American public theology in relationship to the discourse of the natural sciences as well as the human studies. I discuss two types of naturalism in this chapter, modern scientific naturalism and pragmatic naturalism, and I commend the latter as a frame for an African American public theology. In addition to my discussion of naturalism, I also sketch out some of the theological implications of a pragmatic naturalist frame, taking up discussions of spirituality and process metaphysics.

Embracing a form of naturalism raises challenges from both classical theistic theologians and positivist philosophers of science. From a theological perspective, my phenomenological-empirical approach raises questions about how African American public theology understands the relationship between a transcendent God and the immediacy of the observable natural environment. From a positivist perspective, my approach raises questions with respect to the validity of my knowledge claims about the state of nature. Thus, in addition to a discussion of naturalism, this chapter also discusses the cojoined topic of epistemology, looking at the status of hermeneutical and theological claims from the perspective of both logical positivist and pragmatist conceptions of truth and rationality. The status of theological claims has become especially questionable in public debate given the cultural logic of the sovereignty of technological rationality, itself a reflection of the epistemological sovereignty of positivism.

I describe how the totalization of the positivist frame requires one to bracket and suspend phenomenological as well as theological discourse. African American public theology rejects the *sovereignty* of positivism as an epistemological frame. Until the thinking of figures like Hans-Georg Gadamer (1900–2002) and Clifford Geertz (1926–2006), many positivist social scientists remained blind to their own use of symbols to represent social facts.[1] This chapter rejects positivism and finds that pragmatic naturalism and an attendant hermeneutics of world are appropriate epistemological and cosmological frames for African American public theology. These frames allow for the disclosure of aesthetic and truth value from humanistic and religious languages in the description of human experience. From such descriptions, the possibility arises for an African American pragmatic theology.

The Technological Age, Logical Positivism, and Modern Scientific Naturalism

While the empirical method is standard fare in the social sciences, the approach as deployed in theology raises questions of verifiability in the technological

---

1. See W. James Bradley and Kurt C. Schaefer, *The Uses and Misuses of Data and Models: The Mathematization of the Human Sciences* (Thousand Oaks, CA: Sage, 1998), 182. Also see Brian Brock, *Christian Ethics in a Technological Age* (Grand Rapids: Eerdmans, 2010), 10. One might also mention Wilhelm Dilthey and Martin Heidegger, among other philosophers of hermeneutics.

age. We saw in chapter 2 how policy analyst Deborah Stone and social theorist Mitchell Dean described the sovereignty of technological rationality (also called *technique*), where cost-benefit analysis has come to dominate state, national, and global market policy.[2] We can briefly expound on this description of the sovereignty of technological rationality with insights from critical theorist Herbert Marcuse and social theorists W. James Bradley and Kurt C. Schaefer. Marcuse wrote in the context of Nazi Germany and was part of the German critical theory school of social thought that also included thinkers like Max Horkheimer, Theodor Adorno, and Walter Benjamin. Marcuse defines technological rationality as the rationality of efficiency. "The efficient individual is the one whose performance is an action only insofar as it is the proper reaction to the objective requirements of the apparatus, and his liberty is confined to the selection of the most adequate means for reaching a goal which he did not set."[3] For Marcuse, technological rationality is about making human behavior itself into standardized efficiency for purposes of industrial-technological systems of production. Human behavior is outfitted with the rationality of the machine process, operating according to the laws of mass production. He critiqued the way that technological rationality functioned as an invisible instrument of control and domination, one that erodes individual freedom as it makes persons more efficient for the machine. "In the course of the technological process a new rationality and new standards of individuality have spread over society."[4] For Marcuse, self-interest in technological society is only achieved by compliance and conformity, rather than through autonomy as critical reflection and action.

Ultimately, the scientific age, or the technological age, as it is also called, culminates in mathematical thinking and mathematical metaphysics. For philosopher Martin Heidegger (1889–1976), Isaac Newton's *Philosophia Naturalis Principia Mathematica* (1686) inaugurated the technological age, where modern physics lays a perceptual grid over all of reality. Energy and motion are posited as convertible and interchangeable, and the ideal of circular movement comes under criticism as linear movement comes to be venerated. A Newtonian theory of motion itself colonizes every area of contemporary life. Time itself becomes technological, that is, disconnected from particularity and abstracted. Modern time is "linear . . . irreversible . . . the bearer of the irretrievable." Quantitative social sciences are modern technologies, as they are grounded in

---

2. Also see Bradley and Schaefer, *The Uses and Misuses of Data and Models*.
3. Herbert Marcuse, "Some Social Implications of Technology," *Philosophy and Social Sciences* 9 (1941), https://tinyurl.com/y9eux55b.
4. Marcuse, "Some Social Implications of Technology."

a modern account of knowledge (experimental method) and in the attempt to control and predict the energies and motions of humans. Scientific method is not itself technique, but positivist methodology seeks algorithmic explanations of phenomena. Its domain of study is typically aspects of nature that can be described by laws. Practitioners often claim that all of reality can be explained in terms of nomothetic laws.[5] The recent use of data models thus facilitates technique, a method of thinking that reduces activities to routines that then can be made efficient and optimized.[6] These are the hallmarks of the modern technological age, where the term "technology" no longer simply signifies its traditional meaning as "tool" but also points to technology as organizing metaphor for all of life. Technological rationality increasingly characterizes our relations with all things, culminating in understanding the world and humanity itself as raw material. Technological thinking assumes predictive powers and gives the appearance of precision and objectivity via numerical tools.

Epistemologically, technological rationality can be traced to the sovereignty of logical positivism in human and social studies. Positivism was outlined most definitively by eighteenth-century French philosopher Auguste Comte and then emerged again in the early twentieth-century "Vienna Circle" philosophical school. Comte believed that the certain approach to knowledge of human affairs was the empirical method, to the exclusion of theology and metaphysics altogether. He called his method the "positive" method, where the "search for origins and causes, along with the quest for absolute knowledge, is abandoned ... [in order to] discover the actual laws of phenomena."[7] Comte's vision was

---

5. Brock, *Christian Ethics*, 12, 40, 80.

6. Indeed, as sociologists W. James Bradley and Kurt C. Schaefer note, in the twentieth century scientific methodology was the oracle of the Western world (*The Uses and Misuses of Data and Models*, 3, 24–25). The scientific method justified data produced via intelligence tests (e.g., the SAT, PSAT, or Armed Forces Qualification Test), personality inventories, and Myers-Briggs tests used to measure the way people interact with others. Under the influence of positivism, these social sciences generate observations and measurements to the exclusion of metaphysical speculation; measurements guided instead by positive, formal, and quantitative data. Social scientists thus frequently model data, mathematically abstracting characteristics crucial for understanding behavioral, institutional, and technical relationships from the complexities of the real world. Yet, Bradley and Schaefer question the formalization of social sciences with the use of data models. Data and models have the potential to provide great social benefits, yet they also fail to take account of contextual norms in any given situation. Many math-powered models define their own reality and use it to justify sometimes destructive results.

7. See Auguste Comte, *Introduction to Positive Philosophy*, trans. Frederick Ferre (Indianapolis: Hackett, 1988).

taken up in the early twentieth century Vienna Circle in Austria, resulting in logical positivism, produced by philosophers like Rudolf Carnap and Victor Kraft and mathematicians Olga Hahn-Neurath and Gustav Bergmann. Logical positivism is best known for its "verifiability principle" of meaning, where all statements, symbols, and models that cannot be verified (and in principle refuted) by direct sensory experience are held to be meaningless.[8] Statements are only meaningful if empirically verifiable; if a statement cannot be sensed, it cannot be discussed. Positivist social scientists use methods resembling the natural sciences to understand (human) nature and society. Questions of modality, space, time, of the mental and the physical, of "free will" and determinism are all answered according to modern scientific accounts of the world. With positivism, all human studies must embrace methodological individualism, a.k.a. rational choice theory, where individuals are driven primarily by self-interest and make conscious decisions about their actions based on rational considerations of consequences. Efficiency and profitability are central values. For logical positivism, the idea of "instrumental rationality"—that we act to satisfy desires—is a universal "law of nature."[9]

Logical positivism discloses a materialist cosmology that rejects immaterial or supernatural views of nature as meaningless. In the positivist view of nature, nothing exists except for matter and its movements, and language should attend only to the particularity of individual bodies. Philosophers Mario De Caro and David Macarthur describe this cosmology as "modern scientific naturalism." "Here," say De Caro and Macarthur, "the world consists of nothing but the entities to which successful scientific explanations commit us. It follows that scientific inquiry is, in principle, our only genuine source of knowledge or understanding."[10] The world for the modern scientific naturalist is *ultimately*, if not actually, able to be explained in terms of patterns or processes that occur with such regularity that they begin to look like inbuilt "laws." Yet these laws have no creator, at least none beyond those of the material and efficient causes of nature. Again, the modern scientific naturalist believes that only natural, as opposed to supernatural, laws or forces operate in the world. De Caro and Macarthur emphasize its *modern* character, noting that it is opposed philosophically to "any form of Platonism about norms, i.e., that normative facts

---

8. Bradley and Schaefer, *The Uses and Misuses of Data and Models*, 49.

9. Mario De Caro and David Macarthur, "Science, Naturalism, and the Problem of Normativity," in *Naturalism and Normativity*, ed. Mario De Caro and David Macarthur (New York: Columbia University Press, 2010), 2. Also see Lina Eriksson, *Rational Choice Theory: Its Potential and Limits* (New York: Palgrave Macmillan, 2011).

10. De Caro and Macarthur, "Science, Naturalism, and the Problem of Normativity," 2–3.

hold wholly independently of human practices." Here De Caro and others are referring to the early modern decline of the Scholastic Aristotelian-Ptolemaic view of nature. Medieval thinkers drew from Aristotle, Ptolemy, Augustine, and others to argue for a cosmological perspective constituted by "complex webs of interconnections," which were also a "chain of being." Philosopher Alexander Rosenberg traces logical positivism's scientific naturalist cosmology to the thinking of David Hume (1711–1776).[11] Hume's appeal to the verifiability principle made interpretive as well as symbolic theories meaningless. With logical positivism, technological rationality reigns supreme, both as tool and also as metaphor, value, and symbol for life.

Pragmatic Naturalism and the Hermeneutics of World

Thus, the use of the empirical method raises questions about the conception of the natural world as well as the value of theology in such a conception. This book is located within the philosophical tradition of American pragmatism, including early twentieth-century thinkers such as Charles Sanders Peirce, William James, and John Dewey, and contemporary thinkers like Cornel West, Sheila Davaney, and William Dean. The pragmatic method serves as a means to test the practical consequences of our moral discourses as a means for the cultural fulfillment and flourishing of our public practices, institutions, and life together. "The pragmatic method," says early twentieth-century philosopher and pioneer psychological theorist William James, "is primarily a method of settling metaphysical disputes, (i.e., disputes about reality that lie beyond or behind those capable of being tackled by the methods of science) that otherwise might be interminable. Is the world one or many?—fated or free?—material or spiritual[?] ... The pragmatic method in such cases is to try to interpret each notion by tracing its respective practical consequences. ... Whenever a dispute is serious we ought to be able to show some practical difference that must follow from one side or the other's being right."[12] Thus, pragmatist Victor Anderson notes that the pragmatic approach "favored the experimental disposition and method in the justification of knowledge and value judgments."[13]

---

11. Alexander Rosenberg, *Philosophy of Social Science*, 4th ed. (Boulder, CO: Westview, 2012), 14.
12. William James, *Pragmatism and the Meaning of Truth*, introduction by A. J. Ayer (Cambridge, MA: Harvard University Press, 1975, 1994), 28.
13. Victor Anderson, *Pragmatic Theology: Negotiating the Intersections of an American*

Pragmatism thus tests the veracity of truth claims by looking at truth's practical consequences. It rests largely on the judgment of common sense and social sympathy. Francis Bacon (1561–1626) argued that we should build our knowledge on sense experience because it extends our knowledge of nature in ways that practices and argumentation do not. He also said that science extended beyond its limits when it pursued "the ambitious and proud desire of moral knowledge to judge good and evil."[14]

At best, the pragmatist sensibility reflects a respect for what is believed to be known and for what is not known. Our knowledge of the world is always limited and at least partially constructed. This orientation is reflected in the "critical realist" perspective held by pragmatist thinkers such as Victor Anderson and Tyron Inbody. The former holds that there is a fundamental opacity to our knowledge.[15] Indeed, human knowledge is generated as human abilities to perceive and identify the other as an object in experience are stimulated by an other's contact with the human, or vice versa.[16] Consciousness is not an object but a cooperative, creative, psychical, and reflexive process, knowledge being only one of its functions. Objects and states of affairs such as the external world, the past and the future, and other bodies exist independently of our own minds. Yet reality is the totality of undifferentiated matrices of experience, continual streams of thoughts and actions rather than atomistic.[17] In turn, experience is the content of consciousness and statements. Religious experience is also linguistically structured and not beyond the scope of ordinary human knowledge. As we receive impressions from objects, we cognitively intuit them through apperception. That is, we bring our languages, symbols, paradigms, and other ideal constructive artifacts to bear on objects in an attempt to understand them. As theologian Tyron Inbody notes, "experience is never 'pure experience.' . . . It is always derived from, shaped, and interpreted in a social context, both a natural environment of interrelationships and interdependence (nature) and a cultural environment of language, symbol, and myth (tradition). Language arises and develops in the context of an organism

---

Philosophy of Religion and Public Theology (New York: State University of New York Press, 1988), 3.

14. Francis Bacon, "The Great Instauration," in *The English Philosophers from Bacon to Mill*, ed. Edwin A. Burtt (New York: Modern Library, 1994), 13.

15. Victor Anderson, *Creative Exchange: A Constructive Theology of African American Religious Experience* (Minneapolis: Augsburg Fortress, 2008).

16. Anderson, *Pragmatic Theology*, 72–74.

17. Anderson, *Pragmatic Theology*, 72, and also Douglas Clyde Macintosh's *Theology as Empirical Science* (New York: Macmillan, 1919).

encountering a complex environment in experience, and tradition shapes and reshapes the experience of an organism in its (natural, social and cosmic) environment through language, symbol, and myth."[18] This means the possibility for both foreclosure and transcendence.

African American public theology not only requires a theory of knowledge that brackets and suspends logical positivism, but one that also comes to terms with modern scientific naturalism. One such view that seeks to bring phenomenological perspectives into rhythm with empiricism and naturalism is theorized by pragmatist philosopher D. S. Clarke.[19] Clarke argues for an approach to nature beyond scientism, which cannot accept religion's metaphysical and theological language, based on a version of pragmatism freed from the tyranny of positivism. As with positivism, Clarke's "pragmatic naturalism" is rooted in empiricism. Yet in distinction from positivism, pragmatic naturalism argues that the truth of a sentence is not to be judged by its usefulness to one who accepts the isolated sentence. Rather, the truth of a sentence is judged by its usefulness relative to the entire discourse framework in which the sentence is formulated, along with its attendant rituals and ethics. Clarke's pragmatic approach to the question of naturalism enables him to acknowledge a panpsychic "mentality" that pervades nature. "Mentality pervades all of nature in the form of perspectives of countless individuals, and is eternal, in *collective* but not *individual* form . . . every organized body has some element of this mentality."[20] Clarke's nontheistic panpsychism preserves basic aspects of the religious attitude. That is, he believes that the eternal deserves priority over the individual and over that which is transitory. Mentality is eternal. Though every particular locus of it is finite in duration, mentality in the collective sense is eternal. Since mentality is eternal in this generalized way, there is no need to explain its origins or its "emergence." Panpsychists revere the host of finite creatures whose past strivings have made our lives possible rather than a single theistic God. Clarke's version of naturalism thus goes beyond the more limited vision of the frameworks of scientific naturalism and positivism to acknowledge the coexistence of spirit and matter, a.k.a. mentality. It reaches beyond spirit/matter dualisms that might sever the two; spirit and matter are connected.

---

18. Tyron Inbody, *The Constructive Theology of Bernard Meland: Postliberal Empirical Realism* (Atlanta: Scholars Press, 1995), 232, as quoted by Victor Anderson in *Creative Exchange*, 3.

19. D. S. Clarke, *Essays on Pragmatic Naturalism: Discourse Relativity, Religion, Art, and Education* (n.p.: D. S. Clarke, 2016), 204.

20. Clarke, *Essays on Pragmatic Naturalism*, 237–38.

Nature, then, consists of more than natural science's interpretive framework of material and efficient causes. This perspective captures only one aspect of the natural world. The natural world also consists of the supernatural, to the extent that the supernatural is accounted for linguistically, and with attention to the question of mental agency, since mentality pervades all of nature. Thus, describing supernaturals such as God or ancestral spirits with mental language and attributing supernatural agency to them enables us to include the supernatural within the transactional web characteristic of human communities.[21] Religious languages, much of which points to the supernatural, push us beyond the use of mathematical models and technologized time in the representation of human and other relationships. Pragmatic naturalism recognizes human as well as spiritual agency. It focuses on events that may or may not be replicable. Rather than abstracting events to find mathematical patterns, laws, or algorithms, it contextualizes them.

Clarke's turn to pragmatic naturalism is indicative of a larger movement in the discourses of philosophy of science and philosophy of nature to acknowledge the limits of scientific naturalism. For example, philosophers Mario De Caro and David Macarthur make a similar turn to hermeneutical modes of naturalism with their "liberal naturalism."[22] Liberal naturalism is less a precisely defined credo and more a symbol encompassing a range of perspectives that reject scientific naturalism as the conclusive account of human life at both the methodological and ontological levels. Liberal naturalists like De Caro and Macarthur attempt to do justice to the sciences by freeing perspectives on nature from positivist claims to epistemological sovereignty and acknowledging nonscientific, supernatural understandings. Liberal naturalism occupies the space typically overlooked between scientific naturalism and supernaturalism. Philosopher Huw Price has shown that a science of linguistic functions can itself show us that there are nonscientific modes of knowing and understanding.[23] From an anthropological point of view, commonsense realist talk of values only requires the availability of a nonrepresentational function for such talk. Truth cannot be ascertained with the logician's tools, but can only be understood once we know its role in the "game" being played at the time. Thus, technical reason's "neutral" perspective on truth must be understood in

---

21. Eric S. Nelson, "Life and World," in *Routledge Companion to Hermeneutics*, ed. Jeff Malpas and Hans-Helmuth Gander (New York: Routledge, 2016), 378.

22. De Caro and Macarthur, "Science, Naturalism, and the Problem of Normativity," 9.

23. See Huw Price, "Truth as Convenient Friction," in De Caro and Macarthur, *Naturalism and Normativity*, 229.

light of the game of technique, which reduces human activities to routines to prioritize the values of efficiency and productivity.

Ironically, technique and routinization often yield information overload and detachment from reality.[24] Thus, liberal naturalists like De Caro, Macarthur, and Price, and pragmatic naturalists like Clarke, have made space for interpretive social scientists and religious scholars who look beyond mechanistic and mathematical causality to see symbol and meaning in language.

Pragmatic naturalism's approach to questions of knowledge and truth allows for the possibility of world disclosure in both natural scientific and aesthetic terms. The pragmatic naturalist perspective on nature thus does not reject modern science but understands modern science as a discourse that offers statements on nature of a different kind than those offered by phenomenological and religious statements. Here, I draw on the thinking of Gadamer, who argues that discourse on the state of nature may be one of two types, scientific or hermeneutical. The first type, the scientific, refers to discourse on the natural environment.[25] Gadamer defines "environment" in purely natural scientific terms, to the intentional exclusion of social environment or milieu. The study of the natural environment sees nature as a collection of objects upon which human beings are to impose their will and with the scientific approach to the study of nature, the scientific method is appropriate. Human life is characterized by its closeness or proximity to nature, such that humans are understood in relationship to the organization of biotic communities and the cosmological view of physics. In this view, one does not need a personal, existential, or aesthetic connection with the object of study to arrive at a truth. In Gadamerian terms, one does not need "world and language" to possess an environment. Environment, or habitat, is something that *all* living beings possess, and the objective features of an environment may be discovered by way of the physical and biological sciences. Gadamer uses the example of early modern astronomer Nicolaus Copernicus, whose heliocentric theory of the solar system showed that Earth revolves around the sun rather than vice versa. This argument implies that any talk of the "setting sun" or of the sun "setting in the evening" is scientifically, that is, objectively and verifiably, false. The sun doesn't actually "set" in the evening sky.

Alongside natural scientific discourses on the state of nature, pragmatic naturalism also acknowledges aesthetic and phenomenological-hermeneutic ones. In aesthetic perspective on nature, Gadamer's description of nature as

---

24. Bradley and Schaefer, *The Uses and Misuses of Data and Models*, 12.
25. Hans-Georg Gadamer, *Truth and Method*, 2nd rev. ed. (New York: Continuum, 2006).

environment is replaced by the description of nature as language and world. Here, language refers to the literary and poetic dimensions of language over against the modern philological and linguistic ones. Gadamer understands language to be an art rather than a science, and he sees the art of language as an indication of humanity's fundamental freedom in spite of the seeming determinacy of environment. Gadamer uses the language of "freedom from environment" to describe this feature, but I prefer to use language of compatibilism. Gadamer is arguing that although the environment exercises determinacy with respect to human existence, and although language is handed down as tradition, language nonetheless shows us our collective freedom to transcend environment to "world" with language. "World" is thus not an objective reality like environment but an interpretive horizon of meaning constituted through language. Here the scientific method simply will not do. There must be an existential point of contact with the reader rather than a scientific distance, so that the reader is moved to creatively respond to a subject rather than to dominate and control an object. Gadamer again uses the example of early modern astronomer Copernicus, but this time to show how Copernicus's heliocentric theory is *hermeneutically* false, even if scientifically true. "We can see things from the rational viewpoint of the Copernican theory. But we cannot try to supersede or refute natural appearances . . . because the truth that science states is itself relative to a particular world orientation and cannot at all claim to be the whole."[26] Nature as world thus has its own truth and own mode of understanding alongside but apart from that of nature as environment.

World, then, signifies the interpretive horizon of meaning that may include, but extends beyond, the environment of natural science. World is linguistically constituted, and as such, world may not be collected and studied as an object of natural science. This is the case because of the limits intrinsic in expressive and artistic language itself. World cannot become "being-in-itself" because language itself never allows for that possibility. We cannot "step outside" of language itself. To quote Gadamer, "there is no point of view outside the experience of the world in language from which it could become an object."[27] World thus has an independent existence apart from individuals' creation and participation in it. Gadamer will say that language is essentially a worldview: *"a language-view is a worldview. . . .* Language is not just one of man's possessions in the world; rather on it depends the fact that man has a *world*

---

26. Gadamer, *Truth and Method*, 446.
27. Gadamer, *Truth and Method*, 449.

at all."[28] The world of hermeneutics is the world of factualness as opposed to the environment of objectivity. World is conceived of as "being-in-itself" (although by definition it cannot be), as a horizon of truth that gives meaning and significance to existence. Thus (new) facts are made to conform to this horizon of truth as we engage in dialogue with others. These matters of fact aren't really "objects," but what exists comes to language in statements. Thus, world offers us conceptions of time, order, and history by which to order our lives and identify ourselves among human communities. Worlds give us a sense of the whole of reality, of being in itself, even as the being of language is itself rooted in dialogue, in coming to understanding. Worlds remain open to new facts and novel interpretations of the facts. Natural science exerts its will on objects, but world makes first contact and begins a dialogue of existential truth with the interpreting subject.

Thus, pragmatism, pragmatic naturalism, and the hermeneutics of world provide a pathway for discourse on the state of nature for African American public theology. Pragmatism offers a critique of logical positivism, opening the epistemological circle to standards for evaluating truth other than the principle of verifiability. Pragmatic naturalism argues against the *totalization* of the mechanistic and atomistic view of reality produced by scientific naturalism. Pragmatic naturalism argues for the reality of collective consciousness in organized bodies in the natural world. This implies that organized bodies are not simply objects but possess some degree of subjectivity. I find this claim compatible with that of the hermeneutics of world, where one discerns the truth from within a linguistically mediated world by way of dialogue with an alterity subjectivity rather than through manipulation of an object. The hermeneutics of world understands truth symbolically and aesthetically. Here is another point of convergence with African American public theology, which may also deploy symbols and make use of aesthetics in its descriptions of the state of nature. Unlike the natural sciences, scientific naturalism, and positivism, which operate with causal theories that enable prediction and control, literary, cultural theoretical, and religious languages seek to explain behavior by rendering it meaningful or intelligible. They uncover its meaning and significance by interpreting what people do, and the interpretation of human behavior is not fundamentally causal. If life for the scientific naturalist is solely a physical and biological phenomenon, life for the pragmatic naturalist is also physical and biological, but with the added transcendent dimension through psychological, hermeneutical, and spiritual experiences. Environment is empirical;

---

28. Gadamer, *Truth and Method*, 440.

world is constituted through dialogue. Truth becomes tied to world-givenness, world-formation, and world-disclosure.

Pragmatic Theology, Process Metaphysics, and the Ontology of Participation

Pragmatism tests the veracity of our truth claims by looking at the practical consequences rather than their adherence to a mathematical formula or any other sovereign rational principle. It rests largely on the judgment of common sense. But is common sense really enough for theology? The claims of pragmatism and pragmatic naturalism come into direct conflict with the (Christian) theological doctrines of supernaturalism and theism. The classic theist believes in the existence of one supreme God that creates and yet transcends the cosmos. God in classic theism not only intervenes in the world by way of occasional miracles but also providentially guides all of time, nature, and history. Theism is wedded to the doctrine of supernaturalism, where God is portrayed as transcending the world's patterns, processes, and ordinary events and is not subject to or affected by the world. Feminist theologian Elizabeth Johnson explains that the classical theist perspective is a relatively recent development, birthed during the time of the Renaissance. "The concept of God developed by medieval and early modern theology in close contact with classical metaphysics . . . [is one where] God is not to be identified with the world . . . [and which] views God as the Supreme Being who made and rules all things, but is unrelated, unaffected by the world."[29] For Johnson, classical theism places an emphasis on divine transcendence and neglects discussions of divine immanence, that is, of how God is present, active in, and affected by the natural world. God's transcendence is so *absolute* in the classical theist view that God is often portrayed as "God solo," apart from any relationship to even Jesus Christ or the Holy Spirit. For Johnson, this portrayal of God, built on the images of ruling men, undermines human equality and fails to capture the Trinitarian economy of relationships that defines the life of God. Thus, supernaturalism and theism are not only oppressive for some feminist theologians. Supernaturalism and classical theism are also unable to come to terms with either pragmatism or pragmatic naturalism, except as symbol.

---

29. Elizabeth Johnson, *She Who Is: The Mystery of God in Feminist Discourse* (Chestnut Ridge, PA: Crossroad, 1992), 19–20.

I find that the process metaphysics of John B. Cobb Jr. and David W. Griffin offer an appropriate naturalist frame for a rendering of world in a pragmatic African American public theology. Cobb and Griffin understand the state of nature as a state of essential relatedness, where all things have real relations with each other, and these relations belong to their respective essences. Here, Cobb and Griffin follow the thinking of process founder Alfred N. Whitehead, who prioritizes ontological interdependence as an ideal over ontological independence (ethical independence is promoted). Thus, ironically, the state of nature is always in a constant state of change and thus may be defined as a process. "The notions of process and essential relatedness do tend to support each other.... If things have real relations with each other, and these relations belong to their respective essences, it is difficult to understand how these essences can be unchanging."[30] Process indicates an evolutionary process of complexification from simpler things and forms to those more complex. Cobb and Griffin say that this process occurs by way of "gradations of value, and some actualities are capable of greater enjoyment than others. Roughly speaking, more complex actualities enjoy more instrumental value than simpler ones.... The direction of the evolutionary process on the whole is toward more complex actualities."[31] Although nature is defined as relatedness and evolutionary process, where more complex forms of things can only come after simpler ones, it is also the case that the more complex forms presuppose and in many ways remain in relation to simpler forms. Thus, the essential relatedness of process metaphysics promotes an ecological attitude that stresses "the interrelations and hence interdependencies among things" as well as "respect or even reverence for, and perhaps a feeling of kinship with, the other creatures."[32]

Process is thus fundamental to reality. Although not *everything* is process, reality is process and all actual and real individuals and events are process. For Cobb, process is not a single smooth flow, nor is time. Yet process remains, in the most general sense, a rectilinear and directional event, moving in a straight line from past to future. Process constitutes temporality by moving from occasion to occasion. Process metaphysics thus recognizes the importance of time alongside the importance of relatedness and process. Time undergirds one's sense of history, which thus also moves along a rectilinear path for Cobb. On his account, time flows asymmetrically from the past through the present into the

---

30. John B. Cobb Jr. and David Ray Griffin, *Process Theology: An Introductory Exposition* (Louisville: Westminster, 1976), 19.
31. Cobb and Griffin, *Process Theology*, 64–65.
32. Cobb and Griffin, *Process Theology*, 76.

future. There can be no denial of the reality of time, *and for Cobb*, the movement of process from simple to more complex forms means that time cannot be or possess "any doctrine of its circularity."[33] For Cobb, because every moment is new and none can be repeated, time can only be a rectilinear and directed movement. One occasion succeeds another. The past is composed of those events that have occurred, and the future is radically different, since it contains no occasions. The present is the occasion that is now occurring. The present is influenced by the past, and it will influence the future. "The *relativity* definition of the past and future is incorporated into process thought: the past is the totality of that which influences the present, and the future is the totality of that which will be influenced by the present."[34] In a later chapter I return to the question of process thought and time as a hermeneutical concept, informed by African American musicology, to discern the viability of both rectilinear and curvilinear movements of directed time from simple forms to more complex forms. It is important to note that for Cobb, the transition from one form to another is primarily a *bodily* transition.

Cobb's metaphysics of nature as relatedness and process rests on an ontology of mutual embodied participation. This means that although all individuals have a mentality, or capacity for self-determination, they aren't monads, unable to experience anything beyond themselves. We are affected and influenced by one another, and although this begins as bodily experience, it has existential impact. In this way we are part of one another's bodies, in that we mutually participate in one another's influences and responses to the environment. Each of us influences the natural environment, and the world feels our influence and reacts to it. Cobb explains that "hitherto, the prevailing view has been that the body (that is to say, the matter that is *incommunicably* attached to each soul) is a *fragment* of the universe—a piece *completely detached* from the rest and handed over to a spirit that informs it. In the future, we shall say that the Body is the very Universality of things, in as much as they are centered on an animating Spirit, in as much as they influence that Spirit—and are themselves influenced and sustained by it."[35] For Cobb, the body and the spirit influence one another, rather than the spirit maintaining a hierarchical relationship over the body. The ontology of mutual participation sees the body as continuous with the environment: "The body is the more intimate part of the environment."[36] The body cannot be reduced to technological or cost-benefit value as it is the totality of the universe as possessed by me in part. I find Cobb's

33. Cobb and Griffin, *Process Theology*, 16.
34. Cobb and Griffin, *Process Theology*, 23 (emphasis added).
35. Cobb and Griffin, *Process Theology*, 115, quoting Pierre Teilhard de Chardin.
36. Cobb and Griffin, *Process Theology*, 116.

account of reality as process amenable to both the natural scientific explanation of environment and the phenomenological-hermeneutical understanding of world. Cobb's ontology of participation is rooted in bodily participation by way of environment, while Gadamer's account of participation is rooted in language by way of an interpreted world. Both are important for participation.

Public Theology, Creation as Art, and the Movement of Spirit in World

In embracing a hermeneutical approach to world alongside an empirical approach to environment, African American public theology satisfies the conditions of verifiability for public discourse and debate. Thus, the argument made by positivists that theology should be excluded from public discourse is refuted to the extent that it embraces a pragmatic naturalist frame. In this final section of this chapter, I sketch out some initial implications of pragmatic naturalism and process metaphysics for public theology, with the understanding that this sketch will be filled out in part 2 of this book. The first implication of pragmatism for public theology is publicity itself. The pragmatic approach to knowledge allows theological discourse to enter into publics beyond the church and the theological academy. The very language of publicity implies that public theology is both deprivatized and depoliticized. As a deprivatized public theology, theological discourse must be aware of both the three publics that constitute American public life and how truth claims are established on different terms in each of these different publics. David Tracy argues that American public life is constituted by three publics—church, academy, and society. Although all of these operate under the authority of the state (or techno-economy), each public has a different method for verifying truth as well as different taken-for-granted assumptions that shape how it communicates truth. The public theologian must be aware of this feature of publicity. Public theology also means that theology is not political, in the Schmittian sense of "the political," where one draws a hard-and-fast line between friends and enemies that only the second coming of Christ can undo. Schmitt argued that nothing in art, economics, or even ethics and religion could move him to accept some people as friends or neighbors. The best of public theology speaks *against* the political, and for respectful engagement in democratic life.

In modern scientific culture, one of the primary things that publicity means for theology is a pragmatic orientation to naturalism. This book embraces a process metaphysics as theorized by Whitehead, Cobb, Griffin, and others, and understands this metaphysics to be amenable to both natural scientific explanations of environment and hermeneutical understandings of world. As applied to our discussion on the discourse of theology in this chapter, this means that the doctrines of classical theism and supernaturalism are no longer viable. God no longer stands transcendent over the world as sole creator and judge. Yet shall we now rejoice, or lament, that God is dead? This, too, would be a mistake, for it implies the objective reality and truth of another absolute, the negative of the life of God, namely, the death of all existence. But language cannot ever take us to absolute truth, and so the decline of classical theism is not a crash but now appears as a motion, one that necessarily involves a motion of return, response, or exchange. Cobb gets at this feature of theology with language of "dipolar theism," and Johnson with "dialectical theism." It is an understanding of God as one moving back and forth in activity, rather than a static, permanently elevated God. The back-and-forth motion of God implies that divine attributes are constantly being negotiated, rather than absolutely and permanently retained. God is simultaneously transcendent and immanent, both actor and sufferer, both creativity and responsiveness, both power and responsive love. Each of these attributes (and others) has the ability to operate with great force. Yet somehow an attribute never extinguishes its opposite. Love never extinguishes power, nor power, love. Agency doesn't extinguish one's role as sufferer, nor does suffering, as exhibited in divine play, take one's life as an exchange. This dialectical approach to theism raises questions about God's relation to world.

The hermeneutics of world allows world to emerge as nature, and nature as a creation of divine activity.[37] In process theological perspective, the world as nature is a creative evolutionary process that emerges from the creative play of God. This means that the world as nature has its own capacity for generative and other types of creativity even as it also remains with the web of God's own creative actions as world. Creation is a unique act, but we may use analogies from human experience to describe it. Theologian Daniel Migliore offers several models to depict God's creative activity, including generation (creation as a procreative act), emanation (creation as an overflowing or flowing out of God), and body of God (creation as God in intimacy and reciprocity). Yet Migliore's analogy of creation as artistic expression seems most appropriate for my approach to African American public theology. One reason for that is that my phenomenological-hermeneutical method already centers aesthetics and the play of hermeneutics as key steps in the construction of an African American public theology. From the perspective of God's activity, creation as artistic expression reflects both the

---

37. See W. David Hall, "Does Creation Equal Nature? Confronting the Christian Confusion about Ecology and Cosmology," *Journal of the American Academy of Religion* 73, no. 3 (September 2005): 781–812, https://tinyurl.com/5csvpwma.

freedom of God in play and the intimacy of God in play. Creation as artistic expression appreciates the work that goes into composition but sees the language of *work* as potentially too tied to routine, as unpleasant, and as coerced labor. Creation as play suggests that the purposes of creation are not reducible to instrumental values or purposes but possess (aesthetic) value in, of, and for itself, having a certain independence apart from its creator like all works of art. Nature is the art by which God has made and governs the world. Creation as artistic expression means that creation stands as its own horizon of meaning and invites us into its back-and-forth play between our own horizons and its own.

Finally, the hermeneutics of world as nature and nature as creation opens us up to the movement of the spirit in the world. The theological doctrine of the Spirit in creation is an aspect of the dialectical transcendence and immanence of God in the world. The Spirit is thus always already inscribed within at least two economies, one natural and the other divine, neither of which is ever completely separated from the world nor reducible to one another. Thus, the Spirit is necessarily incarnate, bodily, and earthly, even as it also necessarily somehow transcends bodily form alone. This does not mean that humanity participates in the divine economy. The economy of nature and the divine economy remain two distinct economies. As part of the divine economy, the Spirit interacts with, relates to, responds to, and creates for the Trinitarian economy. As part of the economy of nature, the Spirit interacts with, relates to, and creates for the natural economy. Yet while the two economies remain distinct and while humanity does not participate in the divine economy directly, the natural economy does have *indirect* participation in the divine economy by way of the Spirit. This means that humanity participates in the divine economy through divine representatives. In turn, this implies that the natural economy might somehow indirectly perceive the logic of the divine economy of exchange, and that such perception opens us to a new rationality of exchange. Yet even as this perception is not truly perception, neither is this rationality truly reason, because it is a bodily, incarnate rationality, and as such, fails the positivist and natural scientific tests of validity for rationality. All of this suggests that we may find this rationality at the places where Spirit has met with nature and engaged in an irrational, invisible, bodily exchange marked by acts of relation, interpenetration, and call and response.

Part Two

African American Religious Thought

4

Mind, Body, and Spirit

On African American Spirituality

ACCORDING TO ALBERT RABOTEAU, the European-led early modern forced migration and enslavement of West and Central Africans in the United States resulted in the death of the African gods in the New World. "Under British North American slavery, it seems that the African religious heritage was lost."[1] The subsequent emergence of African American spirituality raised questions regarding the status of African retentions in African American religion and culture. A central question concerns the extent to which African American spirituality contains efficacious elements of African culture that have enduring significance for African American, and perhaps even American, religious experience. For some, like sociologist E. Franklin Frazier (1894–1962), the process of deculturation during the Atlantic slave trade led to the complete eradication of elements of African culture in African American culture. The harsh and oppressive realities of the New World not only separated Africans from their homeland but also separated them from any and all African cultural retentions. This thesis was argued most notably by Frazier in both his *The Negro Church in America* (1964) and *The Negro Family in the United States* (1966). Frazier found that African traditions and practices had not survived in the United States and that slaves "had only a vague knowledge of the African background of their parents."[2] The plantation slave system had destroyed all remains of African culture and left the Negro with no past other than one of primitive savagery. Yet not everyone agreed with Frazier. Another view,

---

1. Albert J. Raboteau, *Slave Religion: The Invisible Institution in the Antebellum South* (New York: Oxford University Press, 2004), 47.
2. E. Franklin Frazier, *The Negro Family in the United States* (Chicago: University of Chicago Press, 1966), 7.

put forward by anthropologist Melville J. Herskovits (1895–1963), was that some African cultural retentions survived the ordeal of European contact and conquest. In Herskovits's *The Myth of the Negro Past* (1941), he stresses the continued presence of African retentions in African American culture. US slavery did not defeat "the retention of African customs in generalized form."[3]

This chapter analyzes key figures in the discourse on African American spirituality with attention to the question of African cultural retentions, even as I simultaneously continue to ask my core questions about the "state of nature" doctrine and the cultural logic of sovereignty. I discuss the state of nature doctrine of three figures as exemplary of three types of African American spirituality. The first figure is mid-twentieth-century mystic and Baptist clergyman Howard Thurman, whose own reflections on the "spirituality of hunger" opened an avenue for interracial dialogue and advancement at both Boston University and the Fellowship of All Peoples Church. Next, I analyze the discourse on African American spirituality as represented by contemplative theologian Barbara L. Holmes, whose contemplative spirituality offers yet another distinctive approach. Finally, I ask the same questions of ecowomanist scholar Melanie L. Harris, who roots her understanding of African American spirituality in ecowomanist spirituality and what she calls "ecomemory" rather than Thurman's spirituality of hunger or Holmes's communal contemplative approach. Before this, I begin the chapter with a discussion of popular traditional African religion, whose central feature, in naturalist frame, is African ancestral legend. I ultimately find that the discourse on African American spirituality remains vexed with respect to the problem of the cultural logic of sovereignty. Yet I also find that within the discourse itself, there is movement of the Spirit from a collectivist, environmental spirituality among the peoples of West and Central Africa, to a personal, mystical spirituality in Thurman, to a communal contemplative form of the Black church in Holmes, and finally to nature and the environment in Harris's thinking, where the Spirit is in the world, in the Sacred Earth, and in the lives of black women experiencing oppression.

African Ancestral Spirituality, the Legendary Constitution, and the Logic of Descent

Traditional African religion identifies the High God, the Spirits, and the ancestors as key features of religious cosmology. These features are highlighted by Raboteau and also by others like West African religions scholar Eugene L. Mendoza, and traditional African religions scholars Laurenti Magesa and Dor-

---

3. Melville J. Herskovits, *The Myth of the Negro Past* (New York: Harper, 1941), 296.

cas Olubanke Akintunde. "Common to many African societies," say Raboteau, "was belief in a High God, or Supreme Creator of the world and everything in it."[4] This High God was and is usually understood to be almighty and omnipresent. Mendoza explains that among the Yoruba of the southern Nigeria rain forest, the "high-*Olodumare* is the Supreme Being or Sky God" with the power to both create and delegate.[5] Magesa notes that among the Dogon people of Mali, the High God or Divine Force lives at "the top of the hierarchy of the universe . . . , [as] the primary and ultimate life-giving Power God the Creator and Sustainer."[6] Magesa goes on to explain that the Dogon people take for granted God's ultimate significance and superiority. They honor the High God as "the Great Ancestor." Among various cultures, the High God is given many other names. Among the Yoruba, the High God is named Olodumare, while s/he is named Nyame among the Akan, Omukama among the Ganda, Leve among the Mende, and Unkulunkulu when named by the Zulus. Each of these terms may be loosely translated in a collective sense as "Supreme Creator," indicating that many West and Central African traditional religions believed and continue to believe in a Supreme Creator God. In the United States, it is likely that a modicum of integration and syncretism occurred with respect to belief in the High God and the Christian doctrine of God the Father and Supreme Creator. "Adapting to the foreign culture of the Europeans meant for the Africans not the total abandonment of their own cosmologies, but . . . integrating the new into the old."[7]

Although traditional African religions confess belief in a High God and Supreme Creator, most adherents understand this Supreme God to be radically transcendent, so that there is great distance between the Supreme God and the world. Although other Spirits are active in the human world, the Supreme God is not immanent, present, or directly involved in the world of human affairs. Molefi Kete Asante and Emeka Nwadiora isolate this as a key feature of traditional African religion. "What is believed all over the continent of Africa is that this Supreme Being, who could be male or female, created the universe . . . but soon retreated from any direct involvement in the affairs of humans."[8] Thus, for many traditional African religions, the Spirits and the ancestors take

---

4. Raboteau, *Slave Religion*, 8.

5. Eugene L. Mendoza, *West Africa: An Introduction to Its History, Civilization, and Contemporary Situation* (Durham, NC: Carolina Academic Press, 2002), 89.

6. Laurenti Magesa, *African Religion: The Moral Traditions of Abundant Life* (Maryknoll, NY: Orbis Books, 1997), 40.

7. Raboteau, *Slave Religion*, 126.

8. Molefi Kete Asante and Emeka Nwadiora, *Spear Masters: An Introduction to African Religion* (Lanham, MD: University Press of America, 2007), 2.

priority as the primary spiritual agents that interact with humans and involve themselves with human concerns. The ancestors are those who in their lives achieved some high status in the eyes of a family, clan, or nation.[9] They are dead but continue to maintain a presence among the living, as in West African religion, the dead don't return to God in heaven but rather live on spiritually in a world similar to our own, but one without pain. Ancestors generally remain tied to the families or clans from which they come. In day-to-day life in West and Central Africa, the ancestors form the principal strands for the fabric of life. The ancestors aren't omnipotent, but they are superhuman, with the power to protect society and punish offenses. They are regarded as the moral watchdogs of the community and the authority figures that maintain social and moral norms. With respect to traditional African religion, the continued presence of cultural and familial ancestors offers the community a sense of moral tradition and wisdom that might be of assistance against contemporary social issues or dilemmas. One prays to the ancestors on a daily basis, as well as in times of great need or of special thanksgiving.

One of traditional African religions' most distinctive traits is animism, which plays an integral role not only for continued existence of the ancestors but also for conceptions of the state of nature. The Supreme God has left creation in the hands of other spiritual beings, and these continue to operate as the spiritual causes of material events. Following Asante and Nwadiora, I understand animism as referring to traditional indigenous religions that believe in spirit beings. Belief in spirits, gods, and lesser gods, and unseen personalized forces, is prevalent among the adherents of traditional African religions. "All PTARE [Popular Traditional African Religion Everywhere] expressions are in the end expressions of spirit conquering matter. It is, as the ancient Egyptians believed, the bringing of maat [order, harmony] into the world that makes all things possible . . . there are some things that humans can do simply by applying one's self thoroughly into an idea, a project, a plan, and allowing the spirit of the situation to conquer any material obstacle."[10] For example, in Yoruba cosmology, man is constituted by both body and spirit. This spirit derives ultimately from Olodumare and comes to fulfill a purpose in the world. Thus, the spirit rules, guides, and controls the life and activity of a person, and the person will one day be judged for the person's actions during this life, most significantly by death, which is a "debt that everyone must pay." Among the Dogon people of Mali, spirits may be human or nonhuman. Nonhuman

9. Asante and Nwadiora, *Spear Masters*, 74.
10. Asante and Nwadiora, *Spear Masters*, 70.

spirits are often associated with natural phenomena such as the sun, rain, lightning, thunder, rivers, lakes, streams, trees, or even spears. These spiritual powers are more or less identical to these natural realities. Spirits below are generally considered to be weaker than spirits from above, but all spirits are often referred to as gods. Spirits are omnipresent, so that there is no place on the earth, no object or creature, without spirit.

In traditional Nigerian Yoruba society, this animist cosmology serves as the backdrop for women's labor and caregiving.[11] For example, herbs may act as agents of healing and are observed and memorized by women healers, known as *onisegun* in Yoruba. Plants and trees are also observed and eventually play a part in the work of healing. For example, plants, roots, and herbs are sometimes used in traditional Yoruban medicine for prenatal as well as postnatal care of women and infants.[12] Herbs and elements are also used in orthopedic treatments. The Yoruba medicine woman may use *egbogi* (the roots of trees), *ero* (balm), *ase* (herbal commands), or *epo* (palm oil), among other natural elements. The elements also play a role in healing, and even in the creation of life itself. The West African traditional religion of Yoruba acknowledges the orisha, supernatural and natural deities that have emanated from the supreme being Olodumare, as divine forces behind these natural elements. For example, Yemoja, the goddess of *omi* (water), holds power over all rivers, lakes, lagoons, and seas. She is the source of human, animal, plant, and even divine life, and thus also a symbol of motherhood and fertility.[13] Disciples of Yemoja may operate near rivers or natural springs and may be known to wash adherents in cold water. According to Nigerian religion scholar Dorcas Olubanke Akintunde, in contemporary Nigeria syncretism between traditional African religions and Christianity is prevalent. For example, traces of Yemoja may be found in Aladura churches, which use blessed or baptismal waters, alongside prayer and the Holy Spirit, to cleanse or transform believers. The Yoruba believe that the water receives power when one prays or speaks into it, for there is power in words and the water. Thus, the animism of traditional African religion imbued nature with spiritual forces of the ancestors and the lesser gods.

Thus, a cursory analysis of traditional African religion discloses the world as a world of interconnected forces similar to a spider's web, where action

---

11. Dorcas Akintunde, "Women as Healers," in *African Women, Religion, and Health: Essays in Honor of Mercy Amba Ewudziwa Oduyoye*, ed. Isabel Apawo Phiri and Sarojini Nadar (Maryknoll, NY: Orbis Books, 2006), 159.
12. Akintunde, "Women as Healers," 162.
13. Akintunde, "Women as Healers," 165.

at one end of the web causes vibrations throughout the entire network.[14] Causation flows in all directions to maintain life in the universe, and all creatures are connected with each other in the sense that they may influence one another. Yet in the most general sense, the older forces and more animate creatures are always perceived as the stronger forces. The older forces tend to dominate the younger forces, and this can be seen especially in the authority and power of the ancestors to operate as the moral fabric of society. Philosophically, this marks the authorities of tradition and experience as key sources for the moral wisdom of traditional African religions. While it would thus be uncommon for an adherent of traditional African religion to make a moral appeal to the will of the Supreme God or to use language of "natural law" that is more common in Western moral discourse, it would be quite common and even expected to make moral appeals to ancestral custom, as the still-existing ancestors were vital as the spiritual guardians of African moral tradition and social order. Mendoza refers to this bond between the living and the dead as a "legendary constitution," that is, an orally and ritually established contract between the living and the dead and extending both outward to others in society and backward and forward in time.[15] In this way, new people could always be incorporated into the community, perhaps not always as kin, but in ways that established reciprocal rights and duties between parties. Much of African religion and culture is marked by a strong collectivist or communal moral sense. Contemporary theologians like Desmond Tutu describe this as *ubuntu*, "I am because you are." More generally, the legendary constitution implies that the good of the community is placed ahead of that of the individual.

With respect to the cultural logic of sovereignty, traditional African religion tends to place a strong value on the phenomenon of clan descent, tending toward preferential treatment for particular clan groups. It is difficult to tell how the preferential treatment or option for one clan group over another impacts the rights or duties of the other clan. Mendoza argues that, *politically*, Africans have evolved into a strong, relatively egalitarian and communalistic civic culture. He understands the culture as marked by a series of "checks and balances" that effectively discourage the rise of despots apart from Western influence. Yet, although African societies may have rejected sovereignty politically in a general sense, traces of sovereignty as a cultural logic remain, especially in the notions of descent and consanguinity. Descent indicates that clan members may claim descent from a distant ancestor, and perhaps even a lesser god.

14. See Magesa, *African Religion*, 38–40.
15. Mendoza, *West Africa*, 88.

Descent is thus the foundation and cornerstone of social organization in West Africa, serving as a basis for culture and as a paradigm for various unchanging roles of superiority and subordination as well as unity and division. The language and logic of descent justify the rule of the elders over the youth as well as one clan's claims against those of another, yet it is unclear whether this rule may ever become absolute, eternal, or unchecked. As is the case with language of descent, so is it also with language of consanguinity, which is used to convey that certain members of society have "one blood." This language, in both its real and fictive forms, creates a corporate descent group that is set off from others in society by exclusive rights and duties. These corporations define the identity of individuals such that they cannot be seen apart from these. Thus, the concepts of descent and consanguinity possess the potential to reproduce the cultural logic of sovereignty, even within the contours of *ubuntu* and the legendary constitution.

Finally, in addition to the concepts of descent and consanguinity, the specter of the cultural logic of sovereignty also appears in the principle that recognizes the supremacy of the community over the individual. This dynamic is expressed with clarity by Nyambura J. Njoroge, who calls attention to the lack of women's and children's rights in countries like Zimbabwe and Ghana.[16] For Njoroge, although African society may be perceived as integrated into the moral fabric of the ancestors and the spirits, it is also constituted by a social reality marked by issues in women's health care and access to resources. Although women are responsible for most of the production and processing of food crops, men control the means of production, land, cattle, and reproduction. Furthermore, the relations among the leading men are marked by a competitive patriarchy. "In fine," says Akintunde, African culture is a two-edged sword "that provides deep religious and cultural roots for community life, while at the same time it also binds women."[17] Akintunde explains that the ideology of corporate personality almost always takes priority over the personhood of the individual, especially women. On the underside of society, there is the dialectic of hiding as other women were hidden from the dehumanization of the chains and patriarchal social system. Many women's lives thus remain marked by extreme poverty, chronic hunger, systemic violence, and, today, the social injustices of globalization. For both Dorothy B. E. A. Akoto and Dorcas Akintunde, women's health is a state constituted by bodily, mental,

---

16. Nyambura J. Njoroge, "Let's Celebrate the Power of Naming," in Phiri and Nadar, *African Women, Religion, and Health*, 59–76.

17. Njoroge, "Let's Celebrate the Power of Naming," 51.

and spiritual well-being. This not only requires appropriate medical care but also requires the healing of broken human and environmental relationships as well as the recognition of women's and children's rights.[18] "Women's health in Africa should be synonymous with the rights of children and women," says Akintunde, a "basic right" for women.

The Spirituality of Hunger, the Racially Reconciled Community, and the Disinherited Jesus

Thurman's perspective on world is predicated on a type of rational mysticism that takes the practitioner on an inward journey to the discovery of God and self. Thurman's mysticism emerged in the mid-twentieth century in the wake of a range of interdenominational and interfaith Christian encounters that included education at a Baptist high school, study with Quaker philosopher Rufus Jones, and church leadership with Presbyterian clergyman Alfred Fisk at the Fellowship of All Peoples. Thurman believed that the social reality of American society was too riddled with the ethos of segregation, insecurity, and materialism to be of any spiritual help. During his times in Atlanta, Washington, DC, and San Francisco, among other places, Thurman saw that America implemented techniques of control over Black life, for example, in "the form of policy in business, in the church, in the state, in the school, in the living zones."[19] Thurman saw this will to segregate present both before and after the 1960s civil rights gains, so that as late as 1976 he would write in his famous *Jesus and the Disinherited* that "for the most part, Negroes assume that there are no basic citizenship rights, no fundamental protection, guaranteed to them by the state, because their status as citizens has never been clearly defined. There has been little protection from the dominant controllers of society and even less protection from unrestrained elements within their own group."[20] Thurman was all too aware that under *ordinary, everyday* circumstances, the Negro is at most "a citizen, second class." Finally, Thurman criticized the economic consumerism and materialism that characterized late capitalist American society. He acknowledged that people had material needs but argued that a focus on

---

18. Dorothy B. E. A. Akoto, "Women and Health in Ghana and the *Trokosi* Practice," in Phiri and Nadar, *African Women, Religion, and Health*, 96–112.

19. Howard Thurman, "The Will to Segregation," in *A Strange Freedom: The Best of Howard Thurman on Religious Experience and Public Life*, ed. Walter Fluker, Catherine Tumber, and Martin E. Marty (Boston: Beacon, 1998), 214.

20. Howard Thurman, *Jesus and the Disinherited* (Boston: Beacon, 1976), 34.

"bread and bread alone" crowded out the voice of the Spirit. He thus believed that it was a spiritual error to give oneself over to materialism.

For Thurman, the natural environment offers a clue to the human religious constitution and thus a clue to spiritual freedom. Humanity may reliably infer something about their own spiritual life from an investigation of the environment. Thurman was fascinated by the laws of nature identified by the physical and biological sciences and believed that a mystical approach could identify the natural laws of the human spirit. There seem to be two primary natural laws that appear in Thurman's writings, namely, those of hunger and prayer. He believed that all persons possessed within themselves an existential hunger for God, and that this hunger was itself God and a confirmation of the givenness of God. He described this spirituality of hunger as the movement of a person's heart toward God. The movement of hunger is spiritual, which means that it was established by means other than the body, the senses, by reason or logic. The movement of hunger is the movement toward God, and this spiritual hunger may only be satiated by a "centering down," by a disciplining of the body, a quelling of the senses, and the calming of the mind through the rigors of silent prayer. "The most natural thing in the world for man, then, would be to keep open the lines of communication between him and the Source of his life. . . . Prayer. . . . I am always impressed by the fact that it is recorded that the only thing the disciples asked Jesus to teach them how to do was to pray."[21] Thurman did not see his mysticism as disconnected from America's social realities of economic materialism, segregation, and insecurity. Yet the movement to change these realities was an existential one, rather than a social or environmental one. "Segregation is a mood, a state of mind. . . . The wall is in the mind and in the spirit. . . . When the walls are down, it is then that the real work of building the healthy American society begins."[22] Thus, Thurman's spirituality of hunger and prayer.

Thurman's hermeneutical world is constituted by the horizon of reconciled community of racial difference. The community is the mind of God at work, providing spiritual nourishment to persons. Yet Thurman argued that this spiritual nourishment was for the particular purpose of racial integration and reconciliation. The fundamental unity of life itself serves as the grounds for this goal. It provides hope for the reconciliation of broken relationships, for mutual honoring, and for mutual understanding. In turn, racially integrated, reconciled community is the realization of potential life. Although the com-

---

21. Thurman, "Prayer," in Fluker, Tumber, and Marty, *A Strange Freedom*, 82.
22. Thurman, "Excerpt from *The Luminous Darkness*," in Fluker, Tumber, and Marty, *A Strange Freedom*, 242.

munity is the mind of God at work, this does not preclude human action. This sense of belonging provides a basis for identity with a cause, a purpose, and values more significant than individual survival. Thurman embraces an ethic of care, arguing that we must be intentional in our caring for one another in such a community to the effect that all members have a sense of belonging.[23] Reconciliation is a shift from hate, understood as the will to nonexistence, to love understood as the desire to acknowledge another's existence and to care for another. Thurman saw the mind of God distinctively at work in creativity toward this goal: "the mind of God at work is expressed through authentic creativity, whether through the order in creation and the orderly disorder of 'random activity,' [or] the concepts in the (sense-bound) human mind, esp. humanity's ability to create, conceptualize, to plan, to function with purpose."[24] The Church for the Fellowship of All Peoples in San Francisco was Thurman's successful attempt to make such a vision concrete, working alongside Alfred Fisk. The membership was open to anyone willing to participate in Thurman's and Fisk's established programs and to share in the church's responsibilities. The church conducted fellowship dinners, fellowship camps, and monthly arts programs as it worked toward reconciliation.

Thurman's world horizon of reconciled community of racial difference oriented toward the church but also included American society within a global community. In fact, Thurman's vision for reconciled community of racial difference was brought into focus during his visit to India in the 1930s, which included meeting Gandhi, but also a particular experience that gave Thurman an understanding of the social function of his Fellowship of All Peoples. Thurman scholar John H. Cartwright recounts this vision, noting that the "watershed experience in [his] lifelong work was the event at Khyber Pass" in northwest India.[25] Thurman sat with his entourage on a mountain cleft in northwest India facing northward, thus sitting in India but overlooking Pakistan, and seeing even to the north of Pakistan into Afghanistan:

> Near the end of our journey, we spent a day in Khyber Pass on the border of the northwest frontier. It was an experience of vision. We stood looking at the distance into Afghanistan, while to our right, and close at hand, passed a long camel train bringing goods and ideas to the bazaars of North India.

---

23. Thurman, "Reconciliation," in Fluker, Tumber, and Marty, *A Strange Freedom*, 163, 167.
24. Thurman, "Concerning the Search," in Fluker, Tumber, and Marty, *A Strange Freedom*, 105–6.
25. John H. Cartwright, "The Religious Ethics of Howard Thurman," *Annual of the Society of Christian Ethics* 5 (1985): 79–99, https://tinyurl.com/2afce8wa.

Mind, Body, and Spirit

Here was the gateway through which Roman and Mogul conquerors had come in other days bringing with them goods, new concepts, and the violence of the armed might. All that we had seen and felt in India seemed to be brought miraculously into focus. We saw clearly what we must do somehow when we returned to America. We know that we must test whether a religious fellowship could be developed in America that was capable of cutting across all racial barriers, with a carryover into the common life, a fellowship that would alter the behavior patterns of those involved. It became imperative now to find out if experiences of Spiritual unity among people could be more compelling than the experiences which divide them.[26]

Thurman's analogy of the movement of reconciled community of racial difference into the American public is that of the flow of market goods. Thurman imagined that the spiritual riches of the Fellowship of All Peoples would begin to flow out into the city of San Francisco, transforming the culture in the process. Thurman sometimes talked about the public effect of the Fellowship as creating an ethos of "neighborliness" in America. This, too, was the mind of God at work, coming to God's self in a collective sociopolitical sense. For Thurman, this was the true soul of America, the godly soul as opposed to the economically materialistic and consumeristic soul that kept America spiritually weak and socially divided. He saw in America a prescient purpose, since America's pluralism, hinted at as early as the eighteenth century in the Declaration of Independence, represented the diversity of the emerging global civil society during Thurman's own time. America's problem of diversity had become the world's problem of diversity. "It was as if the Creator of existence wanted to discover whether or not a certain ideal could be realized in time and space," says Thurman, "in anticipation of a time when time and space would be reduced to zero; when the whole planet would be as one little neighborhood in one little town. . . . Yet 'school is now out' and the test is how neighborly our interactions are . . . the degree to which the enforced experience of neighborhoods . . . can be a living, practicing part of neighborliness, which is the fulfilment of the dream."[27] America must begin from the fact of cultural difference and build a new nation that acknowledges the equal worth of all peoples.

Thurman understood the reconciled ecclesial community of racial difference and the neighborliness of America as implicit critiques of all forms of

---

26. Thurman, quoted in Cartwright, "The Religious Ethics of Howard Thurman," 87.
27. Thurman, "America in Search of a Soul," in Fluker, Tumber, and Marty, *A Strange Freedom*, 266–69.

racial and national sovereignty. Thus, Thurman's 1971 essay "The Search for Identity" argues against American nationalism, postcolonial sovereignty, and Black nationalism as all complicit in the perpetuation of the will to segregate. For Thurman, state sovereignty is a symbol that "provides a sense of belonging, thus answering questions of man's alienation and isolation from nature as a result of exploitation, plunder, and rape with impunity."[28] Yet this symbol was only used to build more walls between peoples. For example, Thurman saw the symbol of state sovereignty as necessarily cojoined to the symbol of the minority. "Minorities are further symbols of sovereignty, and this disrupts the minority's sense of national belonging." Likewise, Thurman saw African American calls for self-determination in response to white American practices of state sovereignty as equally problematic. These calls for self-determination from African Americans were problematic because they were simply substitutes for claims to self-sovereignty, requiring voluntary separation and the erection of existential walls. Even the new global postcolonial states reflected this will to segregation. "The emergence of the new African states in the arena of world states and their place of influence in the United Nations must not be separated from the new concept of community appearing in the black community."[29] All of these were evasions of the true mind of God for Thurman, which was the reconciled community of racial difference. Ecclesiastically, Thurman's understanding of the true mind of God took form as the Fellowship Church of All Peoples, and socially, the true mind of God was the ethos of neighborliness. These imbued Thurman's world horizon with a sense of belonging and a sense of kinship to life.

One of Thurman's most significant contributions to the discourse on African American religion is the primacy of individual and personal religious experience. "I asked myself," says Thurman, "how I may find a clue to God's purposes in the world? How may I sense Him at work? Already I am aware of Him in the hunger of my heart; this is a crucial clue. In the depths of my own spirit, then, I may be aware of His presence."[30] The work of reconciliation cannot be separated from the phenomenon of personal religious experience. In religious experience, one has a sense of being touched at one's inmost center, at one's very core, and this awareness, says Thurman, sets in motion the process that makes for integration and wholeness. Cartwright argues that Thurman's

---

28. Thurman, "The Search in Identity," in Fluker, Tumber, and Marty, *A Strange Freedom*, 276.
29. Thurman, "The Search in Identity," 278–79.
30. Thurman, "Prayer," 84; Thurman, "Reconciliation," 179.

mysticism can be classified according to the three types of church organization that were theorized by early twentieth-century theologian Ernst Troeltsch. Troeltsch argued that, historically, the church has taken three general forms. The first is the church proper, which has established some kind of established working relationship with society. Doctrinally the church usually focuses on the objective realities of grace and redemption and tends to downplay matters of personal holiness. The second form is the sect, a smaller, more disciplined Christian society under the objective reality of law rather than grace and redemption. The sect lives apart from the world and society rather than as a part of it and anticipates the coming kingdom of God. Troeltsch's final type was the mystic, whose faith was grounded in personal and inward experience rather than orthodoxy. Religious worship remains for the mystic but becomes formal and loses much of its significance along with doctrine. Thurman argued that personal experience allowed one to see one's true, inward self beyond the divisiveness and lies of larger collectives. Thurman's account of personal religious experience remains an invaluable contribution.

Although Thurman's spirituality of racially reconciled community is rooted in the concept of hunger, his hermeneutical world remains fundamentally a movement away from nature. The search for one's true spiritual self is only begun with the silencing of the body. Thurman's world is a world apart from nature and the environment. The spirit is described as the mind of God without reference to the body of God, and the reconciled community of racial difference only springs forth with the personal disciplining of nature. God is mind over body, order is mystic experience over the flesh. This disembodied spirituality is ironically most apparent in one of Thurman's most celebrated and indeed truly valuable images, that is, the image of the Jesus of the disinherited. Thurman explained that one of the reasons that he liked the character of Jesus was because the "striking similarity between the social position of Jesus in Palestine and that of the vast majority of American Negroes is obvious to anyone who tarries long over the facts.... The masses of men live with their backs constantly against the wall. They are poor, the disinherited, the dispossessed."[31] Thurman saw Jesus as a poor Jew and a member of a minority group without citizenship rights. Yet Thurman understood Jesus's intervention in the world to be a primarily psychological and existential one. Thus, Thurman simultaneously affirms the body in his depiction of Jesus as one of the disinherited but also denies it any property or goodness. In turn, this leaves the masses of men to which Thurman refers in a disinherited state. Jesus's "message focused on the urgency of a

---

31. Thurman, *Jesus of the Disinherited*, 13, 34.

radical change of inner attitude of the people ... the 'inward center' [was] the crucial arena where the issues would determine the destiny of his people."[32] Thurman doubled down on his attack against any social religion in "The Idol of Togetherness," placing "a curse on him who relies on man for human aid. He is like a desert scrub that never thrives."[33]

Finally, Thurman's spirituality leaves us with an ambiguous legacy of understanding the work of the Spirit in the world as progress. On the one hand, Thurman believed that the Spirit's work in the world was seen in progress toward racially reconciled community. In this way, salvation history and social progress were interconnected for Thurman. Thurman was no romantic idealist and acknowledged that "the bloody carnage of fratricide is a part of the sorry human tale."[34] Thus, progress was not possible without suffering. People must suffer as part of the experience of freedom, and Thurman believed that without suffering there was no freedom for man. Yet with spiritual discipline, progress toward racial reconciliation is possible. Thurman seems to conceive of this progress as more of a flow than a straight line. The flow of progress moves from the individual to the individual in a multiracial church of all peoples and finally from the church, indirectly out into the neighborhood by way of emanation or a focused channeling of spiritual energies. Yet Thurman's progress remains fundamentally dehistoricized.

Progress toward reconciliation and neighborliness is possible only to the extent that it is dematerialized and largely disembodied. Thurman talks of the "moving finger of God upon human history" as if God were disinclined to touch history. The impulses and desires of humanity remain an "indispensable part of the defect of [one's] spiritual vision."[35] Thurman's view of progress is fundamentally ascetic, as he believes that this disposition will enable the mystic to resist economic materialism and consumerism as well as the violence cultured within various nationalistic groups. Thus, his understanding of spiritual progress toward racial reconciliation and freedom is fundamentally existential rather than social or economic. Nor does Thurman discuss how spirituality gives us a different understanding of nature or the environment.

---

32. Thurman, *Jesus of the Disinherited*, 21.
33. Thurman, "The Idol of Togetherness," in Fluker, Tumber, and Marty, *A Strange Freedom*, 23.
34. Thurman, "Suffering," in Fluker, Tumber, and Marty, *A Strange Freedom*, 44–45.
35. Thurman, "Mysticism and Social Change," in Fluker, Tumber, and Marty, *A Strange Freedom*, 111.

Contemplative Spirituality, the Contemplative Black Church, and Nature's Spiritual Void

As with Thurman, for womanist theologian Barbara Holmes, spirituality is rooted in practices that allow one to "center down" into an experiential connection with God's divine presence. Holmes commends a range of traditional contemplative practices within the Black church. Practices like communal contemplative prayer, baptisms, the "holy hush" of silent meditation before worship, and ecstatic singing facilitate the collective transcendence and transformation of the Black church beyond the sense of spiritual emptiness toward joy unspeakable. Dance, song, drumming, dreaming, and divination are portals to a world beyond, yet tied to, the ordinary. Powers and principalities are recognized by the Black church in everyday activity but are also specifically invoked during designated rites. Contemplative spirituality acknowledges an unresolved dialectical tension between the seen and unseen worlds. We live within the limits of the seen world even as we are able to transcend the limits of space and time via ritual. Sometimes at the mourner's benches, or at all-night prayer shut-ins, or during the humming of a song during baptism or communion, the community experiences collective ascendancy to that "third heaven . . . [and enters] into joy unspeakable."[36] If Thurman emphasized the personal dimensions of transformative contemplation, Holmes stresses the communal ones. "The key to [crisis] contemplation in the black church seems to be its emergence as a communal practice. . . . In this ethnic context the word *contemplation* includes but does not require silence or solitude" (42). Each person must explore the inner reality of his or her humanity, facing unmet potential and catastrophic failure with unmitigated honesty and grace. Yet, contemplative practices are identified in public prayers, meditative dances, and musical cues that move the entire congregation toward communal listening and communion with God.

With respect to the state of nature doctrine, Holmes's communal contemplative spirituality exhibits a dissonance whereby nature is both spiritually endowed and spiritually impure. On the one hand, Holmes argues that the world is spiritually energized. This aspect of her thought is rooted in African traditional religions and contemporary African scholars of religion. The research of African scholars like John Mbiti, Muse Dube, and Mercy Amba Oduyoye

---

36. Barbara A. Holmes, *Joy Unspeakable: Contemplative Practices of the Black Church* (Minneapolis: Augsburg Fortress, 2004), 54. Hereafter, page references from this work will be given in parentheses in the text.

points to a cosmology that embraces multiple realities without clear demarcation between everyday life and the spirit realm. Holmes acknowledges that "the universe of African reality includes powers and principalities, ancestors and the cosmos... they are sharing an animate life world that is fully imbued with energy" (25). Many African perspectives include the belief that everything has life and spiritual interiority. Holmes even notes that this African-based contemplative perspective is deeply ecological. Yet even as Holmes argues that the world is spiritually energized on the one hand, on the other hand, she remains silent as to the substantive content of that spirituality. Instead, Holmes offers an account of spirituality almost exclusively as experienced in the contemplative ritual practices of the Black church. God is present in the world, but the world is primarily understood as the contemplative Black church. History is the history forged by the situational and fragile accomplishments of the Black church. Trajectories of contemplative consciousness thus propel African Americans forward as various freedom movements, whether these movements be antislavery or civil rights movements. "History has taught us that oppression is cyclical and overcoming is situational and often temporary. Every gain is seeded with just enough destruction, personal and communal, to deflate and nullify the sense of accomplishment" (xxxviii). The world is spiritually energized but also oriented toward oppression.

Holmes's dissonance with respect to the normative status of the state of nature results in an implicit assertion of the sovereignty of the Black church over a market-saturated, religiously charismatic, and spiritually empty world. Nature's sacred transformative power as acknowledged by indigenous cosmologies is almost exclusively incorporated into the contemplative Black church. For Holmes, the world becomes reducible to two basic halves, that is, the contemplative Black church and the charismatic Black church. These two modes of consciousness face off against one another, and for Holmes, the contemplative Black church is the true sovereign, while the charismatic Black church is the church imposter. Her conception of the contemplative Black church thus has a "meta-actual" rather than historical form. "It inhabits the imagination of its people in ways that far exceed its [historical] reach ... it will always be invisible to some extent because it embodies a spiritual idea.... The black church is, in a sense, 'virtual' space created by the worship practices of the congregation" (xxiii). In the end, Holmes's idealism is tempered by a type of realism, so that she concludes with a lament of longing for the return of the king. "Things have changed; African American communities and churches are not as homogenous as they seemed during the years of sanctioned cultural oppression. Instead, both are becoming more and more diverse....

The question is whether the current generation will pass on a legacy rich in the diversity and complexity of the historical black church or whether one type of charismatic [evocative] worship will obliterate all of the creativity we have inherited" (xxiv–xxv). While Holmes does acknowledge the normative dimensions of nature as based in indigenous worldviews, her implicit assumption and deployment of the cultural logic of sovereignty result in a sovereign contemplative Black church over against the state of nature, which is seen as spiritual void.

Ecowomanist Spirituality, the Fullness of the Earth Community, and the Sacred Earth

Ecowomanist spirituality offers an understanding of the world that places a strong emphasis on both the presence of the Spirit in nature and the sacredness of the earth. This leads to an understanding of the earth as a type of spiritual agent whose actions are marked by an ecological orientation and a view of life as fundamentally interconnected. In turn, the interconnectedness of life, the presence of the Spirit, and the sacredness of the earth drive us to seek our true fullness in a global, earth-conscious human community. Ecowomanist theorist Melanie L. Harris's vision is cast against the multidimensional oppressions that frustrate the life chances of Black women, both in Africa and in the global African diaspora. The compounded issues that frame Black women's lives are a consequence of white supremacy's impact on environmental policy, perspective, and understanding. White supremacy, itself driven by the logic of domination, attempts to devalue the lives, worth, and dignity of Black women and communities of color. Yet Harris sees a connection between the logic of domination that justifies the enslavement of Black women and the logic that justifies the domination of nature and other animals. The logic of domination present in white supremacist ideology thus gives rise to both the multidimensional oppressions that frame Black women's lives such as sexism, racism, and classism, as well as the parallel oppressions between the destruction of Black women and the destruction of the natural world. In the modern age, both Black women and the natural world have been systematically and continuously instrumentalized, abused, and destroyed under the logic and regime of white supremacy. For example, both Black women and nature experience structural violence, that is, physical, psychological, or spiritual harm or injury as a result of the unequal distribution of power and the regularized exploitation of African peoples, lands, and knowledge.

White supremacy and the logic of domination are falsehoods in that they deny the circularity and web-like nature of life, where spirit, nature, and humanity are connected and interdependent. Thus, Harris notes that "any ethical or unethical behavior conducted by humans impacts the other aspects of the cosmological order positively or negatively. According to this framework, one could argue that since ancestors are believed to reside in many aspects of nature, any human behavior that diminishes and dishonors nature of the earth can have a devastating impact on the relationship between the human and the ancestor."[37] Harris explains that African cosmology functions in a circular manner, such that human beings are a vital part, but not the center, of the universe. Ecowomanism also acknowledges the reality of the Spirit and understands it as a religious, interreligious, and intrareligious spiritual presence that marks an element of the transcendent.[38] The Spirit may present as a "Mighty Rushing Wind" but may also come like a gentle healing breeze. Harris discusses the work of Alice Walker, who writes pointedly about the "healing breeze" of the earth and how this breath restores physical strength as well as emotional fortitude and hope. "As my mother looked out over the immense acreage still to be covered, she felt so ill she could barely lift the hoe.... Coming to the end of a row, she lay down under a tree and asked to die. Instead, she fell into a deep sleep, and when she awakened, she was fully restored. In fact, she felt wonderful, as if a healing breeze had touched her soul. She picked up the hoe and continued her work."[39] Nature communicates the essence of the spirits. The spirits are in the plants; the spirits are in the land, water, stone, and animals. Nature speaks to us, even as the Spirit endows us with agency and a sense of interconnectedness to nature. God's sustenance is seen in the rain and the sunshine. God gives what is sufficient.

In ecowomanist thought, the inspirited earth is the Sacred Earth. Harris highlights the Nankani women of northern Ghana as one example, whose belief in the sacredness of the environment promotes an ethical mandate to care for the earth. "[For] many African communities ... the spiritual is as much a part of the physical, as the physical is part of all aspects of their daily lives.... This includes the natural environment."[40] The Nankani women practice various key rituals of pacification and restoration that honor the unseen natural

---

37. Melanie L. Harris, *Ecowomanism: African American Women and Earth-Honoring Faiths* (Maryknoll, NY: Orbis Books, 2016), 14.

38. Harris, *Ecowomanism*, 26.

39. Harris, *Ecowomanism*, 33–34. Also see Alice Walker's *Anything We Love Can Be Saved: A Writer's Activism* (New York: Ballantine, 1997).

40. Harris, *Ecowomanism*, 98.

order of the universe, and these rituals recognize the reality of entities such as *Wine*, the creator/creative *will*, the *yan'duma* (ancestors), and *baga* (spirit entities). For the Nankani, *paa'la* (destiny) is shaped by *Wine*, the creator, who sustains the earth and the whole universe, including the relationships between human beings, the earth, and the spirit realm, even apart from human agency. The Akan women, also in Ghana, name God as "Nana, the good parent . . . the source of lovingkindness and protection."[41] God's sustenance is seen in the elements and provisions of nature, such as water, fire, wind, and the bounty of earth. Harris argues that the notion of the sacredness of the earth, present in both African cosmology and African American cultural history, creates a tension and paradox when placed alongside the multiple oppressions caused by the logic of domination. For Harris, this "beauty to burden paradox" constitutes much of African American (environmental) history. African American people's experiences of connection to the earth occur within a history that also includes racial hatred and brutality, and for Harris, the cultural memory of this history places an ecological burden on African Americans. The beauty of the sacredness of the earth, when combined with the burden of a cultural memory of economic and environmental suffering, provides Harris with the fuel for African American struggles for freedom and ecological justice.

In Harris's hermeneutics of world, nature is understood to be primarily a product of divine emanation. While Harris succeeds in drawing attention to the significance of nature, the earth, the body, and their rhythms, her conception of the Spirit is ultimately conflated with that of nature, such that the Spirit seems to exercise little agency beyond that which is already mundane and naturally occurring. The Spirit is not only in nature but also emanates nature. Thus, Harris understands the Spirit to be fully present in *and* as the environment, for example, in *and* as the rhythmic cycles of nature like the seasons and animal migrations, and animal and plant relations of mutuality. In this way, the environment becomes the "Sacred Earth," that is, the environment as known to modern natural science with the added element of religious purpose. The notion of the Sacred Earth is the product of the combination of the idea of the Spirit emanation of the earth and that of the environment. The Sacred Earth is thus predicated on a transcendent act of consciousness that includes environment within the hermeneutical frame of nature. Yet Harris ultimately looks to the environmental frame for conceptions of sacred time and sacred order, with the result that the natural environment becomes a totalized metaphysic. The benefit of the environmental frame is that it draws attention to

---

41. Harris, *Ecowomanism*, 103.

the possible religious significance of cyclical time. Thus, agricultural time is mapped onto the imagined ideal object of the Sacred Earth, and human time becomes defined as a curvilinear path rather than a rectilinear one, that is, by repetition rather than by progress, since agricultural environmental time is cyclical. This curvilinear notion of time challenges Western rectilinear time, and calls all of us to reconsider the value of cyclical time. Yet in Harris's perspective, spirit has no agency to move history forward beyond the repetitive rhythmic patterns of environment. It only moves cyclically.

While Harris's approach offers a rich reflection of African American spirituality, her accounts of moral order and of the cosmos remain unfinished in key respects. This is significant because it leaves the question of the cultural logic of sovereignty unanswered, giving a foothold to imperial claims to supremacy in matters of moral authority. This ambiguity in moral order can be seen most clearly in Harris's account of the relationship between the ancestral, traditional aspects of Black spirituality and the modern, liberal, personal ones. On the one hand, Harris argues for the authority of the tradition of the ancestors and associated ritual, cosmological, and moral beliefs and practices. As I discussed in the section on African ancestral spirituality, this cosmology assumes a strong collectivist moral consciousness as well as a strong emphasis on the authority of tradition in moral and social matters. On the other hand, Harris also commends the ethical value of freedom, as well as the values of land rights, civil rights, and human rights, all of which acknowledge the natural right of the individual over against all other entities. How is the relationship between the ancestors and the individual mediated? On the one hand, it is mediated by social rituals, and on the other, by individual rights. Closely tied to this question of moral order is that of the agential status of nature. Harris describes the earth as both sacred and subject to human rights. In one view nature is home to the spirits, and in another, nature is an object that may be manipulated for personal human use. These ambiguities leave the question of the cultural logic of sovereignty unanswered, thus giving a foothold to willful claims to supremacy in matters of moral authority. Harris's ethics of recognition attempts to offset this, acknowledging the impact of white supremacy on environmental movements, but the relation between recognition and rights remains unclear.

Conclusion

In concluding with Harris's thought, we also see the contemporary state of African American spirituality within a larger historical trajectory marked by

Mind, Body, and Spirit

a fourfold transmigration of the spirit. This transmigration began in traditional African spirituality as a collectivist, environmental, ancestral spirituality among the peoples of West and Central Africa. By the twentieth century, as represented in the thinking of Howard Thurman, this spirituality had primarily come to function as a personal, mystical spirituality. Thurman's spirituality focused on the interiority of the soul to the exclusion of the natural world, which Thurman saw as largely devoid of the spirit. Thurman's emphasis on personal religious experience was expressed alongside an ascetic silencing of the body, a calming of the soul's raging seas. In the thinking of Barbara Holmes, Thurman's contemplative spirituality is taken as a model and then expanded into communal contemplative form as Holmes resources the contemplative practices of the Black church. For Holmes, this is where the Spirit may be found. Finally, in ecowomanist thought, the Spirit as conceived in African American spirituality has made a "return" to nature in an attempt to reproduce aspects of traditional African spirituality. The ecowomanist Spirit is found in the world, and especially in the forms of the Sacred Earth and in the lives of women and others experiencing oppression.

5

Covenant, Law, and the Sound of Jazz

On African American Theology

THE PREVIOUS CHAPTER EXAMINED the questions of the state of nature doctrine and the cultural logic of sovereignty in the discourse on African American spirituality. This chapter takes up the state of nature doctrine and the problem of sovereignty as theorized in contemporary African American theology. I engage the writings of theologians Vincent Lloyd, J. Kameron Carter, and Willie J. Jennings to unearth their natural theologies and theologies of creation. My study finds that their views may be represented as aligning with three types of approaches to the state of nature doctrine: natural law, covenantal theology, and the new cultural politics of intimacy, respectively. Lloyd, Carter, and Jennings thus offer unique angles of vision on the state of nature doctrine, and each of their perspectives has implications for the problem of the cultural logic of sovereignty. Yet in the final analysis, each approach falls short, so that the question of the cultural logic of sovereignty remains unanswered, and the problem lingers. Lloyd, Carter, and Jennings do not write in a vacuum but represent the emergent generation of African American theologians after the dominance of the Black theology of liberation in the North American theological academy. I begin the chapter with a discussion of this context, primarily as represented in the thinking of Dr. James Hal Cone. In the discussion, I give attention to Cone's theology of nature, with special attention to the way that his theology is shaped by his narrative approach as situated within the African American literary and cultural tradition. Cone's ideological critique of white supremacy and his emphasis on God as liberator of the oppressed signal his fundamental thrust against sovereignty. Cone's theology freed up the discursive space for theology to begin to think anew about the question of nature, a question that had been literally subjugated, silenced, and "tamed" in white Anglo-Saxon Protestant theology.

The Election of the Oppressed and the Liberation Dialectic

Black theology of liberation grew out of the post–civil rights African American revolutionary energies that began to spread in the late 1960s. Key events that informed the birth of the academic discourse were the 1966 statement by the National Committee of Negro Churchmen, the 1967 Detroit riot, and the deaths of the vanguard of the US freedom movement. According to theologians Frederick Ware and Dwight Hopkins, the summer of 1966 signaled the formal beginnings of the Black theology movement, marked by a manifesto from the National Committee of Negro Churchmen published in the *New York Times* on July 31.[1] The manifesto stressed a need to move beyond the civil rights discourse of "love and justice" to a revolutionary one of Black power and liberation due to the continued silence of many white middle-class Christians about social problems like racism and poverty in the inner city. For many members of the National Committee of Negro Churchmen, the Civil Rights Act of 1964 and the Voting Rights Act of 1965 did little to move the needle of Black freedom forward, and they desired an agenda that also addressed economic and educational problems as well as police brutality. The 1967 Detroit riot seemed to confirm many of the Churchmen's concerns. The riot, precipitated by a police raid of a local African American bar, was the longest and bloodiest of the summer of 1967 and one of the most violent in all of US history. Among other key events that also shaped Black theology were the deaths of key leaders in the US civil rights movement, symbolized by the demise of both the Reverend Doctor Martin Luther King Jr. and Robert F. Kennedy, assassinated in the same year, about two months apart. These events precipitated the rise of Black revolutionary energies aimed at the goal of liberation from the entire system. It was in this context that James Cone came into his own as a leading thinker for the Black theology of liberation.

In Cone's perspective, academic theology played a key role in US social conflict, and its silence on the issue of anti-Black racism in America only facilitated Black oppression. Cone saw this silence as both a theological and

---

1. See James H. Cone, *Black Theology: A Documentary History* (Maryknoll, NY: Orbis Books, 1979), and Dwight Hopkins, *Introducing Black Theology of Liberation* (Maryknoll, NY: Orbis Books, 1999).

a methodological issue. That is to say that white American theology's silence about the problem of anti-Black racism required a theological as well as a methodological conversion. In terms of method, Cone argued that *all* theology, including white American theology and Black theology, should begin by acknowledging the social element in its reasoning. Theology is produced from within particular social contexts, and thus, to some degree, reflects the interests of a group or groups within that context. In this way, our social environments function as a "mental grid" that filters what data is and is not important, and consciousness itself functions as a social product. To ignore the social fact of the social determination of thought is to fall prey to ideology, and to ignore this fact in America is to fall into the sin of racism, since racism is deeply rooted in US culture. "While God may exist in some heavenly city beyond time and space, human beings cannot transcend history.... Therefore, [theology is] limited by their social perceptions and thus largely a reflection of the material conditions of a given society.... Because white theologians live in a society that is racist, the oppression of black people does not occupy an important item on their theological agenda."[2] Cone accused white American theology of actually being ideology, that is, deformed thought that was *nothing but* the function of the interest of white American society. In their attempt to deny the social element in the formation of their thinking, white American theologians ignore the fact that they are part of the ruling class in America. Thus, their thinking turns ideological, where claims to truth are fundamentally rooted in class interest and the preservation of current social arrangements.

Cone argued that US academic theology should be rooted in the social contexts and experiences of oppressed and poor Blacks. This would give theology a different contour. In America, "black existence cannot, indeed must not, be taken for granted,"[3] as witnessed in Blacks attending "separate but equal" schools, going to the balcony when attending a movie or church service, or drinking water from a "colored" fountain. Cone criticized how Blacks were systematically excluded from US society and how the uniqueness of the Black experience in America was often ignored. For Cone, Black experience was marked primarily by a life of humiliation, poverty, and suffering within a system of white racism and was also uniquely defined by the way that Blacks had been brought to this land.[4] Black theology emerged out of this experience because of the failure of white theologians to confront racism and to relate

---

2. James H. Cone, *God of the Oppressed* (Maryknoll, NY: Orbis Books, 1975, 1997), 39.
3. Cone, *God of the Oppressed*, 2–5.
4. See James H. Cone, *A Black Theology of Liberation* (Maryknoll, NY: Orbis Books, 1986).

the life of Jesus to Black experience. Black theology emerged so that Blacks might see the gospel as inseparable from their humiliated condition. Cone conceived of the poor as God's glory: "The poor are Yahweh's own, special possession. These are the people the divine has called into freedom."[5] Although the poor are enslaved, they will come to recognize that their fight against poverty and injustice is "not only consistent with the gospel but is the gospel of Jesus Christ."[6] Although Black experience was marked primarily by suffering, in the 1960s it had also been marked by a growing call for Black power. "I did not recognize the methodological implication of [being a Black theologian] until the summer of 1966 when Willie Ricks sounded the cry of 'black power' and Stokely Carmichael joined him as the philosophical spokesman."[7] The test of the validity of this starting point "is found in the One who freely granted us freedom when we were doomed to slavery."[8] Divine revelation alone was the test of epistemological validity.

Cone's description of Black experience, one completely marked by suffering, was extended and repeated in future texts, most notably *The Spirituals and the Blues* (1991) and *The Cross and the Lynching Tree* (2011). "In the Spirituals, the black slaves' experience of suffering and despair defined for them the major issue in their view of the world.... They wondered not whether God is just and right but whether the sadness and pain of the world would cause them to lose faith in the gospel of God."[9] Cone's interpretation of nature in the Spirituals reduces the world to sadness, pain, burden, and grief. While Cone sees God as present in the world, God is present in a world that is fundamentally defined as suffering and evil. Cone desires to argue that the Spirituals are not merely "otherworldly" documents, and that they have implications for liberation in this world as well. Yet, Cone continues to describe the world only as suffering, and he also continues to describe faith as faith in a supernatural, otherworldly God in a way that reproduces the faith/world dichotomy. This reproduction of a dichotomy between faith and world can be seen in Cone's own text, where his most substantive engagement with questions about the world and the state of nature is taken up in his discussion of blues music rather than in his discussion of the Spirituals themselves, and Cone labels blues music "secular spiritual," reproducing the faith/world dichotomy once more. More, Cone's discussion of

---

5. Cone, *God of the Oppressed*, 64.
6. Cone, *God of the Oppressed*, 75.
7. Cone, *God of the Oppressed*, 4.
8. Cone, *God of the Oppressed*, 75.
9. James H. Cone, *The Spirituals and the Blues* (New York: Orbis Books, 1992), 57.

nature as present in blues music is also rather thin, depicting Black life in the world primarily through the themes of suffering, sex, and social protest. These themes are certainly present in blues music, and it is important to emphasize them in descriptions of black experience in the world. However, Cone's reading of the Spirituals as primarily identifying the world as a place of suffering and death appears at first glance as reductionistic.

Cone's critique of white American theology as ideology is an implicit and explicit critique of culturally dominant ideas about the state of nature in the United States, especially those that depict the state of nature as a place of total chaos, or as a place only rightly guided by a natural law. If white American theology is indeed ideology, then its ideas about the state of nature are also deformed and primarily a function of the interest of white American society rather than an accurate reflection of the world. In their attempt to deny the social element in the formation of their thinking, white American theologians ignore the fact that their doctrines about the state of nature may not be objectively true but may serve the interests of the ruling class in America. Thus, notions of indigenous Americans and Africans as "godless," a "mission field," or a "frontier," and of African Americans as lazy, ugly, criminal, and unintelligent, must also be ideology, and we must turn anew to the question of the state of nature. Cone transforms the rejection of the state of nature into the divine election of the oppressed, and this is the closest that Cone will get to discourse on nature given his Marxist-informed belief that capitalist societies are in many ways alienated from nature and simultaneously indistinguishable from nature. Philosopher David Leopold explains that in Marxist thinking, human productive activity mediates the evolving relationship between humankind and the natural world.[10] As humans struggle to change the material form of nature to better reflect and satisfy their own needs and interests, both the natural world and humankind are transformed. On one hand, the natural world becomes less "other" as human beings continue to express themselves, that is, "objectify" themselves, in concrete forms. On the other hand, the poor become alienated from nature as they live more in the city rather than the country and according to industrial schedules rather than circadian rhythms.

Cone thus transforms discourse on the state of nature into discourse on the divine election of the oppressed, who are caught up in a cosmic liberation dialectic. God is liberator of the oppressed, and from God's initiative, the divine enters our social existence and reveals God's self to be with the oppressed.

---

10. David Leopold, "Alienation," *Stanford Encyclopedia of Philosophy*, Winter 2022 ed., https://tinyurl.com/bdzccdds.

This can be seen in the exodus narrative in the Old Testament. "This is the dialectic of Christian thought: God enters into the social context of human existence and appropriates the ideas and actions of the oppressed as God's own."[11] Through this dialectic, the story of the liberation of the oppressed becomes God's story, and the people's struggle for freedom becomes God's struggle, too. We see this not only in the exodus narrative but also in Jesus's life and ministry, where Jesus preaches on behalf of the liberation of the poor. Cone explains that when this event of liberation occurs, the very words and actions of the oppressed become the word and action of God. "They no longer belong to the oppressed. . . . The oppressed have been elected, not because of the intrinsic value of their word of action but because of God's grace and freedom to be with the weak in troubled times."[12] In this way, Cone can talk about the blackness of Jesus. If the presence of the living Christ is real, then in the modern world, Christ must be Black in order to remain faithful to the divine promise to bear the suffering of the poor. To claim that Jesus is Black means both that Jesus is literally Black and that God has never abandoned the oppressed in the struggle. Thus, to be chosen by Yahweh involves liberation from oppression and also service to God as well as a willingness to suffer in the struggle for freedom, if necessary, in order to establish justice in the world. The divine election of the poor is a call to freedom, a call to service, and a call to a willingness to suffer with God for justice. The poor are God's glory and elected to freedom and service by way of the liberation dialectic.

I read Cone's approach to theology as a narrative approach rooted in African American–signifying religious and cultural practices. Philosophically, Black theology of liberation is rooted in narrative theory, which rejects the attempt to ground truth in universalizable rational justifications and acknowledges that truth is often communicated through story. On this point, Cone finds agreement with established theologians like Stanley Hauerwas and George Hunsinger and philosophers Paul Ricoeur and Alasdair MacIntyre. Yet Cone tells the story from a position of Black marginalization and poverty rather than from a position of white privilege. Cone's narrative approach is also shaped by a narrative practice particular to African American religion and culture, namely, the practice of signifyin' narrative. Theologian Kelly Brown Douglas explains that Black prophetic testimonies in the United States have historically been more than a counternarrative to America's narrative of Anglo-Saxon exceptionalism. They have also been signifyin' practices, where one turns the

11. Cone, *God of the Oppressed*, 90.
12. Cone, *God of the Oppressed*, 90.

nation's or the church's identity back upon itself, holding it accountable to its own religiously legitimated chauvinistic claims. "Signifyin has been an ongoing tool within the black culture of survival and resistance to the oppressing power of cherished white property. Signifyin takes a variety of forms ... [e.g.] the form of double talk or coded language, as seen in the Spirituals and the blues. Sometimes it is simply 'repetition with a difference.' [It is also] one of the ways in which black people have spoken truth to power."[13] Cone's discussion of divine election signifies on a nation whose own historical claims to divine election have also been rooted in the exodus narrative. Cone now transposes that language of election and covenant onto the Black poor in such a way that white American theology is called to task and criticized for not fully living into the exodus narrative that it claims to embrace.

Even as Cone's theorization of Black theology of liberation offers a helpful focus on the social conditions of the oppressed in North America, some questions remain with respect to his doctrine of the state of nature and the cultural logic of sovereignty. Cone embraces a Marxist approach to criticism, yet he only takes the historical materialist method so far. Cone's primary target of criticism is white American theology as ideology, yet Cone does not extend criticism to the topics of either money or commodities. Furthermore, Cone does not analyze Black experience as the experiences of workers in a capitalist social arrangement. For Marx, sovereignty presents itself in the tripartite forms of ideology, money, and commodity products.[14] While Cone rightly targets ideology, his writings remain devoid of an explicit account of how the money system impacts African Americans or how products, commodity fetishism, and conspicuous consumption may or may not play a role in the sociopolitical subjugation of African Americans. Nor does Cone discuss the ways that Black workers are treated like machines, subjected to inhuman work schedules and production quotas, and with little to show for their efforts other than meager wages. Overall, the "worker becomes all the poorer the more wealth he produces.... The worker becomes an even cheaper commodity the more commodities he creates."[15] To the extent that Cone does not attend to questions of the sovereignty of money and the sovereignty of commodities in African American social relations, his work leaves an opening for the reemergence of these forces over African American life, thus reproducing the very social

---

13. Kelly Brown Douglas, *Stand Your Ground: Black Bodies and the Justice of God* (Maryknoll, NY: Orbis Books, 2015), 208.

14. See Robert C. Tucker, ed., *The Marx-Engels Reader*, 2nd ed. (New York: Norton, 1978).

15. Tucker, *The Marx-Engels Reader*, 71.

conditions that Cone wants to criticize. Finally, one may question how Cone's goal of Black liberation relates to the communist goal of the abolition of both the bourgeois and the proletariat. Does the abolition of the proletariat mean the abolition of Black consciousness?

Black Natural Law

In the remaining pages of this chapter, we analyze contemporary African American moral-theological discourse on the state of nature. Philosopher of religion Vincent Lloyd answers questions of nature with Black natural law as moral guide. The source of Black natural law is located in the lived experiences of African American heroes like Frederick Douglass, Anna Julia Cooper, W. E. B. Du Bois, and Martin Luther King Jr. "I argue," says Lloyd, "that each of these figures *performs* natural law, offering words or texts that exemplifies the characteristically human capacities to reason, to feel, and to create."[16] For Lloyd, the undergirding performative pattern that is Black natural law appears less as a unique miracle and more as a series of revelatory events within ordinary, everyday practices of African Americans. While European natural law understands human nature to be basically *rational*, Lloyd's Black natural law understands humans as creatures that think, feel, and imagine, and ultimately as beings that defy all description. Black natural law makes it evident that labels used to degrade Blacks (slave, Negro, prisoner) do not capture the true dignity of Black humanity. Black natural law makes it equally evident that we should honor a higher law, one that *does* acknowledge Black humanity and that calls all peoples to use social movements to challenge systems that fail to recognize Black personhood. "My claim in this book," he says, "is that this process, when engaged in collectively, catalyzes social movements and offers a critique of the wisdom of the world . . . as a style of political and ethical engagement." These performances call attention to and criticize the limits of the mainstream American liberal tradition and religious traditions. Lloyd argues that Black natural law overcomes the supersessionist logic implicit in American political life by destabilizing the narratives of God's "grace" produced by various Christian denominations.

For Lloyd, then, Black natural law takes us beyond supersessionist logic, that is, the cultural logic of sovereignty, by opening our eyes to the tensions

---

16. Vincent W. Lloyd, *The Problem with Grace: Reconfiguring Political Theology* (Stanford, CA: Stanford University Press, 2011), xii.

between the traditional values of Black natural law and their malpractice in ordinary life. Supersessionist logic is dominant in the discourse on political theology. It suggests radically "overturning one world and replacing it with another."[17] Supersessionism implies a "Gestalt switch," that is, a radical switch where old social standing is lost in commitment to an allegedly "revelatory" event that introduces an entirely new axis of meaning. A redemptive force replaces the old, tragic world; the immanent is superseded by the transcendent; and law is replaced by grace. This is the problem with grace, for Lloyd. Ideas such as grace, transcendence, and "hopes for a redeemed world" carry a suppersessionist logic that justifies (new) hierarchies of oppression and blind us to the injustices of the status quo. In ordinary life, there is a tension between our professed values and their (mal)practice. Oftentimes, our social practices fail to live up to our norms, laws, and ideals. Our emphasis on grace unwittingly makes reality simulacral. Instead of focusing on a mystically graced reality, we should redirect our desires to the natural law found in ordinary spaces. "To represent the everyday as the ordinary is to display the distinct planes of norms and practices that were always there, just obscured."[18] Overturning supersessionism does not offer relief through grace; it exposes the messiness of the world from which there is no escape. Our task as humans is to accept life as it is, as ordinary. "That what is to be done will not be done, what is done is not what was to be done." We are to give beauty, dread, and power to those novel practices that emerge in everyday, ordinary life for which there is not yet a norm, to those revelatory events that show us the limits of our laws and social norms.[19] These ordinary revelatory events (also called liturgy and sanctity) have the potential to criticize and alter established norms. They facilitate faith, love, and joy as we live in and navigate the world.

Lloyd's turn away from supersessionism to Black natural law is rooted in a deconstructive method that he calls the "rhetoric of tradition." The rhetoric of tradition functions as historical *a priori*, providing the conditions of possibility for understanding and becoming oneself in the world. For Lloyd, tradition is the means by which one is woven into "cloth" meet for the world. In fine, the rhetoric of tradition has two aspects: the "eloquence tradition/tradition

17. Lloyd, *The Problem with Grace*, 11.
18. Lloyd, *The Problem with Grace*, 204.
19. For example, show how our norms create "The Kafkaesque"—the condition of being trapped in a never-ending maze that offers no hope, only alienation, where one lives on the plane of norms untethered from practice, where norms can't be contested, only repeated, where there is not reality, only simulacrum, and where the virtues of faith and love are unnecessary or necessarily misapplied.

of rhetoric" and the "rhetoric of contrast." On the one hand, the eloquence tradition, stressing similarities between peoples, is represented by the image of a weaving shuttle, "an invisible shuttle is guided by the speaker . . . lifting the warp and interlacing the weft, familiar threads are combined in unfamiliar patterns . . . as with any cloth, to distinguish between rational and affective components is to introduce confusion." On the other hand, rhetoric of contrast establishes stasis, structure, distinctions, and delineations. If eloquence fuses, contrast emphasizes difference. Tradition is thus not a monolithic set of norms or rules but acknowledges *both* insular communities whose lives are exotically different from ours *and* a story that embraces us and all of our worlds, a story in which we are to affirm the common humanity of all.[20] The strategy of the rhetoric of tradition even shows the disparate constitution of tradition itself. Tradition is made up of a range of different and often conflicting voices and communities, even as it is also woven together. The "rhetoric of tradition as political strategy" method thus operates deconstructively. That is, one turns to "tradition" not to venerate traditional values but to imaginatively toy with and reconfigure the logic of traditional norms. One turns to tradition not to recover and lift up its original core, or to show the norms implicit in practices, but to show where practitioners of the tradition have failed in sometimes comedic and often tragic ways.

Lloyd's approach unearths key insights for African American public theology. For example, the relationship between religious discourse on grace and American exceptionalism is often overlooked. Lloyd discloses how talk of "God shed his grace on thee" causes one to lose sight of America's oppressive and antidemocratic aspects, and how the language of grace can find itself unwittingly entangled in the cultural logic of sovereignty. Lloyd is also correct in his gesture beyond a communitarian and nationalist ethic toward a transcultural moral vocabulary. "To put the claim strongly," he says, "black natural law offers the best way to approach politics, not just for blacks but for everyone. It is the approach that ought to be taken . . . all ethical and political theory ought to start with the insight of blacks, rather than relegating them to a final chapter."[21] According to Lloyd, the history of Black natural law is a tragic one, where a once heroic Black natural law tradition has fallen out of vogue in the wake of late twentieth-century pragmatism and literary criticism. Yet human attributes like emotion, thought, feeling, affect, imagination, and sense represent the universal shared human condition and stand in place of God's divine law. Thus, Black natural

20. Lloyd, *The Problem with Grace*, 91–92, 102.
21. Lloyd, *The Problem with Grace*, ix–xiii.

law, which Lloyd understands as "ideology critique and social movements," is the liturgy by which progressive American culture might come to call its own social norms and laws into question. Yet for all of its accomplishments, Lloyd's language of natural law is inadequate for the postmodern context, where universal laws of any kind, including the so-called natural law, have fallen under critical gaze. Indeed, Lloyd's talk of Black natural law presents African American moral thought with a dilemma not unfamiliar to Catholic thinkers, who have struggled to convey the continued relevance of the natural law in the modern period. Also, is it necessary to throw out language of "grace" altogether?

Christ's Covenantal Economy of Redemption

As with Lloyd, theologian and religious studies scholar J. Kameron Carter approaches questions regarding the state of nature from an African American theological perspective. While Lloyd's method was the rhetoric of tradition, Carter's, like Jennings's, is genealogy. As a reminder, the *Oxford Dictionary of Philosophy* notes that genealogy can be understood to have two aspects: part historical reconstruction of the way certain concepts have come to have the shape they do, and part "rational reconstruction," or story about the function they serve, which may or may not correspond to historical evolution. In fine, Carter's *Race: A Theological Account* (2008) tears down the modern cultural monument of "race" operative in anthropological discourse. According to Carter, race discourse has justified a political economy of white supremacy since at least the time of Kantian Enlightenment philosophy (1724–1804). Thus, Carter interrogates Western philosophical discourse in ways that Jennings does early modern theology. For Carter, in the political economy of white supremacy, "white" signifies superiority, while "race" and "black" signify Black or Jewish inferiority. Kant's discourse of race is the political unconscious that forms the backdrop for Kant's vision of autonomous, cosmopolitan, "Enlightened" subjects. "Race," Carter says, "controls Kant's ostensibly egalitarian politics of global civil society and domestic civil society in its functioning under the auspices of modern democracy ... in such a way as to require the subjugation of the racial alien outside the West as well as the racial alien ... *within* the Western political order." Carter's genealogy thus shows how modern race discourse makes possible enlightened, cosmopolitan society and remains at its core.[22]

---

22. J. Kameron Carter, *Race: A Theological Account* (New York: Oxford University Press, 2008), 96. Hereafter, page references from this work will be given in parentheses in the text.

Carter's genealogical research finds that the monument of "supersessionism," in addition to that of "race," must also be destroyed. Here is where Carter's research shares a basic commonality with Lloyd's. Both identify supersessionism as the fundamental issue that needs to be addressed in theology and religious studies. However, Carter's account is distinguished from Lloyd's in that Carter produces a theological understanding of supersessionism: "the notion that Christians replace Israel as God's people, that God discards the Jews in favor of the Christians" (27). For Carter, the "modern racial imagination and modern theological imagination articulate each other," and theology is plagued with the problem of supersessionism. "I show contra Foucault, that the story of the modern invention of race had everything to do with the modern invention of religion; that both of these stories were of a piece with the story of the rise of the modern nation-state as a new form of political economy or sociopolitical governance, and that the so-called Jewish problem was a key subtext of all of this" (76). Theology "aided and abetted" the processes by which "man" came to be viewed as a racial being; "modernity's racial imagination has its genesis in the theological problem of Christianity's quest to sever itself from its Jewish roots" (372). Race functions to support the formation and sustaining of modern society and public culture, but Carter sees matters of race, religion, and the modern state as the organizing form of civil society as fundamentally connected. Thus, the social order of white supremacy is not only a philosophico-anthropological problem, but primarily a theological problem. "Embedded within the social imaginary of the civilizations of the West," he concludes, "is the theological problem of the *Rassenfrage*." Since Kant, Western social imaginaries are constituted by casting Jews as a race group in contrast to Western Christians.

For Carter, we cannot correctly take account of the state of nature without understanding the person and work of Jesus Christ, the first-century Galilean Jew. Christ is significant because he "recapitulates" (*anakephalaiosis*) creation, that is, nature, including humankind, so as to "imprint a new modality of existence on it, a modality of the cross, the ascetical mode of life that refuses to tyrannically possess the world" (28). Christ is "the Word of God . . . at work from the beginning of creation," and in the cross of Christ, the whole case of humanity is reinstated. The entirety of creaturely life, nature, and history is brought together in one vision so as to make the particularities of these lives and histories more meaningful. In turn, creation and Christ are read through the mediating term of Israel. For Carter, the particularity of Christ's flesh is the material horizon within which creation is ordered toward the God of Abraham. This is the case because Jesus, as the Israel of God, *is* the living reality of the covenantal promises of the God of Israel. Thus, this same Christ is the discourse and *logos* of all creation, the living, enfleshed rationality in which all different (words of) creation inhere. The logic of Christ's covenantal flesh and his economy of redemption have the power to overcome racism and supersessionism. Carter points to New World Afro-Christian texts, especially the writings of African American Methodist minister Jarena Lee (1783–1864), as paradigms that enflesh this vision of Christ. For example, when Jarena Lee uses the symbol of "Zion-Pentecost" to rename herself, it reflects Christ's covenantal economy of redemption in ways that signify YHWH's covenant and ongoing election with the people of Israel. In this way, Lee accounts for both Christ's "humanity and his interhumanity that constitutes a new, intrahumanity" (8, 353). The modern state of nature was marked as racially other by Kant, but Christ's covenantal economy of redemption rejects this heresy.

Carter focuses on a Christologically redeemed nature, then, rather than nature's inherent "laws." The covenantal economy of redemption holds that human beings are most fully themselves only as they receive themselves from other human beings in shared, nonidolatrous ways. All human beings in this perspective become "icons" or bearers of God in their humanity. Carter's theological-anthropological claims are largely targeted against those of eighteenth-century Prussian philosopher Immanuel Kant. Although Kant did not self-identify as a theologian, Carter argues that Kant's philosophy is rooted in a heretical understanding of Jesus Christ, one severed from Jewish culture. Kant's project of "cultural rationalization" was simultaneously a project of "de-Judaization," where moral religion worshiped a "rational Christ," that is, "a Jesus who, rather than disclosing YHWH or the God of Israel as the ground of redemption for Jews and Gentiles alike, instead affirms . . . that the human species should make itself into a moral creature," that is, an autonomous creature (107). The modern state is thus rooted in a hierarchical anthropological system that is itself "pseudotheological" in character. Christology was "problematically deployed to found the modern racial imagination. For at the genealogical taproot of modern racial reasoning is a process by which Christ was abstracted from Jesus, and thus from his Jewish body, thereby severing Christianity from its Jewish roots. Jewish flesh . . . was converted into racial flesh, positioned within the hierarchy of racial-anthropological essences, and lodged within a now racialized chain of being" (6–7). The loss of a Jewish-inflected account of (Christian) identity thus cleared the way for whiteness to function as a replacement to the doctrine of creation. "White" now not only signifies pigment but is also a stand-in for God within a regime of political and economic power for arranging the world.

Carter's genealogy offers much insight regarding modern racial thinking as well as the problem of the cultural logic of sovereignty, or in his terms, supersessionism. By way of his analysis, we see how the technological age is entailed in racist discourse and rooted in an Enlightenment-framed, "rationalized" Christology. The technological age, that is, the age of "cultural rationalization," was also the age of the racially scaled system of human rank. Western perceptions of race, nature, and the world are indirectly connected to theological perspectives, even in the age of reason. Carter also shows how the authority of modern reason justified the cultural logic of sovereignty, a logic that stripped Jews and the African diaspora (and others) of their power to interpret, name, and identify themselves and that cut Christianity's links to its Jewish roots. The denigration of Christ's flesh was thus also the denigration of the material order, of the darker races, of creation, and embodiment. Carter's recovery of Christ's covenantal flesh gestures toward a "material horizon" that orders creation toward the God of Abraham. It offers us a *taxis* that is a material arrangement of freedom that discloses the historical transcendence of God. Yet Carter's own turn to an ethic of love seems to remain wedded to some type of rationalist anthropology, and thus fails to adequately give an enfleshed account of the state of nature, one that might serve as conditions for the possibility of transcontextual morality. Carter defines love as both "a virtue and a cosmic or ontological reality . . . held together within a theological-spiritual vision of reality" (346). Yet in the fleshly, natural world, love presents itself as *ascetic detachment* from the things of this world. Since love values knowledge of God above all created things, it requires asceticism and rigid control of the self and passions. If Christ has redeemed nature, where might we see God active in the state of nature?[23]

The New Cultural Politics of Intimacy

Shifts in modern Western society and culture toward the cultural logic of sovereignty cannot be fully understood without also noting changes in modern theological discourse. Theologian Willie James Jennings tells the story

---

23. Carter does have an understanding of covenant that mediates the relationship between God and humanity. In fine, covenant occurs between God and humanity. It signifies that the line of supposed "purity" between God and people is already intersected, rendered "impure," or contaminated. Yet this theology of peoplehood and intrahumanity still says little with respect to nature.

of the fundamental shift experienced in modern Western theology such that European and North American societies no longer acknowledged God's active presence in the natural world, and instead began to speak of God as an immutable, distant, and disembodied will. "In the colonialist moment, the pedagogical vision of Christianity lost its Christological center in *participatio Christi* and its *imitatio Christi* and became . . . docetic. . . . [The] divine presence was denied while demonic presence was claimed in the places and peoples of the new worlds." This shift can be understood by an all-too-brief comparative analysis of modern Western theology with a late medieval Catholic perspective on the question of divine presence in the world. According to Saint Thomas of Aquino (1225–1274), one participates in the grace of the living God by way of the sacraments of the church or through the "natural law, both revealed in Scripture and discerned by reason." Nature itself, represented by the passions, remains unordered and tends to veer toward sin and vice, but Jesus touches our lives through sacraments like baptism, the Eucharist, and anointing the sick. Sacraments are thus not only signs of Jesus's presence in our lives but also a means of participating in the life of Christ. In the modern context (ca. 1500), the state of nature is understood to be entirely evacuated of any signs of divine presence, save through the assertion of one's will to dominate a world of unlimited resources. The West came to see this as the immutable will and presence of God. There was a shift from seeing divine presence as the virtue of *caritas* to that of *dominium*. For the West, it signaled evolutionary progress away from the "primitive" state of nature to a civilized and rational Christian empire.[24]

Jennings engages the discourse on political theology and the state of nature by way of genealogy in his *The Christian Imagination: Theology and the Origins of Race* (2010). Unlike the historian, who conceives of history as continuous, linear, and objective, the genealogist sees history as ruptured, fractured, and contingent.[25] To the historian, history's narrative is an open book accessible to any rational and patient mind. Genealogies like Jennings's reject this humanist understanding of the self, since it only masks the fact that human reason is always already overwhelmed by the forces of nature and history. Jennings thus writes to unleash these forces of "effective history" upon the reader so that it

---

24. Willie James Jennings, *The Christian Imagination: Theology and the Origins of Race* (New Haven: Yale University Press, 2010), 106–12.

25. See Michel Foucault, "Nietzsche, Genealogy, History," in *The Essential Foucault: Selections from the Essential Works of Foucault, 1954–1984* (New York: New Press, 1994). Also see Vincent P. Pecora, "Nietzsche, Genealogy, Critical Theory," *New German Critique*, no. 53 (Spring–Summer 1991): 108, https://tinyurl.com/2rybb4pd.

disrupts our notions of historical continuity, razes our historical monuments, and introduces discontinuity into our very being. Jennings's genealogy reaches back to the Renaissance age, to figures like Portuguese royal chronicler Gomes Eanes de Zurara (ca. 1410–1474) and Italian Catholic missionary Alessandro Valignano (1539–1606). Jennings writes to disrupt the West's "diseased social imagination," which he discovers as early as the fifteenth century. This diseased social imagination is itself a sign of thwarted patterns of intimacy, a sign that the West has to date been "unable to grasp either the true logic of Christian theology or the logic of indigenous thought." Instead, Europe and the United States have tried to control (and misrepresent) dark bodies. "I argue here that Christianity in the Western world lives and moves within a diseased social imagination . . . theology lacks the ability to see the profound connections between an embrace by very different people in the chapel and theological meditations articulated in the classroom, between connecting to the earth, to strangers, and to the possibilities of identities formed and reformed precisely in and through such actions."[26]

According to Jennings, early modern Christianity provided the conditions for the possibility of the "diseased social imagination" and modern race discourse. This was accomplished as theology took on certain features, especially the doctrine of "theological isolationism," a.k.a. divine impassibility, where God's "disinterested" providential care stands in as a poor substitute for communal care. Theology also embraced the doctrine of ex nihilo—the notion that God creates the world out of/from nothing and owns all of creation. This ex nihilo theology would later become secularized as the metaphor of technology and

---

26. Jennings, *The Christian Imagination*, 149–54. To show this, the genealogist writes in three specific modalities of history: parody, dissociation, and sacrifice. Parody seeks to exaggerate and push to absurdity those achievements normally lauded by monumental history, to disclose the "concerted carnival" of historical monuments. Dissociation is opposed to that aspect of history that seeks to unearth a collective identity by way of a native land, native language, or native laws. If history seeks to cultivate and preserve these heritages, genealogy reveals the moment of arising (*Entstehung*) of this myth and "the heterogeneous systems that, masked by the self, inhibit the formation of any form of identity." Finally, genealogy shows how the "subject of knowledge" is sacrificed to the "will to knowledge." One shows how the (collective) will to knowledge (i.e., the desire to know truth) transforms into a passion that risks human lives. "Where religions once demanded the sacrifice of bodies," says Foucault, "knowledge now calls for experimentation on ourselves, calls us to the sacrifice of the subject of knowledge . . . [knowledge] loses all sense of limitations. . . . For knowledge . . . no sacrifice is too great." Through these three modalities of history (parody, dissociation, sacrifice), the genealogist conjures the force of effective history against the knowledge productions of historians. (See Foucault, "Nietzsche, Genealogy, History.")

the technological age. Alongside theological isolationism, a docetic Christology emerged in the thinking of persons like Spanish Jesuit missionary José de Acosta (1539–1600). Christ's materiality and full humanity were denied, and doctrines such as *participatio Christi* (humanity's ontological participation in the life of Christ) and *imitatio Christi* (imitation of Christ) were lost to the emerging hegemony of a racial optic. Human beings were gauged according to a racial calculus, and Africans thus became trapped in the West's diseased social imagination. This diseased imagination "enables an insularly economic reading of the New World ... [such that] God had prepared the Spanish and this New World for their intercourse.... God is responsible for colonial desire."[27] The West acts out its colonial desires, replete with violence, on the New World and interprets these desires within a Christian narrative that evacuates modern colonialism of any sense of wrong. For Jennings, this diseased imagination is a distorted vision of creation and the state of nature. The West's "white-to-black" order of existence signifies not only the modern order of existence but also that there is a fundamental error in theological discourse. Political theology must thus reimagine itself to move beyond the modern diseased social imagination.

Jennings argues that a religious narrative of "divine disruption" and a new cultural politics of intimacy can move us beyond the diseased social imagination. Our knowledge of God should begin with the biblical story of Israel. For Jennings, it is the story of divine grace and divine election that disrupts supersessionist logic. In Israel's story, we see a people struggle to emerge "beyond the agonist vision of ethnic destiny" as it encounters the presence of the living God. God disrupts Israel's narrative and brings into judgment and submission the claim that land—the land of Egypt—has upon Israel's being. In disrupting Israel's link to the land, God also challenges their identity that was formed in the place of bondage. They are no longer slaves, but free, and this freedom breaks down the logic of sovereignty. "The distinction between the elect and nonelect," Jennings says, "between those of Israel and those not of Israel, is not easily discerned in the Scripture.... All those who entered Israel's land entered the space of God's claim."[28] God brings divine disruption to Israel again in the person of Jesus Christ. God's election of Jesus breaks open Israel's story and challenges natural and cultural forms of election and selection like birth, family, and lineage. Jesus has the power to release people from social hierarchies, and he demands that those in the land of Israel choose a new household with God. The story of Jesus (being driven into the wilderness and resisting temptation) also offers hope that humankind might resist temp-

---

27. Jennings, *The Christian Imagination*, 112. Also see 25, 92–93.
28. Jennings, *The Christian Imagination*, 250–80.

tations to power, security, and isolation. "The narrative draws us into the awful condition of our collective weakness, yet the wilderness struggle and victory anticipates a possibility: a people joined to the body of Jesus who can overcome the temptations of evil." Finally, the work of the Holy Spirit signals God's new reality of relationship and communion, where life is lived in submersion and submission to another's cultural realities.

Jennings's hermeneutic of divine disruption provides the pathway for a new cultural politics of intimacy that resists supersessionism and forges new networks of kinship. We see in Scripture, in places like Acts 10, how God desires to create social spaces of communion and intimacy in the world. In Acts 10, Peter encounters God's new reality of God's intimacy with all nations. "You yourselves know that it is unlawful for a Jew to associate with or to visit a Gentile; but God has shown me that I should not call anyone profane or unclean" (Acts 10:28 NRSV). "I truly understand that God shows no partiality, but in every nation anyone who fears him and does what is right is acceptable to him" (Acts 10:34–35 NRSV). God desires for peoples to join together to constitute spaces of kinship and fellowship, and this is accomplished with the disruption of people's settled narratives of identity. These divine disruptions usher in a new cultural politics, where our cultural distinctions are undermined, and where peoples are "transformed from two to one," effecting a rebirth of peoplehood. For Jennings, this new cultural politics of intimacy alters the shape of supersessionism. Supersessionism is not extinguished altogether. Instead, supersessionism shifts from "Israel replaced by the church" to "one form of Torah drawn inside another, one form of divine word drawn inside another form—that is, the word made flesh." In other words, supersessionism exchanges the logic of sovereignty for that of inclusion. For Jennings, Torah still accomplishes its central purpose, namely, the formation of a new humanity. It does this whether it is in its original form or transformed into the living word of God in Jesus Christ. Jennings's new cultural politics of intimacy provides the framework for the possibility of renewed sociopolitical and artistic-literary spaces even as it calls into question modern racial and economic classifications and the diseased social imagination of the West.[29]

In the thinking of Willie Jennings, then, we are presented with the challenge of the diseased social imagination and the solution of the new cultural politics. The diseased social imagination and modern race discourse have wreaked havoc on African Americans and others. Yet we must remember that they did not emerge from within a vacuum. Modern race discourse is an effect of a diseased theology, one that emphasizes divine impassibility, a docetic Christ, and a "white-to-black" order of existence. The new cultural politics offers us hope. It is

---

29. Jennings, *The Christian Imagination*, 272.

predicated on a series of key divine disruptions that indicate that God's will is to join peoples together by disrupting their settled narratives of identity. One group is not destined to triumph over another, each is to be drawn inside the other. Jennings's analysis is an insightful addition to the contemporary conversation on African American political theology, as it brings attention in an explicit manner to theology's complicity in racial thinking. Jennings also presents us with a theology that is intentional in its inclusion of Jewish culture and religious thought. However, in terms of the question of the state of nature, Jennings's thinking remains largely silent, only noting that God acts to disrupt it and goad it toward unity. Said another way, Jennings offers provocative and constructive religious criticism with respect to cultural politics, but his theology of nature remains rather thin, so that while Jennings's God inspires culture, God's presence is still absent from nature other than in the form of disruption. This leaves questions regarding the ontological, theological, and moral status of creation and the state of nature. What kind of state of nature doctrine is involved in the new cultural politics of intimacy? What doctrine of nature moves us beyond the diseased imagination and modern racial thinking to anticipate and even realize God's presence, and thus God's future for the good of all peoples, and for the world?

The Lingering Problem of the Cultural Logic of Sovereignty

Although Lloyd, Carter, and Jennings use different methods, each makes an intervention in the discourses on political theology and the state of nature on the problem of supersessionism. Each thinker is concerned in his own unique way about the phenomenon of displacement and replacement, that of setting something aside for another, of taking the place of, wherein an inferior is forced out (of use) by a superior. Yet they conceive of supersessionism in a slightly different manner. Lloyd identifies supersessionism as a radical event of enchantment, a "Gestalt switch," or threshold moment (e.g., the "big bang," creation event, revolutions, etc.). He rejects such events and instead emphasizes an understanding of events as processes, sequences, or networks of relations in the messiness of ordinary, human life (e.g., process thought). If Lloyd understands supersessionism as Gestalt switch, Carter conceives of supersessionism as modern antimaterialist rationalism taking the place of late medieval "enfleshed" Christology. The "White Western Christ" forged by Kant stands as supersessionist symbol for an ascetic disembodiment that enables European Christians to replace Israel as God's "chosen" people. Carter rejects this form of supersessionism by way of an incarnational, enfleshed, Jewish

Jesus. All the difference of creation inheres in this material Christ, himself the symbol of "Zion-Pentecost," that is, of YHWH's covenant and ongoing election with the people of Israel. Carter's criticism of supersessionism redirects us to nature and the passions as embodied in Jesus. For Carter, this means that our passions must somehow acknowledge our universal "intrahumanity." Jennings understands supersessionism as ethnocentrism. A diseased desire for ethnic election produces an agonist vision of land and identity. Overcoming supersessionism means allowing our narratives of purity, identity, and land to be disrupted toward a cultural politics of intimacy.

Jennings, Carter, and Lloyd each disclose a unique angle of vision on the problem of the cultural logic of sovereignty. For Lloyd, the cultural logic of sovereignty, that is, of "Gestalt" supersessionism, is overcome by the Black natural law. Lloyd prefers the moral discourse of natural law over that of "grace" when formulating his theology of nature. On his account, the problem with grace is that establishmentarian political theologies often produce narratives of grace to justify the operations of sovereignty in the most depraved religio-military missions of state. Natural law offers a cross-cultural and international moral framework that checks national and cultural claims to sovereignty. Ideology critique and social movements are evidence of a redeemed state of nature that has overcome the cultural logic of sovereignty. For Carter, the cultural logic of sovereignty, that is, a white, rational, anti-Semitic and anti-Black religion, is overcome through Christ's economy of redemption. This redeemed nature comes forth as ascetic detachment that would reject claims to western European supersessionism. Sovereignty, according to Carter, is understood as "the politics of whiteness," where the modern body politic completes the tasks of "de-Judaizing" and "whitening" the body, stamping out all races in the process toward a global cosmopolitan society. In Jennings's thinking, the cultural logic of sovereignty appears as the "narrative of royal religious ideology," the account of God as distant landowner that justifies modern colonial projects. Jennings responds with a vision of redemption as the new cultural politics of intimacy, where sociopolitical structures are reshaped around the logic of communion. Yet Jennings says little in terms of a theology of nature, that is, of a reading of nature that would give roots to his cultural politics. Yet in the final analysis, each approach to the problem of the cultural logic of sovereignty is limited so that the problem lingers.

Part Three

The Spirituals

6

Ring Shout to Heaven, Call and Response

On the Spirituals as Practice and Play

IN THIS CHAPTER, I TAKE ACCOUNT of the Negro Spirituals, first descriptively and then epistemologically. The Spirituals were the primary form of African American musical production during the antebellum period and after Reconstruction. They were the religious music of African Americans during slavery, the earliest form of religious music to develop among African Americans in the United States, and they continue to shape African American musical and cultural practices today. Their significance is not only enhanced by the fact that music pervades the social and communal life of African peoples, but also because music was both the primary art and central religious practice to endure the tragedy of the *maafa*, that is, the North Atlantic slave trade and chattel slavery. Both enslaved and free African artisans in the New World continued to practice several indigenous African arts, including sculpting, architecture, and quilting. Yet the Spirituals played a dominant role in the lives of early African Americans, and as philosopher Alain Locke has argued, have become "a classic folk expression."[1] For the composers, the Spirituals were also religious practices and functioned as communal and personal practical theologies that allowed transplanted African peoples to create meaning as they negotiated the liminality between the death of the African gods in the New World and the subsequent emergence of varieties of African American Christianity. On the one hand, the Spirituals blur boundaries between theology and aesthetics, as the skills of communal dance and song are employed to create

---

1. Alain Locke, "The Negro Spirituals," in *The New Negro: Voices of the Harlem Renaissance*, ed. Alain Locke (New York: Simon & Schuster, 1925).

collective works of musical beauty. The beautiful rhythms and melodies of the Spirituals may also serve as a means to the gifts of divine revelation, or as the Spirituals say, as a means to "hearing from heaven." On the other hand, the Spirituals bring theological signification to bear on aesthetics, acknowledging a divine reality that transcends aesthetics.

Although the songs were collectively composed by African American slaves during Western culture's classical period, they were not put into print until the late nineteenth century. They were put into print primarily for purposes of preservation and pleasure rather than for play and understanding. One of the earliest volumes of the Spirituals, published by William Francis Allen, Charles P. Ware, and Lucy McKim Garrison in 1867, just after the Civil War, was done so in an effort to "collect and preserve their melodies . . . already becoming difficult to obtain."[2] The songs were made, then, beginning in the late eighteenth century but not recorded and collected until the height of the romantic and realist periods. Some in modern rational society sought to recover lost innocence and zest for life by looking for beauty and the sublime in nature. They saw African Americans as savage, barbaric, and as nature in the raw. Others in modern society held a more "realist" perspective and reasoned that the Spirituals ought to be preserved given that African Americans must eventually go extinct in the competition among the races. In either case, the Spirituals were rarely used for purposes of either play or understanding. Following the thinking of Hans-Georg Gadamer and Jean Grondin, play (*Spiel*) is the dialogical act of artistic induction, the back-and-forth movement of question and answer as one is engaged by a work of art.[3] One comes to understanding not by the exclusive use of a scientific method, but through play. "Understanding is less like grasping a content, a noetic (intellectual) meaning, than like engaging in a dialogue." These acts of play and understanding make us conscious of our own finitude and remind us that our subjective consciousness is conditioned by its given place in history. Yet they also remind us that we are not lost to our preliminary understandings and prejudices, and that in play, new understandings are possible.

The composition of the Spirituals tends to be marked by certain features that have impacted, to varying degrees, other African American musical

---

2. See William Francis Allen, Charles Pickard Ware, and Lucy McKim Garrison, compilers, *Slave Songs of the United States: 136 Songs Complete with Sheet Music and Notes on Slavery and African American History* (n.p.: Pantianos Classics, 1867), viii, xvi.

3. Jean Grondin, *Introduction to Philosophical Hermeneutics* (New Haven: Yale University Press, 1994), 116–17.

genres like jazz, the blues, soul, and hip-hop. These features include the "call and response," the orchestral chorus, congregationalism, percussive vocals, and offbeat melodic improvisational freedom. In fine, Alain Locke (1885–1954) is correct to note that the "Spirituals" may be grouped into evangelical shouts, folk ballads, work and labor songs, and prayer songs.[4] This chapter is primarily concerned with the latter, although not to the exclusion of the other types. Although I use the volume published by Allen and others in 1867 as the primary text for the Spirituals, I also consider the 1915 text published through the joint efforts of Hampton Institute, Fisk University, Tuskegee Institute, the Calhoun Colored School, and the Penn School.[5] This breadth offers a sense of continuity and change in the Spirituals over time and allows us to observe how cosmological perspectives located in the Spirituals have endured. Although I am interested in the Spirituals' cosmology, the Spirituals themselves are sonic arts, and as such invite us to considerations of artistic composition. It is difficult to say today whether the Spirituals are classified as folk art, having emerged from Black vernacular culture, or as fine art, as they are now associated with formal training, specialized apprenticeships, and academic inquiries. Yet as music-making practices and productions, the Spirituals were created with attention to questions of composition. In this chapter, I analyze the compositional features of the Spirituals, taking the features as clues to cosmological structure. This involves attending to certain compositional matters such as form, symmetry, dynamism, harmony, and scale. The Spirituals' rendering of musical time, movement, and balance gives rise to an acoustic horizon that may be used to fine-tune an African American theological cosmology.

"Praise, Member": A Quick Thick Description of a Spirituals Service

To hear the Spirituals we must rewind the time, back to the late eighteenth and early nineteenth centuries. This was the time of the second Atlantic trade system, when the Dutch, French, and English had overtaken the Spanish and Portuguese empires in the slave trade. Slaves arrived from West and Central Africa to the United States primarily through the major markets in South Carolina. Their ultimate destination was the plantation, an arrangement of quarters that was closer to a town than a farm or a private home. Although

---

4. Locke, "The Negro Spirituals."
5. Thomas P. Fenner, with Hampton Normal and Agricultural Institute, *Religious Folk Songs of the Negro as Sung on the Plantations* (Hampton, VA: Wentworth, 1915).

slavery existed in the past, this modern form was far more intense, as nations had become mercantilist and proto-capitalist, thus establishing the accumulation of wealth as a central political objective. Plantation economies emerged (ca. 1500s) that were based exclusively on slave labor. With respect to the creation of the Spirituals, this was also the time of the cotton gin, which ironically *increased* the demand for slave labor and for plantations even as it made picking cotton more efficient. Historian Howard Zinn tells us that "[in] 1790 a thousand tons of cotton were being produced every year in the South. By 1860, it was a million tons [per year]. In the same period, 500,000 slaves grew to 4 million."[6] At the close of the eighteenth century, the Methodists and Baptists were advocates for granting more rights and even complete freedom to slaves based on the Christian doctrine of the equality of all believers.[7] Yet over the course of the nineteenth century, racial segregation during worship increasingly became the practice and the law in the South, and the views of the early evangelicals began to fade. By the 1830s, slaves were facing increasingly strict laws about where and when they could gather for worship, and by the end of the antebellum era a growing number of states required whites to supervise the worship of slaves. From the perspective of many slaves and white abolitionist Christians, slavery conflicted with the gospel's message of equality.

Plantation missions to evangelize slaves in the American South began in the late 1820s as a rival to abolitionism, and the Spirituals represented the self-instituted practices of the slaves in resistance to plantation missions. While Christian abolitionists like John Brown and William Lloyd Garrison worked to abolish slavery in the name of the gospel, figures like Charles Colock Jones of the United Evangelical Front and William Caspers, superintendent of missions of the Missionary Society of the Methodist Episcopal Church, preached a master/slave social order. Slave owners in the British New World colonies had been reluctant to convert slaves in part due to fear that baptism would lead to emancipation.[8] The antebellum period saw many slave owners attempt to control slave missions and evangelization. By the eve of the Civil War, Christianity had pervaded the slave community, and the rule of gospel order established. Yet the slave community had an extensive religious life of its own that was virtually invisible to slave owners, consisting of a range of instituted practices, arts, and rituals. Accounts by Albert Raboteau, Gayraud Wilmore,

---

6. Howard Zinn, *A People's History of the United States: 1492–Present* (New York: HarperCollins, 1999), 171.

7. Roger Finke and Rodney Stark, *The Churching America, 1776–2005: Winners and Losers in Our Religious Economy* (New Brunswick, NJ: Rutgers University Press, 2004), 105.

8. Albert Raboteau, *Slave Religion: The Invisible Institution in the Antebellum South* (New York: Oxford University Press, 2004), 98–110.

Ring Shout to Heaven, Call and Response

Barbara Holmes, Diana Hayes, C. Eric Lincoln, and Marla Frederick are instructive. Although slaves were cut off from their West and Central African lands, they established socially autonomous civic and religious associations here in America that were practically invisible to white Americans. While independent Black churches in the North were guided by the principle of freedom, slave worship in the South was predicated on survival.[9] The "invisible institution" was concerned, among other things, with offering hope to keep people's body and soul together, and to maintain their sanity and semblance of humanity. Practices like the Spirituals gave a sense of community and personal worth to people and eased their suffering.

Analytically, the Spirituals are *both* religious practice that combines singing, dancing, and worship *and* a collection or body of songs that has become meaningful or authoritative for many African Americans over the course of time. Although slavery scattered and separated African peoples, religious practices known as "ring shouts" were widely practiced and deeply ingrained in various African American settings across the United States. Sometimes ring shouts were practiced deep in the hollows, under dense brush, and other times on the plantation during revivals at established churches. The name "ring shout" is usually meant to indicate that the practice is rooted in early modern West and Central African religion and culture. Indeed, although many slaves had been converted to Christianity, they also brought their own religious and cultural traditions from places like Senegal, Gambia, Angola, and Congo, as well as their own creativity, to bear on the construction of the Spirituals. Raboteau notes that the Spirituals, "like all folk songs, are hybrids, born of mutual influence and reciprocal borrowing" between African and Anglo-American musical contributions.[10] Before the Civil War, the Spirituals were not only sung but primarily danced, so that the two practices of singing and dancing were often intertwined in the Spirituals. They were thus also frequently called "running sperichils" to indicate that bodily movement and dance were once integral. This, along with other features such as spontaneity, variety, and communal interchange, as well as interplay between the song leader and the chorus, makes the Spirituals a distinctive genre. Another perspective, that of a slave, submits that "their origin no one exactly knows. An old Aunty, questioned on the subject, declared that 'When Mass'a Jesus He walk de' earth, when he feel tired, He sit a-restin' on Jacob's well and made up dese yer Spirituals for his people.'"[11]

---

9. Gayraud Wilmore, *Pragmatic Spirituality: The Christian Faith through an Africentric Lens* (New York: New York University Press, 2004), 52.
10. Raboteau, *Slave Religion*, 243.
11. Fenner, *Religious Folk Songs*, v.

The Spirituals

In making the Spirituals, people would usually gather together in a circle and move single file around a central point, while simultaneously dancing and singing, usually holding hands.[12] The steps of this curvilinear motion are akin to a shuffle. Musically, the purpose of the dance was to establish a rhythm among those gathered, to bring all into the same movements of musical time. Thus, Raboteau discusses slaves who sang "[and] kept time, while [their] feet resounded on the floor like the drumsticks of a bass drum," and who "stand at the side of the room and 'base' others ... clapping their hands together on their knees."[13] Historian Tanya Price explains that, in part because African drums were banned, "either African instruments were created ... or enslaved Africans used their bodies like a drum, clapping and stomping with feet and sticks."[14] This rhythm would provide a bass line for an entire gamut of harmonic and melodic creations. While dancing was considered integral to the practice of the Spirituals in the late eighteenth and early nineteenth century, its significance seems to have decreased for many after emancipation. Yet shouts were documented in Louisiana, Texas, the Bahamas, and Haiti as late as 1934. As early as 1819, Methodist John Watson wrote that "the coloured people get together and sing for hours together ... or prayers lengthened out with long repetitious choruses."[15] He would go on to note a similarity between the circular formation of the Spirituals and that of the "Indian dances," that is, the Sun Dance. As late as 1878, African Methodist Episcopal bishop Daniel Alexander Payne also expressed his disapproval when he observed the dance: "After the sermon, they formed a ring, and with coats off, sung, clapped their hands and stamped their feet in a most ... heathenish way. . . . [Upon request] they stopped their dancing and clapping of hands, but remained singing and rocking their bodies to and fro." In 1845, Scottish natural historian Sir Charles Lyell lamented that slaves continued to practice "sinful" dances, even after conversion: "Of dancing and music, the Negroes are passionately fond. On the Hopeton plantation violins have been silenced by the Methodist missionaries. . . . At the Methodist prayer meetings, they are permitted to move round rapidly in a ring, in which manoeuvre, I am told, they sometimes contrive to take enough exercise to serve as a substitute for the dance, it being, in fact,

---

12. Diana L. Hayes, *Forged in the Fiery Furnace: African American Spirituality* (Maryknoll, NY: Orbis Books, 2012), 53.

13. Raboteau, *Slave Religion*, 69, 71.

14. Tanya Y. Price, "Rhythms of Culture: Djembe and African Memory in African-American Cultural Traditions," *Black Music Research Journal* 33, no. 2 (Fall 2013): 227–47, https://tinyurl.com/mve2wtmu.

15. Raboteau, *Slave Religion*, 67.

a kind of spiritual boulanger."[16] Hampton Institute professor R. Nathaniel Dett recounted a "backwoods 'after-service'":

> It was once the privilege of the writer to attend a backwoods "after-service" at which, when the regular service had "let out," a small group of not more than seven or ten (they were all women if he remembers rightly) grouped themselves together by standing in a ring with a criss-cross clasping of hands. To the strong rhythm of a sort of chant, they violently thrust each other backwards and forwards with an intense fervor. There was no shuffling of feet or rotating of the ring as described by Mr. [James Weldon] Johnson.... But this I soon forgot, for, looking into the faces of the singers, I was struck by evidences of spiritual elevation, and I realized that in some mysterious way these unlettered people, by a common consent, were mutually enjoying a communion with eternal forces by a method of evocation beyond the reach of the uninitiated.[17]

Again, the Spirituals were a combination of dancing along with music and song. Spirituals were not derivations of nineteenth-century evangelical revival hymns, and many nineteenth-century whites condemned the Spirituals. This is because the songs worked "up from one degree of emotion to another, until, like a turbulent, angry sea, men and women ... surged and swayed to and fro."[18] Features such as spontaneity, variety, and communal interchange, as well as interplay between the song leader and the chorus, make the Spirituals a distinctive genre. In practice, a song leader leads off in a recitative style (repeating aloud), and others respond as a chorus. Some Spirituals were made in the moment, while others were made after wrestling with the Spirit in the wilderness. Spirituals were also made when at play or when at work. Musicologists Dena J. Epstein and Rosita M. Sands have discussed how Spirituals were sung in factories: "Work and boat songs continued a tradition that had been common in Africa—integrating music into daily life. Often, the chorus began to sing before the leader had finished his call. Work songs could have religious words. When William Cullen Bryant visited a tobacco factory in Richmond in 1843, the workers sang, but his guide informed him that they only sang sacred music.... The guide commented, 'They will sing nothing

---

16. Raboteau, *Slave Religion*, 67.
17. Nathaniel Dett, ed., *Religious Folk Songs of the Negro as Sung at Hampton Institute* (Hampton, VA: Hampton Institute Press, 1927), xiii.
18. Raboteau, *Slave Religion*, 244, quoting Harris Barrett of Hampton Institute.

else.'"[19] The singing of the Spirituals was most often an occasion of wonder, enchantment, and beauty, not only for slaves but also for white listeners. But even as the Spirituals are beautiful in one sense, in another they express the entire range of aesthetic standards. There is a beauty, but also the ugliness of slavery and injustice. There is the tragedy of lost love and life, and the comedy of jokes, digs, and insults. There are majestic visions of heavenly crowds and low experiences in the lonesome valley. Yet the aim of the Spirituals seems to have been to build social sympathy among the enslaved. In the Spirituals, as a form of the "invisible institution," one person's sorrow or joy became everyone's through song. It was about the community's recognition and support of individual slaves as persons, and it was about individual slaves bearing witness to a communal life that was not absolutely determined by racial discrimination and that was a reflection of their own creative efforts. The practice of the ring shout as performed in the late eighteenth and early nineteenth centuries is lost to us. We are separated from the invisible institution by time and history. What remains are records and collections of the practices, relics of a bygone era. These are not the actual events themselves, but they may still offer cosmological wisdom.

Yet, although the Spirituals desired to bring about a certain effect with respect to social sympathies, this could not occur apart from a change in the consciousness of the slaves. As noted, although the slaves were conscious in many positive ways, they were also marked by an alienated consciousness. One way that the slaves resisted and temporarily transcended this alienation, and transformed social sympathies, was by participating in the invisible institution. Here, participation doesn't simply mean "taking a part in" but, phenomenologically, being open to (something) in a way such that one's (cosmological) vision is interrupted and one experiences transformation. Although the collective imaginary of the slaves as exhibited in the Spirituals was fashioned by the slaves, phenomenologists understand that the social imaginary itself had an existence independent of the slaves' participation in it. The social imaginary conveyed through the Spirituals was something that "stepped forth" from the natural world such that it took on the status of an ontically independent ideal or imagined object. It is possible and likely that this independent object maintained an amount of constancy in the consciousness of slaves to greater and lesser amounts of time. While participation in the practice of the Spiritu-

---

19. Dena J. Epstein and Rosita M. Sands, "Secular Folk Music," in *African American Music: An Introduction*, ed. Mellonee V. Burnim and Portia K. Maultsby, 2nd ed. (New York: Routledge, 2015), Kindle location 1029.

als was limited by time and space, if slaves perceived enough consistency and coherence in these experiences, they could have felt as if they were actually citizens of two equally valid worlds. It is likely that the invisible institution took on more and more of an independent status to the degree that slaves experienced what they understood to be illumination, existential reorientation, or relocation with respect to social significance. In the Spirituals, the invisible institution is also the musical institution. An institution heard rather than seen, one rooted in the sound and the tone rather than vision and the image. One that emerges from the moans and wails of call and response.

"I Hear from Heaven To-Day": On the Spirituals' Epistemology

African Americans drew from a range of sources to make the Spirituals, including the Bible, Protestant hymns and sermons, African styles of singing and dancing, and African Americans' everyday experiences. Although the slaves used these sources to make music with heavenly sounds, they did so based on the reciprocity between ideas and social reality here on earth. Their discourse about the gospel was framed by their social perceptions, quality of life, and social context. In *God of the Oppressed*, James Cone emphasizes the importance of acknowledging the relationship between our ideas and social reality as a critical first step for epistemology. "Theology arises out of life and thus reflects a people's struggle to create meaning in life ... it is appropriate to ask, What is the connection between life and theology?"[20] Cone draws from the sociological thinking of Peter Berger, Thomas Luckmann, and Karl Marx to argue that "it is not consciousness that determines life but life that determines consciousness." In more compatibilist language, I would argue that it is not consciousness that determines life but life that frames consciousness. As Cone says, "While God may exist in some heavenly city beyond time and space, human beings cannot transcend history." The major problem with white theology and with many hermeneutical approaches in philosophy is the failure to recognize the sociology of knowledge in their epistemologies. They don't acknowledge the connection between their ideas and social reality. Sociologist Orlando Patterson has shown how slaves occupied a liminal status with respect to American slaveocracy. "The institution of slavery bestows [upon the slave] an institutional marginality ... [and] its members exist ... in a limbo, neither

---

20. James H. Cone, *God of the Oppressed* (Maryknoll, NY: Orbis Books, 1975, 1997), 39.

enfranchised ... nor true aliens."[21] For Patterson, this alienation produced in the slave a social death. Yet he argued that one social power that the slaves had was religion, as the slaves' liminal status made them something like social oracles, positioned on the boundary between sacred and the profane.

African American vernacular speech itself functioned as a source and norm for the Spirituals. The Bible, hymns, dancing, and everyday experiences that inform the Spirituals became collectively organized under the complex structures of African American semiosis and culture. This primarily meant that they became subject to what cultural linguist Henry Louis Gates Jr. calls the "signifyin' practices" of African American speech and rhetoric. Gates explains that "signifyin'" is "repetition of a sound or word *with a change* denoted by a difference in sound or letter [so that] two different signs are designated by the same signifier."[22] Signifyin' is an iconic or aural reversal of a received sound or image, usually to critique the sign as "the difference that blackness makes." For example, Albert Raboteau notes in his *Slave Religion* that, in the Spirituals, "religious images, such as freedom, were ambiguous. To some slaves they undoubtedly meant freedom from physical as well as spiritual bondage. At certain times, one meaning probably had more urgency than the other ... [was] bolder, [having] more ring, and [lasting] longer into the night."[23] In Raboteau's example, the slaves signified on the idea of freedom by giving the same word a different sound or more frequent repetitions. In the repetition and the sounding, something of the original meaning of freedom is bracketed or aurally released in a "ritual renaming." As a result of this process, a meaning is conveyed that is *other* than the standard meaning. Signifyin' thus signifies the trickster's ability to talk with innuendo, to cajole, to boast, to insult, to "sound," or to "put on blast." It is a relation of difference inscribed within a relation of identity that operates as a technique of indirect argument and persuasion. To wit, Gates's term "signifyin'" is a signification on the standard English "signifying," demonstrating both the constructed meaning of the word and the difference that blackness makes.

The Bible was also central for the Spirituals, as it was for most of antebellum (African) American religion and culture. In the sixteenth and seventeenth centuries, many West and Central Africans responded to "the Bible" with rejection

21. Orlando Patterson, "Authority, Alienation, and Social Death," in *African American Religious Thought: An Anthology*, ed. Cornel West and Eddie S. Glaude Jr. (Louisville: Westminster John Knox, 2003), 111.

22. Henry Louis Gates Jr., *The Signifying Monkey: A Theory of African American Literary Criticism* (New York: Oxford University Press, 1989), 57 (emphasis added).

23. Raboteau, *Slave Religion*, 248–49.

and suspicion. Christianity was not foreign to the continent of Africa. In eastern Africa, the Christian kingdom of Ethiopia had stood since AD 850 and would endure until 1550. Christianity spread through Egypt and North Africa in the first to the fourth centuries. Yet modern West and Central African responses were often responses to Protestant colonizers, whose interpretations of doctrines of *sola scriptura* and iconoclasm devalued African liturgies, rituals, symbols, art, myths, oral traditions, and ancestors.[24] Yet upon the heels of the mass conversions in the eighteenth century, many slaves adopted the Bible as a way to negotiate and understand the New World, to work out their own faith, and to seek their own interest. Vincent L. Wimbush argues that the Bible came to represent a virtual language-world that slaves could enter and interpret in light of their traumatic situation.[25] The Bible was central to the slaves' imaginations, especially as stories were often read aloud and heard in group settings. Wimbush explains that during the antebellum period, slaves created and operated with a folk circle hermeneutic, where interpretation was understood as the "collective freed consciousness and imagination" of the African slaves. They heard and retold biblical stories to reflect their own situations and to give voice to injustices or to visions for a different world. The Spirituals were central to this process, transforming the book religion of the dominant peoples into the renderings and perspectives of Africans who were made slaves. In the Spirituals, biblical stories and symbols functioned allegorically, parabolically, or as veiled social criticism.

The Spirituals were shaped by the everyday experiences of slaves in the United States. They flowed from the lips of people who lived on, worked on, and were buried on American soil. If something of note occurred during the day, the slaves usually sang about it that night at the "prayer meeting." These everyday experiences occurred in relation to various environments, and these environments, predicated on the mimetic consciousness of the slaves, play a central role in the Spirituals. The term "mimetic consciousness" comes from the thinking of critical theorists Theodor Adorno, Walter Benjamin, and Fred Rush, who understand it as that knowledge produced by "physical imitation of external nature."[26] For Adorno, who promoted mimesis as an ethics, this

---

24. See Jacob K. Olupọna, "The Study of Yoruba Religious Tradition in Historical Perspective," *Numen* 40, no. 3 (September 1993): 240–73, https://tinyurl.com/4pb9kewp. Also see John Pobee, "Aspects of African Traditional Religion," *Sociological Analysis* 37, no. 1 (Spring 1976): 1–18, https://tinyurl.com/mt6rmctb.

25. Vincent L. Wimbush, *The Bible and African Americans: A Brief History* (Minneapolis: Fortress, 2003), 23.

26. See Fred Rush, *Conceptual Foundations of Early Critical Theory* (New York: Cambridge University Press, 2004), 154.

imitation, or repetition, of nature helps persons overcome their fear of nature, thus tempering the will to control. "Nature becomes conscious of itself,"[27] and one moves toward reconciliation with nature as one suffers nature. Enslaved and free African Americans lived on several distinctive land formations, stretching westward from the Atlantic Ocean to the Mississippi River. The major regions are the coastal plain; the Piedmont; the Appalachians, including the Blue Ridge, the Ridge Valley, the Appalachian Plateau, and the Alluvial Lowlands. The coastal plain extends about three thousand miles from the Atlantic to the Gulf Coast and consists of lagoons, beaches, swamps, savannahs, and offshore islands. Metaphors in the Spirituals like God as "rock of my soul" are drawn from and reflect these environments. The Spirituals were thus constituted as slaves' collective freed consciousness sought consonance with various inflections of American terrain. In the Spirituals, nature becomes intrinsically related to human affairs and plays a decisive role. Nature does not make nor dominate slave religion. Yet, the environment shapes the Spirituals' understandings of faith, and in the images and sounds of the Spirituals, natural phenomena reverberate with otherworldly depth.

Finally, there are the more formal ritual and liturgical aspects of the Spirituals that mark them off as discrete occasions of sacred time. Formalized ritual and liturgical aspects of the Spirituals direct the body with ordered actions or forms in an effort to center, heal, and strengthen the spirit. Actions like praying or softly humming lead the community into existential and communal spaces of silence, reflection, and meditation. Slaves did not need the experience of slavery to learn to meditate, but they consciously chose to redeem the time by instituting liturgies to fortify individual and communal will. Liturgies like (Black-directed) baptisms, "shut-ins" (overnight prayer), and Spirituals facilitated divine adoration, existential examination, and communal healing. Theologian Barbara Holmes has classified these rituals as *contemplative* practices, that is, practices where listening, repose, and receptivity predominate and where meditation invites the soul and spirit into a deeper union with God. "I've named these practices 'contemplative,'" says Holmes, "because they create intersections between inner cosmologies and the interpretive life of a community.... [They] provide an interpretive grid that synthesizes inner and outer cosmologies."[28] Holmes explains that as one participates in rituals like

---

27. Deborah Cook, "Nature Becoming Conscious of Itself: Adorno on Self-Reflection," *Philosophy Today* 50 (2006): 296–306.

28. Barbara A. Holmes, *Joy Unspeakable: Contemplative Practices of the Black Church* (Minneapolis: Augsburg Fortress, 2004), xiv–xv, xx, 2.

the Spirituals, the border between what one knows as "sacred" and what one knows as "profane" is weakened, so that the ordinary overlaps with the extraordinary. The Spirituals thus inscribe a relation of sacred time inside secular time. "In the midst of worship, an imperceptible shift occurred that moved the worshipping community from intentional liturgical action to transcendent indwelling." Thus, while slaves recognized powers and principalities in everyday life, they specifically invoked them in designated rites like the Spirituals to bring into contemplative focus the unresolved dialectical tension between the everyday and extraordinary worlds.

Another liturgical source for the Spirituals was dance. African Americans would gather not only to sing but primarily to dance the "ring-shout" dance. Holmes notes how a "singer—whoever felt so moved—would step forth from the circle of worshippers. By chanting, dancing, and clapping, the community provided a bass beat upon which the singer would create his or her own distinctive musical text."[29] As I discuss below, dancing, or "shouting," occurred as dancers created, acted out, praised, mocked, or scorned certain religious or social issues. In his analysis of African American shouts, ethnomusicologist Michael Iyanaga argues that ring-shout dances, in addition to being actively and consciously reproduced by consciously motivated actors, are "practiced memories" and "forgotten histories." He calls the dance a vehicle of forgotten histories "embedded in habits, social practices, ritual processes, and embodied experiences."[30] Iyanaga foregrounds ethnography as a methodological step in postcolonial music history and understands that the ring shout holds a historicity beyond the motivations of conscious actors. In so doing, Iyanaga follows ethnographers and cultural theorists like Mieczyslaw Kolinski, Melville J. Herskovits, Pierre Bourdieu, Franz Boas, and Rosalind Shaw. They see culture as socially learned rather than biologically inherited, and in the case of the ring shout, Iyanaga sees linguistic patterns, musical styles, and values "carried below the level of consciousness." These embedded habits resemble Bourdieu's *habitus*, a "product of history [that] produces individual and collective practices, and hence history, in accordance with the schemes engendered by history."[31] However, unlike the homologous and all-encompassing *habitus*, overt manifestations of practiced memories are multiple, circumstantial, and

29. Holmes, *Joy Unspeakable*, 85.
30. Michael Iyanaga, "On Flogging the Dead Horse, Again: Historicity, Genealogy, and Objectivity in Richard Waterman's Approach to Music," *Ethnomusicology* 59, no. 2 (Spring/Summer 2015): 173–201, https://tinyurl.com/mpfcrf34.
31. Pierre Bourdieu, *Outline of a Theory of Practice* (New York: Cambridge University Press, 1977, 2006), 82.

The Spirituals

located in specific social institutions. With dance, an activist consciousness is introduced into the Spirituals' epistemology.

In the late nineteenth century, the Spirituals began to be appreciated by white American culture, and over time this appreciation effected a change in the meaning of the term "Spirituals." The term took on the connotations of white culture and generally came to mean personal piety, moral purity, and anticipation for an immaterial heaven. As a result, commentary on erotic matters in the Spirituals has dried up and gone soft. Thinkers like musicologists Arthur C. Jones and Dena Epstein as well as author Zora Neale Hurston trace this shift in composition to the Harlem Renaissance of the 1920s and 1930s. Hurston coined the term "neo-Spirituals" to signify a conscious effort by African American composers during this time to present musical arrangements of Spirituals influenced by Anglo-American cultural and musical values.[32] This meant a secularization of the Spirituals to the effect that the Spirituals became less erotic, while the more erotic songs already in existence became classified as secular, taking up the mantle of "the blues." Blues artists partly worked to disrupt the norms of a racist culture that sanitized Black sexuality. Jones is turned off by the "relative absence of substantive analyses that center on themes in the songs that relate to sexuality ... and more broadly, physical sensuality."[33] The neo-Spirituals of the late nineteenth and early twentieth centuries cut out certain corporeal elements, most notably dancing and erotic lyrics. Yet early nineteenth-century African American cultural forms like the Spirituals exhibited a consciousness of the erotic, including sex and desire, as an interwoven element of the sacred. One finds in the Spirituals a tension between purity and holiness and eroticism and profanity. Songs range from "You Must Be Pure and Holy" to "Charleston Gals." In an attempt to reincorporate the erotic back into commentary on the Spirituals, this chapter also considers the impact of blues music on African American cosmology.

Even with all the unique sources noted, the Spirituals would still be something altogether different were it not for their being musical productions. Music is a unique form of artistic, aesthetic, and theological production in that music is primarily about making something in time, rather than in space, with the caveat that music is also a spatial art to the extent that it has a significant impact on the physical and spiritual *energy* of a space.[34] In the practice of the

---

32. Arthur C. Jones, "Black Spirituals, Physical Sensuality, and Sexuality: Notes on a Neglected Field of Inquiry," in *Loving the Body: Black Religious Studies and the Erotic*, ed. Anthony B. Pinn and Dwight Hopkins (New York: Palgrave Macmillan, 2004).

33. Jones, "Black Spirituals," 237.

34. János Maróthy, "Rite and Rhythm: From Behaviour Patterns to Musical Structures,"

Spirituals, the various sources that inform the songs and dances are disciplined according to the movements of musical time. As music, the ring-shout dance perceives the timing of soundwaves and sequences and maps them onto both bodily motion and musical form. For all of this, a musical consciousness is required, and the slaves possessed the art of organizing tones moving in time. Philosopher of music Philip Alperson emphasizes that musical sounds are not just sounds but *tones*, that is, sound-units that people recognize as musical, and as such, "[belong] to a system of such sounds and [occupy] a determinate place in that system."[35] Musical tones exist in relationship to one another, and together constitute a musical system. In turn, musical systems are ordered according to pitch, that is, the degree of highness or lowness of a tone. At the same time, musical systems are mathematically organized, as there are ratios between frequencies. In the case of the Spirituals, the concept of musical consciousness is even more significant to the extent that African Americans retained traces of West and Central African tonal languages. Ethnomusicologist and composer J. H. Kwabena Nketia notes how many languages in West and Central African societies use tones as speech surrogates.[36] In other words, tone plays a phonemic role, and different tones function to make *grammatical* distinctions much like the functions of the English sounds p, b, d, or t. Words may be spelled the same but distinguished by tone.

Thus, the Spirituals were rooted in a range of sources, including those noted above. Moreover, this phenomenological-empirical approach acknowledges neuropsychological claims that religious experiences can be partly described by neurological processes. The brain played several roles in the constitution of the Spirituals, from storing and recalling information, to facilitating the narrative imagination, to possibly rewiring after new experiences or practices. Theologian and psychologist David A. Hogue draws from the neurosciences to argue for the reality of a "social brain," predicated on the brain's inherent relatedness. "Human brains relate to each other . . . our brains are built to empathize. . . . Empathy is not an 'add-on,' something we have to force ourselves to do, or to teach each other."[37] The fact that the brain may be rewired and

---

Studia Musicologica Academiae Scientiarum Hungaricae T. 35, Fasc. 4 (1993–1994): 421–33, https://tinyurl.com/yc78bbn4.

35. Philip Alperson, ed., *What Is Music? An Introduction to the Philosophy of Music* (University Park: Pennsylvania State University Press, 1987), 138.

36. J. H. Kwabena Nketia, "The Musical Heritage of Africa," in "Slavery, Colonialism, and Racism," special issue, *Daedalus* 103, no. 2 (Spring 1974): 151–61, https://tinyurl.com/2jdv8pcp.

37. David A. Hogue, "How I Learned to Stop Worrying and Love the Brain," in *Moral*

that genetics may be rewritten by new experiences means that deterministic assumptions about biology, genetics, and the brain are unsatisfactory. Modern scientific knowledge and African American theology are not mutually exclusive. Human consciousness requires the brain. Yet, there is actually no morphological definition of the human "species" that allows us to clearly identify what an anatomically modern human is in biological taxonomic terms. More, a hermeneutical approach also recognizes the "thrownness" of the human condition. Human existence (*Dasein*) means always already finding oneself within a given perspective that guides one's expectations of meaning. Thus, the brain reminds us that consciousness is both mental and corporal, self-aware and unconscious, and contemplative and activist. In the Spirituals, consciousness publicly attains a state of a particular phenomenological quality such that limited participation with various modes of sense perception becomes possible. Thus, the invisible institution emerges as ideal, imagined objects become possible for consciousness.

"Shout On, Children": On Call and Response, or the Rooted Pattern of the Spirituals

The practice of "call and response," or antiphony, is one of the most distinctive features of the shout. Ethnomusicologist Portia K. Maultsby defines call and response as "a song structure or performance practice in which a singer or instrumentalist makes a musical statement that is answered by another soloist, instrumentalist, or group."[38] The pattern is ubiquitous in African American music, familiar to anyone who has sung a word, verse, or sentence *responsively*, that is, with timing and phraseology that answers the lead soloist appropriately. For example, a soloist may start a spiritual: "Swing low, sweet Chariot, coming for to carry me home," and the congregation will respond with the refrain: "Swing low, sweet Chariot, coming for to carry me home." Michael Iyanaga sees call-and-response patterns as a central feature of both African American and African musical patterns, alongside other features like the dominance of percussion and off-beat phrasing.[39] Music historian and literary critic Samuel Floyd has given some of the most sustained attention to the phenomenon

---

Issues and Christian Responses, ed. Patricia Beattie Jung and L. Shannon Jung (Minneapolis: Fortress, 2013).

38. Burnim and Maultsby, *African American Music*, Kindle location 370 of 9843.
39. Iyanaga, "On Flogging the Dead Horse, Again," 179.

of call-and-response patterns in African American music. In texts like *The Power of Black Music* (1996) and *The Transformation of Black Music* (2017), as well as in several articles, Floyd traces the influence of call and response, concluding that it is the "musical trope of tropes." He sees it as the master trope embracing all the other musical symbols and figures in African American music.[40] Floyd says the "Afro-American musical process of call-and-response, metaphorically speaking, might be considered as the musical trope of tropes . . . [an] all-important, all-encompassing concept."[41] The practice of call and response is a relational practice that, with repetition, establishes a pattern, a sequence, or a rhythm that moves the song forward in musical time. It is an art of dynamic struggle, and also of play, with back-and-forth movement that invites participation in music making.

Beyond music, the logic of call and response is one of the most distinctive features of a wide range of African American religious and cultural practices. In addition to the ring-shout dance, it is also in oral traditions, literature, preaching, and rap and hip-hop music. For example, congregants may respond to a sermon *during the act of preaching*. Black church scholar Evans E. Crawford calls this call-and-response dynamic in African American preaching "the hum," as the response often takes the form of someone audibly humming.[42] In addition to humming, sermon responses take other forms: "Help 'em Lord!" "Well?" "That' all right!" "Amen!" and "Glory Hallelujah!" Standing up, waving one's hand, and shouting are also responses. It can also be observed in dancing, hand clapping, and foot stomping. Literary critic Maggie Sale identifies call-and-response patterns as a key characteristic of African American oral traditions, Spirituals, and work and play songs, noting: "Antiphony, or call and response . . . can be thought of as part of the group or communal nature of art. . . . [It] is interactive, process oriented and concerned with innovation rather than mimetic, product-oriented, or static."[43] Sale goes on to explain that call-and-response patterns offer a model that relies on audience performance, improvisation, and tone inflection—not only what is said but *how* it is said—ensuring that the art will be meaningful to the community. One key

---

40. I understand Floyd's language of "call and response" as distinct from his more specific coinage of "Call/Response."

41. Samuel A. Floyd Jr., "Ring Shout! Literary Studies, Historical Studies, and Black Music Inquiry," *Black Music Research Journal* 22 (2002): 49–70, https://tinyurl.com/7j34xaau.

42. Evans E. Crawford, *The Hum: Call and Response in African American Preaching* (Nashville: Abingdon, 1995).

43. Maggie Sale, "Call and Response as Critical Method: African American Oral Traditions and Beloved," *African American Review* 26, no. 1 (Spring 1992): 41.

The Spirituals

distinction between Sale's work and my own is that while Sale uses call and response as a critical method in literary studies, I understand it as the root logic in the formation of the invisible institution and in African American slave culture, that is, as social reason. As it emerges in the practice of the Spirituals, call and response is an inductive musical logic that is indicative of a wider social consciousness. The cultural logic of call and response implies a corpus composed by both individuals and collectivities, by one and many, as they sound to one another back and forth in the deep, offering call for response to establish rhythm in the chaos.

Upon analysis, the logic of call and response is dialectical, inductive, informal. It emerges from a context of collective, embodied, rural musical practices rather than atomized, disembodied, urbanized linguistic or rational practices. The musical movement of call and response begins with the soloist's declarative call, which can also be called a making known, or revelation. Once made, this declaration awaits and depends upon the response of the chorus, and thus the soloist's musical declaration comes forth as a predicate, that is, as a fragmented expression capable of connecting with other terms to make a sentence, but incapable of expressing truth on its own. The declarative call of the soloist expresses a condition that the chorus may or may not satisfy. It requires recognition by the congregation. The congregational response is an attempt to satisfy the soloist's expressed conditions, thus constructing a "true" or "well-formed" musical sentence and also achieving a recognition of its own. The operations call and response may appear to be solely cooperative or conjunctive, but this logic can also operate as disjunction (e.g., signifyin' on swing as "swang"), material implication (e.g., humming, rather than singing, the response), and negation (e.g., singing "then ride high"). The logic of call and response is oriented toward the musical birth of the collective consciousness of the invisible institution. It is social reason birthed within a musical *ethos*, that is, by the Spirit, musically, but not to the exclusion of either *pathos* (the passions) or *logos* (reason). Yet, even as the musical practice of call and response is inductive, there is also a formal aspect to the logic of the Spirituals, especially when considering matters of musical meter and scale. In this respect, the soloist's call is not a declaration but a putting forth, a proposition. As such, the truth of the soloist's call does *not* depend on the congregation's response but on the soloist's conformity to the structures of musical space-time.

Thus, in the play of call and response in the Spirituals, two opposed shapes of self-consciousness come forth. Each of these forms exists both for the other self-consciousness and for itself. There is recognition between the two, but this recognition is not mutual, as the forms of self-consciousness relate to one another within a dynamic context of asymmetry and opposition. When self-consciousness faces off against itself, there is both a disturbance of one's sense of certainty about themselves and a tonal reassurance. The forces of antagonism and anxiety at play between these two shapes of self-consciousness frequently bring their conflict to head in extreme conditions of face-to-face, or voice-to-voice, combat as well as play. At times, the sound of the call and the sound of the response must enter into this struggle to bring about a sense of tonal certainty of being for themselves. Each must risk its life for freedom, proving that consciousness isn't bare existence. However, these shapes of self-consciousness are also limited in their struggle by the frame and form of the song, which necessarily requires the continued life of competing shape of self-consciousness, that is, both the persisting call of the caller and the continued response of the responder to the call. Therefore, in risking one's life in the call, the risk is, in part, to struggle against the response, and in part, to struggle alongside it. The relation between these two forms of self-consciousness is posited in the extreme terms of a life-and-death struggle, and in the musical movement of the Spirituals this confrontation never diffuses or settles into a permanent hierarchy of relations between the two sides of self-consciousness, so that neither may be called master or slave. This dynamic gives rise to a social exchange within a society shaped by a liminal existence, not only on the margins of US antebellum society but also at the liminal point between modern rational societies and archaic systems of exchange.

7

Nature, Spirit, and Song

On the Aesthetic Dimensions of the Spirituals

This chapter takes up the spirituals as social and religious practice. I ask about the ways in which the Spirituals help us to think about questions of social exchange, then of sacrifice, and finally, of formal aesthetics. These seemingly disparate topics all emerge out of the Spirituals when considered as a social practice. The term "practice" situates the work in contemporary philosophical conversations on practice shaped by Alasdair MacIntyre, Pierre Bourdieu, and Michel de Certeau, among others. MacIntyre's neo-Aristotelian account of human action as practice is applicable here, where practice is understood as a "coherent and complex form of socially established cooperative human activity through which goods internal to that form of activity are realized in the course of trying to achieve those standards of excellence which are appropriate to us, and partially definitive of, that form of activity, with the result that human powers to achieve excellence, and human conceptions of the ends and goods involved, are systematically extended."[1] The Spirituals may be read as a socially established, cooperative activity that taught certain goods. Yet Aristotle's discourse on practices was directed to the Greek aristocracy while the Spirituals emerge from slave culture. The Spirituals can also be understood according to Bourdieu's understanding of practice as "'pure practice without theory'... like the rite or the dance;... which communicates, so to speak, from body to body, i.e. on the hither side of words or concepts,

---

1. Alasdair MacIntyre, *After Virtue*, 2nd ed. (Notre Dame: University of Notre Dame Press, 2003), 187.

Nature, Spirit, and Song

and which pleases (or displeases) without concepts."[2] For Bourdieu, practices cannot be reduced to "structure" or "function," as they produce, reproduce, and use relationships, and are also the product of strategies oriented toward the satisfaction of material and symbolic interests. The Spirituals sit at the intersection of these types, a socially established cooperative human activity, but one on the hither side of words.

Furthermore, the Spirituals may be read as tactical practice. This term is theorized by Certeau, who defines a tactic as a practice "which cannot count on a 'proper' (a spatial or institutional localization).... It has at its disposal no base where it can capitalize on its advantages."[3] The operations of the Spirituals were multiform, fragmentary, and relative to the situation at hand. Certeau reminds us that because it does not own a place, a tactic "depends on time—it is always watching for opportunities that must be seized 'on the wing.' Whatever it wins, it does not keep, and must constantly manipulate events to turn them into opportunities."[4] Slaves frequently transferred any number of settings into "borrowed time" for a prayer meeting, and they had to play on and with a terrain imposed on them and organized by the law of a foreign power. Thus, the Spirituals were practiced with a mobility that accepted the chance offerings of the moment. They were not written down or given formal musical notation by their antebellum composers. They are not predicated primarily on a vision of "the city." Rather, the heroes of the songs are the members of the golden band, a vision that often has disturbing implications for human social arrangements. Finally, the Spirituals were not theorized, and one should not take the view that theorizing the Spirituals will make them more respectable, more civilized, or epistemologically verifiable. In these ways, the Spirituals were tactics rather than strategies, and as such they partially escaped the panoptic procedures and techniques of modern society. Thus, they may offer insight into common sense, a social *hexis*, and a way of life unfamiliar to the modern West, yet in no way primitive or non-Western. This chapter describes the sociological and aesthetic features of the Spirituals, attending to compositional questions of form, proportion, and design.

Ultimately, I am interested in the ways that the compositional and aesthetic features of the Spirituals may be read cosmologically. While music has the

---

2. Pierre Bourdieu, *Outline of a Theory of Practice* (New York: Cambridge University Press, 1977, 2006), 8.

3. Michel de Certeau, *The Practice of Everyday Life*, trans. Steven Rendall (Berkeley: University of California Press, 1984), xix.

4. Certeau, *The Practice of Everyday Life*, xxii.

capacity to represent objects in the physical world, it may also be considered cosmological art, offering insight into the nature of a reality beyond the physical world of appearances. The compositional features of the Spirituals may be used as an ontological and cosmological clue to help us understand the workings of nature and history. Such an exercise must also be an exercise in epistemological humility, as all descriptions of the nature of reality beyond the physical world are linguistically mediated, and thus finite and subject to the limitations of time, history, nature, and culture. We see through a glass darkly. Yet musical experience is grounded in lived, practical experience, and thus ripe for consideration within the area of phenomenology as theorized by Martin Heidegger and Hans-Georg Gadamer as well as phenomenologists of music like Waldemar Conrad, Hans Mersmann, and Bruce Ellis Benson. The antebellum slaves did not relate to music as disembodied minds but as people with both bodily and mental intelligence. Musical intervals and musical orderliness have long been considered keys to the nature of reality. Plato conceived of music as a world soul, where the positions, motions, and velocities of celestial bodies are fashioned and relate to one another musically. Music has thus been related to cosmology, "the study of the origin and structure of the universe . . . especially conceived as ordered and law-governed, whether by destiny, fate, justice, divine command, or rational necessity."[5] The English word "cosmos" is rooted in the Greek *kosmos*, meaning order. In philosophical thinking, cosmos is almost always connected to *logos*, translated from the Greek as "statement, principle, law, reason, or proportion." Logos is that which gives order to cosmos and rationality to the world.

The Golden Band: On the Call and Response and Social Exchange

My cosmological reading of the Spirituals begins with a reading of them as a certain practice of social exchange among the slaves, and it is partially informed by social theorist Marcel Mauss's 1925 study of gift-exchange practices. The study included Polynesia, Melanesia, the Andaman Islands, the American Northwest, and also ancient Rome, India, China, and feudal Germany.[6] Mauss's general finding was that practices of property exchange and contracting in these societies was not based on the idea of free, rational individuals

---

5. *Oxford Dictionary of Philosophy*, ed. Simon Blackburn, s.v. "cosmology."
6. Marcel Mauss, *The Gift: The Forms and Functions of Exchange in Archaic Societies*, trans. Ian Cunnison (n.p.: Cohen & West, 1966).

making an agreement or promise but on the bonds of obligation within webs of clan and family relationships. The exchange of gifts in these societies wasn't voluntary but reflective of archaic systems of exchange that both created and reproduced social relations. In these societies, the web of social relationships itself obligated one to participate in gift exchanges, and since every gift carried with it a set of obligations, it presented a materialization of social relations and the flow of social intercourse. Mauss's key example was the *potlach*, a gift exchange practice with heightened rivalry, violence, and antagonism, predicated on the acquisition of honor. Prestige is bound up with expenditure. One gives in excess, such that a creditor becomes the debtor. Consumption and destruction were virtually unlimited, and the rich man shows his wealth by spending recklessly. This cycle of exchange is constituted by the threefold obligatory sequence of "give, receive, reciprocate." "The threefold sequence of obligation," says sociologist Carl Olson, "forms a never-ending cycle of exchange, a cycle that suggests an orderly system.... This cycle of giving forms a structure that constrains both the giver and the recipient because of the obligations imposed on both parties."[7] "The most important feature," says Mauss, "is clearly [the] one that obliges a person to reciprocate the present that has been received."[8]

Mauss's analysis of the gift-exchange practices brings certain features of the Spirituals into sharp relief, even as the conditions and practices of African American slaves highlight certain features unique to the Spirituals as gift exchange. These features include the demoted social status of the slaves in relationship to Mauss's ancient aristocracies, the unique blend of gift giving and commodity exchange in African American slave culture, and finally, the peculiarity of the gifts exchanged in the Spirituals. Mauss's study did not examine slave cultures but looked instead to the laws of ancient aristocratic societies in an effort to revive an obligatory "aristocratic extravagance" in modern contracts. Mauss saw this as a cure for commodified modern exchange. "As is happening in English-speaking countries and so many other contemporary societies, whether made up of savages or the high civilized, the rich must come back to considering themselves—freely and also by obligation—as the financial guardians of their fellow citizens."[9] For Mauss, gift exchange enhances the status of the donor and feeds the consumption of the recipient. Yet, these ex-

---

7. Carl Olson, "Excess, Time, and the Pure Gift: Postmodern Transformations of Marcel Mauss' Theory," *Method & Theory in the Study of Religion* 14, no. 3/4 (2002): 350–74, https://tinyurl.com/jfsc4xbe.
8. Mauss, *The Gift*, 9.
9. Mauss, *The Gift*, 84.

changes likely meant more extravagant forms of destruction for slaves in these ancient societies, who, in practices of gift exchange, were themselves part of the property and gifts that were donated. In the New World, the US economic system saw Blacks primarily as commodities to be sold on the market rather than as gifts to be exchanged. African American slaves themselves did indeed build and maintain social ties with one another through gift giving. Historian Tamara J. Walker has discussed how US slaves distributed clothing and other gifts to family members on other plantations to cement relationships.[10] Yet slaves also participated in commodity exchange, making antebellum African American slave culture a hybrid culture consisting of both ancient and modern features of exchange.

Another noticeable element of the Spirituals' exchange in relation to Mauss's gift exchange is the seeming absence of an exchanged object. Whether Mauss discusses the Germanic *Gaben*, the Brahmin Hindu *dandharma*, or the Roman *re*, he notes that the "*res*," the service or the thing, is an essential element in the contract. "Re contracts constitute four of the most important legal contracts: borrowing, deposit, pledge, and *commodate*. A certain number of *innominate* contracts also—particularly those we believe to have been, with the contract of sale, at the origin of contract itself: gift and exchange—are likewise said to be *re* ones."[11] There must be a thing or service for there to be a gift, and the thing or service must place one under obligation. *Nunquam nuda traditio transfert dominium*. This *traditio* of the *res* has always been one of the key elements in Roman law. By contrast, antebellum slaves may have exchanged gifts, totems, or trinkets, but such items of property were not culturally established signs of transfer—if slaves were allowed to own property in the first place. Yet in the Spirituals' exchange of call and response, singers participated in the exchange of musical notes and tones. These exchanges were rational to the extent that they were in harmony with one another. These exchanges were also erotic, and in a finely tuned manner, to the extent that they required one to be moved by the rhythm. Finally, these exchanges were also expressive to the extent that they gave wide and ample space to irregular and nonconforming exchanges like improvisation, spontaneity, novelty, and syncopation. The exchanges of call and response in the Spirituals thus suggest an ethos of obligation that is similar to the one noted by Mauss. The ethos of the antebellum Spirituals may be described as "call-response-reciprocate." Yet

---

10. Tamara Walker, "Gift Exchange," Encyclopedia.com, accessed July 2, 2024, https://tinyurl.com/mr2rjy5w.

11. Mauss, *The Gift*, 65.

there are also aspects of rational utility and existential freedom not found in Mauss's *potlach* gift exchange.

The Golden Altar: On Call, Response, and Atonement

The Spirituals' musical system of exchange was not only a system of social exchange but also a spiritual exchange, thus giving rise to the topic of spiritual or religious atonement. To atone is to become reconciled, or to come into unity, concord, or harmony with a thing.[12] Spiritual atonement usually involves making amends or propitiation by doing something to please the gods such that friendly relations are repaired. In religious discourse, the topic of atonement is usually conflated with the topic of sacrifice, such that the two are thought to be the same thing. Yet, in the Spirituals sacrifice was for all intents and purposes impossible, as slaves were legally dispossessed of the animals, property, and even religious agency required to conduct sacrifices. In other words, the practice of religious sacrifice required that one be a legal person, and the enslaved of the US antebellum South were not recognized as such. They were themselves legally identified as property, presenting them with the question of atonement in a way that troubled its relationship with sacrifice. One can also see the enslaved themselves questioning the practice of sacrifice in the Spirituals. One especially notable example occurs in the song "The Golden Altar," which tells of John's revealed vision of a "holy number" sitting on top of a golden altar. The lyrics attempt to console the holy number, who, like those gathered under the holy altar in Revelation 6:10, await God's vengeance: "It's a little while longer yere below, . . . It's a little while longer yere below, Before de Lamb of God!" The lyrics are a response to the martyrs in Revelation 6:10, who have been killed for their witness to the Word of God, and who cry out: "Sovereign Lord, holy and true, how long will it be before you judge and avenge our blood on the inhabitants of the earth?" (NRSV).

In reflecting a general aversion to the practice of sacrifice as a form of atonement, the Spirituals strike a chord with several contemporary thinkers who are also critical of the practice. The notion of spiritual exchanges and their links to sacrifice is a salient point not only for Mauss, but also for late twentieth-century critics of sacrifice like Jacques Derrida, Georges Bataille, and René Girard. Mauss explains: The "connection of exchange contracts

---

12. *Shorter Oxford English Dictionary: On Historical Principles* (New York: Oxford University Press, 1973, 2007).

among men with those between men and gods explains a whole aspect of the theory of sacrifice."[13] For Mauss, sacrificial destruction occurs during a spiritual exchange as the adherent gives something of value to the gods. This sacrifice in the exchange with the gods implies a giving of something that will be repaid. "It is not simply to show power and wealth and unselfishness that a man puts his slaves to death ... he is also sacrificing to the gods and spirits, who appear incarnate in the men who are at once their namesakes and ritual allies."[14] One has to buy from the gods, and the gods know how to repay the price. For Derrida, it is exactly this element of requisite sacrificial destruction that makes spiritual exchanges problematic. Derrida uses the biblical story of Abraham and Isaac to illustrate that one *must* be willing to go to dangerous extremes. These spiritual exchanges demand from the adherent a *double* gift of death to the gods. The double gift of death is "the sacrifice of Abraham and Isaac ... the sacrifice of both of them, it is the gift of death one makes to the other in putting *oneself* to death, mortifying oneself in order to make a gift of this death as a sacrificial offering to God."[15] If for Mauss gift exchanges consist primarily of the sacrifice of objects, especially gifts and property, and in an increase in social ego, Derrida sees sacrifice as a sacrifice both of the thing and of oneself. This self-sacrifice is prerequisite for any sacrificial gift, and for Derrida, the sacrifice of the self cannot be repaid.

If for Derrida the dynamics of spiritual exchange raise the problem of "the gift of death," these same dynamics raise the problem of the scapegoat mechanism for René Girard. Like Derrida, Girard also sees sacrifice as enigmatic due to its sanction of violence. Sacrifice "has to do with emphasizing the transgressive power of violence. It is simultaneously a murder and a most holy act. Sacrifice is divided against itself."[16] Girard sees religious sacrifice as fundamentally rooted in violence, specifically the mimetic violence characteristic of all archaic groups, where religious sacrifice justifies the unanimous lynching of real victims so that the community is protected from its own violence by diverting it onto expendables. Girard sees mimetic violence itself as a product of a universal mimetic desire and rivalry, where "as soon as one of the two reaches for an object, the second anxiously follows suit; soon there are two desires in place of one, two desires bound to collide since they have

13. Mauss, *The Gift*, 13.
14. Mauss, *The Gift*, 13.
15. Jacques Derrida, *The Gift of Death*, trans. David Wills (Chicago: University of Chicago Press, 1995), 69.
16. René Girard, *Sacrifice* (East Lansing: Michigan State University Press, 2011).

Nature, Spirit, and Song

the same object."[17] The scapegoat mechanism occurs when mimetic rivalry reaches a point where it fastens on to a single victim and the scapegoating mechanism destroys the sacrificial victim to quell the rivalry. Girard observed the structure of the scapegoat mechanism in Vedic texts of the Hindu tradition, but the same structure can also be observed both in US antebellum society's relationship to African Americans and in the Spirituals' musical exchange of call, response, and reciprocate. Girard's description of rivalry applies to both of these exchanges: two, three, then four antagonists (i.e., the congregational response) form an alliance against a fifth (i.e., the soloist's call), and little by little, mimetic rivalry mounts, to the ruin of the one arbitrarily selected antagonist. The system of exchange and mimetic rivalry thus "tips over" into sacrificial violence against a single adversary. For Girard, the scapegoat mechanism is too rooted in mimetic rivalry to offer a just distribution of sacrifice.

Thus, an analysis of the structure of exchange in the Spirituals' practice of call and response shows us its ambiguity. On the one hand, the call-and-response structure of exchange gave shape to social relationships and discloses the outlines for a potential alternative social economy. On the other hand, the call-and-response structure of exchange is involuntary, and threatens participants with scapegoating and death. The cruel irony is that the Spirituals were made as African Americans were themselves scapegoated, sacrificed, and put to death by an enlightened, Anglo-Saxon Christian nation that had allegedly evolved beyond such "archaic" practices. For Derrida, the ideal "gift of death" is the mortification of the soul resulting in love for God *without reserve*, rather than the "double death" of both soul and the sacrificial offering of one's only son. His ideal sacrifice is the decision to sacrifice without the act of sacrifice, as God has suspended the act and reinscribed the act back into the economy as a reward. Derrida's God is not the God that requires the act of sacrifice, but the God who challenges the strict economy of exchange, of payback, and of an eye for an eye. God desires "to give back life, to give back the beloved son, once he is assured that a gift outside of any economy . . . has been accomplished."[18] If Derrida challenges the strict economy of exchange, so, too, does Girard, as he argues that a thoroughgoing critique of the scapegoat mechanism requires a "scape-*logos*," that is, a form of rationality that has incorporated the idea of the exclusion and the expulsion, a form of reasoning altogether foreign to Greek thought. The scape-*logos* is a space opened up by questioning the socio-symbolic. The antebellum Spirituals offer a unique case

---

17. Girard, *Sacrifice*, 17.
18. Derrida, *The Gift of Death*, 96.

of gift exchange in that they are a case where the slaves made musical tones and musical time for God, an intangible gift consisting of musical notes rather than real property. With the Spirituals, atonement comes forth most directly in the form of musical tones. The music produced by the antebellum slaves possessed a form, logic, and balance that have implications for questions of social exchange.

"Lean on the Lord's Side": On the Formal Features of the Spirituals

According to Alain Locke, the Spirituals were made within an orchestral context, such that the entire (invisible) institution participated in the composition. Other features of the Spirituals, such as rhythm, harmony, and melody, are often stressed such that their original orchestral form is easily overlooked. "It must be realized more and more," Locke says, "that the proper idiom of the Negro folk song calls for choral treatment . . . orchestral choral style, with its intricate threading in and out of the voices."[19] As indicated by the orchestral choral form, the Spirituals as music-making practice are sung in such a way that the tones of a song are continuously modified by the singers and musicians. They are attuned to matters of balance in volume and metrics, and they ensure that all voices and instruments are adequately tuned and blended to attain the right compositional texture. The Spirituals' orchestral form is a collective sorting of voices, pitches, tones, and rhythms to discern the best form of organization of each instrument, voice, and body for the band. Different participants take on different roles within various sections, all toward the making of sweet music. For example, the percussionists might separate themselves into a group apart from the singers and dancers to test their beats. Instruments like the drum, or dancers who would produce drum-like rhythms with their bodies, propel the song into motion. One might beat an enclosed palm against one's chest, slap an open palm against a thigh, or beat a broomstick against a hardwood floor. Singers or musicians might perfect their performance at certain points in a song, checking for sonic relationships of either consonance or dissonance, or for the harmony or disharmony of tones. Although sectioned, the band remains interdependent, and the goal of the orchestral chorus is to shape sections such that the form of the Spirituals, through the play of call and response, rightly balances unity and variety, sameness and difference.

19. Alain Locke, "The Negro Spirituals," in *The New Negro: Voices of the Harlem Renaissance*, ed. Alain Locke (New York: Simon & Schuster, 1925), 208.

Nature, Spirit, and Song

When we ask about the form of the Spirituals, we're asking about their formal structure.[20] The form is that which gives basic shape to questions of composition such as balance, weight, equilibrium, and disequilibrium. As indicated by the logic of call and response, the Spirituals present us with a binary form, where a musical statement—the call—is made by a song leader and the chorus, soloist, instrument, or band makes a response. In music theory, the standard representation of the binary form occurs as "A-B," with A representing the statement and B representing the response. In African American music, the binary form is deployed as "statement and response." Familiarity with other musical systems, such as the Western tonal system's ternary form ("statement-departure-return," or "A-B-A"), may lead the musician to impose this same structure on binary forms, thus interpreting binary forms as underdeveloped or incomplete since there appears to be a statement and departure without a return. Yet musician and professor Earl L. Stewart identifies at least three types of call-and-response patterns that may be created from the binary form.[21] The first type—on display in the aforementioned "Sweet Chariot" example—is *call and confirmation*, where a thematic idea is introduced by a call and then confirmed with a response that essentially repeats the call verbatim. The second type of pattern is *call and completion*. It occurs when the thematic statement given by the response *completes* the thematic statement introduced by the call. For example, different verses in a song may begin with unique calls: "I shouted Hallelujah . . ." or "I heard de angels singin'," and yet find completion with the same response: "Leanin' on de Lord."[22] Stewart's third type, *call and conclusion*, occurs when the "caller" and "responder" are different mediums, for example, a vocal call and an instrumental response. To the extent that call-and-response patterns *are* incomplete, this reflects an intentionally unresolved tension that points toward promise.

An inquiry into the compositional features of the Spirituals discloses not only the contours of their form but also their approach to matters of symmet-

---

20. For an in-depth analysis of music theory, see Joseph Machlis, *The Enjoyment of Music*, 3rd ed. (New York: Norton, 1970). In his study of the philosophy of music in the early modern period, Charles Bouleau argues that certain early modern renaissance artists organized their plastics according to music. Artists like Gian Paolo Lomazzo (1538–1592) and Leon Alberti (1404–1472) believed that musical ratios and relationships could create balance and beauty in ways that geometry could not. They thus argued for musical consonance, that is, that proportions be transferred from music to other arts. (See Charles Bouleau, *The Painter's Secret Geometry: A Study of Composition in Art* [New York: Harcourt, Brace & World, 1963], 85.)

21. Earl L. Stewart, *African American Music: An Introduction* (New York: Schirmer Books, 1998), 4.

22. From the Spiritual "If Ye Want to See Jesus."

rical design. There is a basic rudeness to the Spirituals, made, as they were, from work-worn hands, feet, and voices of everyday, common folk. There is a brokenness to the sounds of the Spirituals, forged yet still somewhat unwrought, finished but with a rough and dull tonality. This rude element is produced in part by their asymmetrical design, where the movements of call and response disclose disproportionalities in the logic and standard pattern of the Spirituals. For example, we see asymmetry in any case of call and response where a musical instrument responds to a human call. Asymmetry can also be noted in the instance of the soloist's call and the congregational response. As we will see, asymmetry also characterizes the structure of syncopated rhythms and polyrhythms, and, as I shall discuss in a future work, offbeat melodies and phraseology. The asymmetrical design of the Spirituals reflects, among other things, a perspective on the passage of time, that is, on the directionality of musical time. In the Spirituals, and in a great deal of African American music, the directionality of musical time exhibits a limited malleability as humans play with and make it, even as it maintains its own independence. Musical time is both relationally determined and independently real. Its reality dictates that time is irreversible and static. Yet its relationality is shown in the range of options for sequential progression and time-dilation techniques. For example, musical time may be made to move along the habitual course of past, present, and future, but its directionality can also take other forms. It can be produced as directed time, that is, still irreversible, yet along an asymmetrical path (e.g., past to future, with no regard for the present), or musical time can have no direction at all (e.g., a jam session).

The Spirituals' asymmetrical structure creates a compositional flexibility with respect to matters of musical dynamism. As we will see, the practice of call and response produces a standard pattern, also called the "ostinato," and then goes on to introduce asymmetry into that very pattern by way of repetition, syncopation, or polyrhythms. For example, syncopation accents rhythmic patterns on weak pulses rather than strong ones to produce the musical sense that strong beats are temporarily overcome, contradicted, or resisted. Syncopation also produces the overall musical effect of the weak pulse playing a decisive role in musical composition overall, not only with respect to matters of dynamism but also with respect to musical time and logic. Professor Earl L. Stewart calls this effect "rhythmic tension," describing it as "dissonance occurring when musical events are unable to form repeated patterns [ostinatos], making up the conflicting part of the plexus."[23] Musicologist János Maróthy

---

23. Stewart, *African American Music*, 13.

Nature, Spirit, and Song

has a similar perspective on rhythmic tension. He argues that this rhythmic tension is an emergent pattern, that it is "something waiting to happen, but is not allowed to play itself out properly.... The standard pattern ... never achieves internal resolution, but is permanently marked by promise, an extensive anacrusis."[24] While the standard pattern, or ostinato, is a unifying force of the music, rhythmic tension offers the musician several options for musical dynamism. One can move by way of progress smoothly to the next note, bar, or meter. One can use syncopation and polyrhythms to create conflicts and clashes in music. Finally, one can use the tension as an opportunity to repeat a beat or bar *ad nauseam*, giving way to the joy of repetition so prevalent in much of African American music, even beyond the Spirituals. The dynamic aspects of African American music, including its rhythmic tension, allow one to play with the tempo and mood of the music, empowering the musician to affect musical dynamics through either progression, conflict, or repetition.

The essential form of the Spirituals offers a general path or plan for the entire process of subsequent composition. Philosopher of music Suzanne K. Langer argues that this general form may be called "the *commanding form* of the work" that only requires subsequent ornamentation and intensification or greater simplicity.[25] Like a living organism, it maintains its identity by staying true to form, "like a statement imperfectly made or even merely indicated." It is the "Idea" of the music, the implicit logic that all conscious artistry serves to make explicit. The form is not essentially restrictive but fecund, opening up a range of options for the musician to compose the song and offering a plan for unfolding the rhythmic and tonal potentialities of the song's harmonies and cycles. It is of note that this form, as it operates in the Spirituals, operates as a *taxis*, that is, as a planned order, but this order is not dictated "from above." Nor is the form shaped without the input of orchestra. In fact, this *taxis* is unique in that it emerges "from below," from the interaction of musically free individuals who began not with a plan but with a reciprocal process of musical exchange. This form thus emerges as a spontaneous evolutionary order, that is, a *kosmos*, where individual plans adapt to the plans of others, rather than as a commanded form. Yet the form of the Spirituals also possesses an objective authority apart from the will and desires of the singers. The form of

---

24. See János Maróthy, "Rite and Rhythm: From Behaviour Patterns to Musical Structures," *Studia Musicologica Academiae Scientiarum Hungaricae*, T. 35, Fasc. 4 (1993–1994): 421–33, https://tinyurl.com/yc78bbn4.

25. Suzanne K. Langer, *Feeling and Form: A Theory of Art* (New York: Charles Scribner's Sons, 1953), 122.

the Spirituals thus exerts power on singers but does not do so in a way that is absolutely deterministic. Thus, the musical form of the Spirituals functions in compatibilist fashion, giving ample space to both the determinacy of design and the free expression of individuals. The imprint of the guiding form of the Spirituals can especially be observed on the formation of musical time and space, where binarism, asymmetry, tension, and antiphonal orchestra give shape to musical content.

"What a Trying Time": On Musical Time and Space

In the Spirituals' back-and-forth play of call and response, they impose and establish a "standard pattern" or rhythm onto sound, ordering it in the process. One hallmark of African American music is its emphasis on rhythm, largely an inheritance from its African roots.[26] Rhythm, as ostinato, syncopated rhythms, and polyrhythms, plays a definitive role in African American music making. As rhythm becomes the standard pattern, it begins to operate like a pulse or a bass line, giving temporal structure to musical sound. Rhythm becomes an ostinato, making and keeping time, and serving as a constant point of reference for musical events. Musicologist János Maróthy explains the language of "standard pattern," describing it as "one of a class of . . . patterns referred to as 'time-lines.' The standard pattern, one of the basic principles of timing, keeps time as it is played as an ostinato. . . . [It] organizes the phrase structure of a song as well as its linear metrics."[27] The standard pattern serves as the tonal center of the music and gives temporal framing to the song's meters, thus providing a resolution point in the music and guidelines for keeping the song's phrases both on time and on key. Musicians call this "the groove." Although the standard pattern can be heard in the Spirituals, it also appears in forms as contemporary as rap and hip-hop. Ethnomusicologist Robert Walser explains that in rap, the "bass plays a repeated pattern that can be heard either as syncopated—it pushes against the metric framework just as the kick drum does—or as polyrhythmic, a layering on of the 3-3-2 pulse (here, in eighth notes)."[28] Also noting the interplay of regular rhythms, syncopation, and polyrhythms,

26. See John M. Chernoff, "The Rhythmic Medium in African Music," *New Literary History* 22, no. 4 (Autumn 1991): 1093–1102, https://tinyurl.com/3c4x6xts.

27. Maróthy, "Rite and Rhythm." Also see Robert Walser, "Rhythm, Rhyme, and Rhetoric in the Music of Public Enemy," *Ethnomusicology* 39, no. 2 (1995): 209, https://tinyurl.com/2489y599.

28. Walser, "Rhythm, Rhyme, and Rhetoric in the Music of Public Enemy," 202.

musicologist Lawrence M. Zbikowski describes the groove as "a large-scale, multi-layered pattern that involves both rhythmic and pitch materials."[29] The groove, or standard pattern, imposes order on sound and organizes it through the interplay of complex rhythms.

A recurring theme in the literature on the Spirituals and on African American music in general is the *cyclicity* of their rhythmic paths. Whether in discussions about ostinato rhythms, syncopated rhythms, or polyrhythms, rhythm in African American music is understood to be cyclical, that is, *repetitive*, suggesting a curvilinear contour as basic to the shape of African American musical sound. Walser talks of bass "grounding the start of each rhythmic cycle." Zbikowski argues that a key feature of "the groove" is its cyclicity: "Rhythmic events are cyclic. Cyclicity coordinated different regularities . . . and characterized [sounds] in terms of proprioception [and] regularity."[30] Here it must be acknowledged that the cycle, or circle, is used as a *musical* symbol, rather than a mathematical one, although we have seen that there may be overlap. More, this musical shape reflects modern Western notational cues, and it is unclear whether it distorts African American music, especially its inability to notate nonperiodic rhythms.[31] Languages of cycle and circle are often used to illustrate the priority of the musical elements of rhythm and meter over those of pitch and harmony, as well as an openness to contextual improvisation over "fidelity to the score" of sheet music. The emphasis on cyclicity discloses a type of musical composition that addresses questions of musical texture, depth, and space primarily by way of rhythm. Harmony, the prime factor for musical unity in Western tonal music, seeks the appropriate distance, simultaneity, and succession between two tones on a rectilinear, diatonic scale. This is usually talked about as tones forming a chord. By contrast, rhythm seeks the right duration, frequency, and regularity of pulses or patterns. Rhythmic musical order isn't primarily about tonal harmonies, but about the right mix of various musical times. This is usually talked about as finding the groove.

The focus on rhythm as central to musical practice also has implications for musical order. John Miller Chernoff explains that while the Western tonal system is based on the harmonic potential of tones, African and African Amer-

---

29. Lawrence M. Zbikowski, "Modelling the Groove: Conceptual Structure and Popular Music," *Journal of the Royal Musical Association* 129, no. 2 (2004): 272–97, https://tinyurl.com/3ekpxjn2.

30. Zbikowski, "Modelling the Groove," 272–97.

31. See Dena J. Epstein and Rosita M. Sands, "Secular Folk Music," in *African American Music: An Introduction*, ed. Mellonee V. Burnim and Portia K. Maultsby, 2nd ed. (New York: Routledge, 2015).

ican musical composition is made from complexes of rhythmic tensions and consonances, and tonal ambivalence and compromise. Musical systems organize tones into intelligible relationships with one another, but while the harmonic system does so by *dividing* time by way of intervals to deduce harmonic ratios, the rhythmic system organizes tonal relationships by *interweaving* time by way of antiphony to induct rhythmic ratios. With tonic organization assigned solely to the harmonic scale, questions of timbre, color, and key signature become central questions for musical order as the musician arranges relationships between white keys and black keys, and between whole notes and flats or sharps. The harmonic musician assigns the roles of tonic, dominant, and subdominant to tones, and tones must travel the predetermined musical path from home statement to departure away, and finally back home. In the rhythmic scheme, tonic organization is addressed with questions of tempo, meter, and rhythmic complexity, as well as how tones relate to one another in relation to the beat. The rhythmic musician assigns the roles of upbeat, downbeat, and offbeat to tones traveling a dialogical, cyclical musical path of call and response, where tensions create conflict, progression, or repetition. Yet, rhythmic organization allows for and even requires timbral and pitch distortions, and quartet harmonies and blue notes also create spaces for tonal asymmetry. Tones are free to play on rhythmic tensions, weaving themselves into patterns of ostinatos, syncopations, or polyrhythms, because the tempo keeps the chorus in organized motion.

While rhythm has been the prime factor in African American musical composition, Locke also notes the significance of its harmonic and melodic features as well. "But as a matter of fact, if we separate or even over-stress either element in the Spirituals, the distinctive and finer effects are lost." African American harmonies, appearing in contemporary styles like jazz and rhythm and blues, first became the center of public debate in the late nineteenth and early twentieth century with the rise of quartet ensembles. In the postbellum context, many African American musicians moved from rural spaces like plantations and cabins to urban settings and to Black colleges and normal and industrial schools like Fisk University, Clark Atlanta University, Southern University, and Hampton University. One ambiguity of emancipation was that political emancipation and educational opportunity effected a transformation in the way that the Spirituals were composed. During this time, the erotic rhythms of folk Spirituals became disciplined by the modern West's rational ladder of musical progression, and the Spirituals became the *arranged* Spirituals. These were also commodified forms of musical production, primarily by Black singers for consumption by white audiences, and for purposes of transactional exchange.

Thus, although the Spirituals contained harmony before emancipation, there is some debate as to what degree current African American harmonic scales (e.g., pentatonic, blues) are authoritative. Yet the distinctive proportions of African American harmonies—the "quartet"—reflect the binary pattern of call and response rather than a triadic form. In African American music, a quartet is not simply four singers but a vocal ensemble of a minimum of four voices and a maximum of six voices singing four-part-harmony arrangements.[32] The quartet is thus a doubling of the call and response.

The harmonic element in African American music introduces both the vertical and rectilinear aspects more directly into considerations of musical space-time. On the one hand, harmonic relationships provide the possibility for musicians to climb up and down "Jacob's ladder" by way of ascending and descending scales. Yet these scales are also rectilinear, in distinction from rhythm's curvilinear path. In African American music, two of the most prominent ways of relating tones are the pentatonic scale and the blues scale. The pentatonic scale refers to the fourth and seventh notes of the diatonic major scale, and fourth, sixth, and seventh notes of the minor scale. As a codified scale, the blues scale is hexatonic, having six notes as opposed to five. It consists of flatted approximations of corresponding naturalized scale steps, typically the flatted third, flatted seventh, and sometimes the flatted fifth, with the flatted third being the most frequently employed. For our purposes, it is significant to note that the constitution of harmonic orders in African American music takes place at the intersection of mathematical objectivity and the practical, dialectical cultural ethos of call and response, between the measured distance between tones and the flexibility and freedom of singers or tones to periodically respond to the harmonic order by a range of dialectical movements, so as to create dissonance or to create harmony by a different progression. From this general principle we get harmonic innovations like the "blue note" and the "grace note." Again, the blue note is a note that falls between two adjacent notes in the standard Western division of octave and is usually the third or seventh degree of a scale. A grace note is a short ornamental note performed as an embellishment before the principal pitch. The blue note challenges the constancy of the harmonic order, and the grace note challenges the priority of the harmonic order.

In African American music, the vertical structure of harmony is framed by rhythm's cyclical polyrhythmic texture, so that the temporal grid of rhythm

---

32. Joyce Marie Jackson, "Quartets: Jubilee to Gospel," in Burnim and Maultsby, *African American Music*, Kindle location 1596 of 9843.

and the spatial grid of harmony intersect to create a certain kind of compositional temporal depth. Geometrically, this combination might produce a range of shapes including the cone, the cylinder, the ellipsoid, the torus, or the sphere. We might also imagine a spiral, especially when verticality is interpreted within a musical sequence of rhythmic progression. The predominance of the rhythmic element in African American music produces harmonies that display rhythmic features of form and symmetry. Again, the quartet reflects rhythmic features in its fundamentally binary pattern. With respect to symmetry, distinctive harmonic features of African American music such as the quartet and the blue note reflect the ever-present space for some type of harmonic asymmetry. For example, David Evans notes how a blue note creates a musical space for tonal ambivalence or compromise. "A blue note . . . [might be] a wavering between flat and natural or two other points within an interval. It might also occur as the simultaneous sounding of the flat and natural pitches, or simply their use at different times in a piece."[33] This tonal ambivalence and compromise mirror the asymmetrical features of rhythm and suggest a harmonic system and musical composition that are fundamentally ordered not by arranging tone colors but by four-part harmonies echoing formal binarism and asymmetry. This harmonic system can also sound asymmetries in hierarchical arrangements, musical or otherwise.

The distinction between harmonic and rhythmic order has ontological implications. As observed in this analysis of the Spirituals, rhythmically ordered musical compositions acknowledge both collective and individual aspects of musical existence, both the one and the many, as temporal entities. The music-making practices of call and response are animated by an orchestral chorus that begins with the soloist's call of the one and a congregational response from the many. Upon repetition, this logic becomes the standard pattern around which the orchestra organizes itself. As left to us in song, the chorus frequently referred to themselves as church, and also as "the band," and their descriptions of the band were woven from a rich tapestry of theological aesthetics. The band no doubt referred to the orchestra, with its musical instruments, voices, bodies, and the collectivity of dancers and singers. Yet the language also meant a gathering of the converted, those whose religious experience of God as redeemer, healer, merciful judge, and worker provoked a revolution from a life of selfish and prideful "false pretending" to one of humility and "bandedness" with creation. Thus, the band also referred to nature as God's call. "My Lord calls me, He calls me by the thunder; The trumpet sounds within a my soul. . . .

---

33. David Evans, "Blues," in Burnim and Maultsby, *African American Music*.

Nature, Spirit, and Song

He calls me by the lightning." And again, "Upon the mountain my Lord spoke, Out his mouth came fire and smoke." The band was sometimes sung about as "the band ob Gideon," linking their own context of oppression to the Hebrew and biblical traditions, and also to the band "ober in Jordan," that is, in heaven. Of heaven, the Spirituals sing of golden harps, of sounding trumpets, and of "angels singin all around de trone." In this way, all of creation is entailed in a cosmic orchestra, whose purpose is to make sweet music by rhythmically interweaving with the groove.

"I Can't Stay Behind": On Musical Progression

Along with the formal structural aspects of the Spirituals like form, symmetry, dynamism, and time, musical composers must also come to terms with the question of musical motion. We have seen how musical form emerges from basic elements of duration, stress, and pitch. The question of musical motion was settled, in part, by both the dialectical logic of call and response and the rhythmic tension in certain dynamics of African American music. Yet the question of the nature of the process of musical movement remains unanswered. As with all music, the Spirituals are musical form *in time* rather than space. This is not to say that music remains independent of its spatial environment, nor to say that music produces no physical responses. Indeed, the composition of the Spirituals is certainly impacted by the types of instruments available to musicians and by whether they sang the Spirituals in cornfields or factories. Also, music is real in that it cannot occur without observable physical processes, such as wavelengths and amplitudes. Music is partly the expression of energy, as vibrating atoms and molecules dissolve particles of matter into waves and, in turn, waves give rise to forms perceived by the senses.[34] Yet, this still tells us nothing with respect to the nature of the aesthetic procedure, course, or series of steps that the music itself is made to undergo as the song is woven and unfolds. The question of musical movement is a question of procedural means, that is, the *way in which* musical motion occurs. Musical motion is ideal motion, occurring largely in the individual or social mind. It can be both explained as an observable formal structure and interpreted and understood as an existential perception of musical change, development, or progression by the listener. There can be no music without the use of some type

---

34. See Juliette Bowles, "A Rap on Rhythm," in *This Is How We Flow: Rhythm in Black Cultures*, ed. Angela M. S. Nelson (Columbia: University of South Carolina Press, 1999), 5–14.

of musical progression, as music itself is motion in time. Without progression the music stops.

Let us take the rhythmic features of the Spirituals as an example in thinking about the question of musical motion. We have seen how the standard pattern, also called ostinato, is built up from compounded cycles of repetition. Rhythm's path is cyclical; it can also be called curvilinear, meaning that the movement of rhythm must travel a path that leads ultimately and repeatedly back to its beginning point. Yet it may be said that there is still a type of rhythmic progression that occurs in musical creations like the Spirituals. First, rhythm in the Spirituals is organized according to meter and measure, that is, to sections or groups of beats that must occur in a particular sequence. Although the path is cyclical, the musician must still progress along the path according to the appropriate measures of rhythmic beats, and failure to do so means that the music stops. Also, we must recall that for the Spirituals, cyclicity implies an openness to contextual improvisation as opposed to fidelity to the score. Repetition, then, may provide the opportunity for either monotony or innovation, for sameness or for difference. There is thus an openness to spontaneity and improvisation within the rhythmic cycles, which means that, ideally, each rhythmic cycle has the potential to create a new sound, a different beat, and a new time. Finally, although rhythm travels a circular path, it is difficult to make categorical statements about the axis, diameter, radius, or circumference, nor about the contours of its shape, as cyclical paths appear in circular, elliptical, and cylindrical shapes. In rhythm, the most basic structural units of the musical form are primary, and there is an up-close look at the details of meter and measure. It is a dynamic movement, from moment to moment, such that one may describe this type of musical motion as successive, where one motion occurs earlier, and another, later, and where there is a movement from moment to moment.

As is the case with rhythm, we can also analyze the features of musical motion in the Spirituals with respect to harmony. If rhythm travels a curvilinear path, harmony travels a rectilinear one. Generally speaking, the harmonic scale, whether classical, blues, or pentatonic, is about the rational ordering of musical notes according to a logic. Harmony reflects the cognitive dimension of music. Harmonic ordering moves away from moment-to-moment motions to consider a collection of notes together. Musical form is not experienced up close and in terms of immediacy, but from the perspective of the whole. The principle of motion in harmonic ordering is accretion, or that of organic growth, which builds up over time. Harmonic ordering suggests some type of gradual progress or process as the musical form is made to flower from a single idea into a continuous motion. Yet social reason that drives the harmonic process in the African American Spirituals is distinct from the *logos* of Western culture that has been inherited from Greco-Roman antiquity. The logic of call and response has incorporated the social exclusion and the expulsion, and indeed is constituted by this "scape-*logos*" such that harmony cannot happen without those notes that are normally silenced in the Western classical harmonic scale. We might also recall that the harmonic scale of the Spirituals is rooted in a bodily rationality, which means that musical progress is led by both body and mind. We might also note that in African American blues and pentatonic scales, harmonic progression is often about reconciling musical tensions, for example, tensions between whole notes and half notes, between half notes and quarter notes. Progress is not a straight line in Black music, but one forged through the struggle of notes seeking balance and harmony. Thus, while successive temporal motions of rhythm carry the beat, the accretions of harmony give spatial depth and dimension to the melody.

Finally, there is the musical movement of melody. In fine, the movement of melody is more appropriately left to discussion about questions of the self, the individual, and the body, rather than questions of the world, the cosmos, and the state of nature. The melody of the "soul" of music, that which makes the widest and most direct appeal. Melody attends to the affective dimension of human and musical experience. Here, the emotion, passion, and sympathy of the singer give rise to a wide range of strategies, tactics, and games of articulation. The Negro Spirituals and much of African American music is known for its percussive melodies and offbeat melodic phrasing. This strong element of percussion in melodic movement is partly a response to the legal prohibition of the use of African drums during slavery in the United States. Through melodic movements of repetition, variation, development, contrast, reprise, and others, the melody plays into and on, and around the patterns established by, musical form, rhythm, and harmony. The movement of melody is the movement of addition, of part to part. It is a secession of single tones that is perceived as a unity as opposed to a set series of tones in a planned scale. The movement of melody may thus be described as agglutination. Melodic movements operate by way of a "clumping" effect, as melodies are triggered to move in certain musical directions, for certain durations, according to certain pitches, by the deeper movements of rhythm and harmony. In ways similar to rhythm and harmony, the melody is also separated into two halves, each constituting a "melodic phrase," and true to form, these phrases are asymmetrical in relation to one another. Yet, unlike the rhythm and harmony of the Spirituals, the melody may be constructed with many different notes of different lengths and flows freely over the meter and measure. Here is the element of freedom not found in either rhythm or harmony. Yet when the three movements coincide, one begins to experience the musical flow.

"I Saw the Beam in My Sister's Eye": On Music in 3D

In the call-and-response exchange, a logic of reciprocation was generated and then woven into the fabric of the Spirituals. In this way, antebellum slaves created a balanced and proportional work of art, which, as we have seen, is a work ironically marked by asymmetry, dynamism, tension, and dissonance. These formal features create the space-time structures where rectilinear ladders of harmony travel through the centers of cyclical rhythms that are themselves superimposed on one another. Alongside these and to be explored in a further work is the improvisational freedom of melody. These basic elements constitute a well-formed musical structure in the antebellum Spirituals. From these sonic structures one may offer a preliminary perception of the contours of a musical understanding of just and appropriate relations and ratios.[35] From rhythm, one may first deduce the significance of the body, of basic needs, of categorical basic goods, and of quality-of-life issues, as well as that of life, of the pulse, and of sustaining ecosystems. The standard pattern's slight off-centeredness conveys the dimension of equality, that is, of maximally similar analogues, even as it aligns segments in ways that convey both similarity and difference, complementation and competition, rather than either the notion of categorical otherness or the notion of absolute sameness that erases differences altogether. From the structures of harmony, one may deduce the dimension of equity, that is, of fairness, and impartiality, and thus of rank and merit, yet one achieved by way of musical reason of call and response and including in its progression notes of dissonance formerly rendered silent. Finally, there is both a rational and an expressive dimension signified by melody, where freedom comes forth as melodic choice, giving rise to values of individuality, conscience, existence, and identity. For the antebellum Spirituals, a well-formed song included these three dimensions.

Mauss's emphasis on gift exchange is an attempt to strengthen social bonds against a creeping cultural individualism, but his absolute rejection of contract

---

35. See Nicholas Wolterstorff, "The Work of Making a Work of Music," in *What Is Music? An Introduction to the Philosophy of Music*, ed. Philip Alperson (University Park: Pennsylvania State University Press, 1987).

theory destroys natural rights. Mauss sees modern systems of law, property, and economy as the key culprit. These systems prioritize the sovereignty of individual interest in exchange interactions. It draws a sharp distinction between obligation and services not given for free, on the one hand, and gifts and charity, on the other hand, thus eroding social bonds. Modern systems of law also depersonalize property. This means that modern systems of law, property, and economy create a conceptual categorical distinction between persons and objects, and in law, between personal rights and real rights. Legal theorist Jens Kersten explains that the "legal person" is one who is recognized as possessing subjective rights that can be enforced in court trials.[36] By contrast, the thing, or property, is not recognized as having subjective rights and thus had no ability to be represented in court. Property is only seen as an instrumental good to be owned or disowned, used or prohibited, and protected or destroyed by law. Kersten explains that these legal concepts of the legal person and real property operate as tools as transferable labels rather than hard-and-fixed descriptions of reality. "Legal systems are free to choose between different legal concepts in order to solve social, economic, and ecological problems."[37] For Mauss, it would be better if we rejected modern individual rights altogether. "There is total service in the sense that is indeed the whole clan that contracts on behalf of all, for all that it possesses and of all that it does, through the person of its chief."[38] The musical structures of the Spirituals suggest that the exchanges therein retained elements of individual interest and modern law, while also creating effective social bonds, as the pattern of call, respond, and reciprocate was formalized in the aesthetic principles of equality, equity, and expressive individualism.

---

36. Jens Kersten, "Who Needs Rights of Nature?," *RCC Perspectives*, no. 6 (2017): 9–14, https://tinyurl.com/bdfpzfpt.

37. Kersten, "Who Needs Rights of Nature?," 9–14.

38. Mauss, *The Gift*, 8.

8

De Lord Is Per-Wide, Rock O' My Soul, and Holy-Ghost the Pilot

On the Trinitarian God of the Spirituals

IN THE LAST CHAPTER, I took up the Spirituals primarily in an empirical fashion asking about both their logic of social exchange and their compositional features. This chapter takes up the Spirituals in a primarily phenomenological-hermeneutic fashion, asking about the Spirituals' theological depiction of the world. According to the Spirituals themselves, such a move requires a "crossing over" of sorts, that is, a conversion that enables one to sense the world on a different register. Theologian Barbara Holmes notes that this shift often occurred during the Spirituals as well as in other rituals of the "invisible institution" such as baptism and prayer "shut-ins." These practices of the Black church ushered in a type of ritual abiding time, where the presence of the Spirit occurs among a collective consciousness with the explicit expressed intention of communication with spiritual entities. "In the midst of worship," says Holmes, "an imperceptible shift occurred that moved the worshipping community from intentional liturgical action to transcendent indwelling."[1] For many in the worshiping community, time becomes sacred time and participants experience the transformative sacred power of God. Albert Raboteau speaks of the "superimposition of human and divine worlds" through the chilly baptismal waters or through the intensity of the dance.[2] Through these practices, the devotee's

---

1. Barbara A. Holmes, *Joy Unspeakable: Contemplative Practices of the Black Church* (Minneapolis: Augsburg Fortress, 2004), xx.

2. Albert J. Raboteau, *Slave Religion: The Invisible Institution in the Antebellum South* (New York: Oxford University Press, 2004), 26.

consciousness can be so transformed that the boundary between the ordinary and the extraordinary becomes blurred. Slaves sang "Give way, Jordan," out of a desire to "go across to see my Lord."[3] They sang that their "head got wet with the midnight dew," or that they "done been to heaven,

> An' I done been tried,
> I been to de water,
> An' I been baptized.

This chapter describes and analyzes the theological contours of the Spirituals. I find that the theological content of the Spirituals is constituted by the three main topics of crossing over, of Jesus, and of God and possible futures. In the first section, I discuss the concept of "crossing over" as presented in the Spirituals. I argue that the concept is a nested metaphor that can mean conversion, entrance into spiritual battle, or death, and that the concept is closely linked to the systematic theological doctrine of revelation. As one crosses over, one enters into new spaces of consciousness that bring with them new insights, and perhaps new questions as well. Although the Spirituals disclose religious insight into the nature of the divine economy, they do so in piecemeal fashion only. In the Spirituals, we see through a glass darkly into the life of the divine. Thus, even as the Spirituals discuss the person and work of Jesus as well as the nature and being of God, they do so in a way that leaves as much hidden as it reveals concerning God. In this way, the Spirituals don't aspire to either apodictic certainty or even exhaustive knowledge about God. They are, instead, primarily cultural works of praise and testimony that also helped the enslaved to both endure and assist in the overthrow of US slaveocracy. Yet they disclose a Trinitarian God that is intimately related to both heaven and earth in ways that facilitate humanity's redemption, physical and existential sustenance, deliverance, and justice. After beginning the chapter with an account of "crossing over," I then discuss Jesus in the Spirituals. I argue that they depict him in three primary images, those of the Lamb, the Rock, and Final Judge, and that each of these images corresponds to a certain work accomplished by Jesus. God is also depicted in three primary images, namely, Deliverer, Provider, and Composer. I conclude with a brief discussion on the eclipse of the heavens as represented in the antebellum Spirituals.

---

3. "Give Way Jordan," in *Religious Folk Songs of the Negro: As Sung on the Plantations*, ed. Thomas P. Fenner (Hampton, VA: Institute, 1973), 131.

Holy Ghost the Pilot: On Crossing Over in the Spirituals

Phenomenologically, the practice of the Spirituals functions as a portal by which one crosses over from ordinary time into the heavens. As portrayed throughout the antebellum Spirituals, heaven itself is primarily an audio and acoustic rather than a solely visual reality. The motion of sound takes the devotee into the presence of the Spirit, and the Spirit serves as a guide into the heavens. Contemporary theologians will use the language of "revelation" to describe this phenomenon, understood as God's gracious partial self-disclosure to the devotee. Revelation, as theologian Daniel Migliore tells us in *Faith Seeking Understanding*, is a threshold moment, where God is revealed even as God remains hidden and a mystery. Although the knowledge gained from revelatory occasions is partial, devotees nonetheless affirm its trustworthiness. This is the case whether such partial divine self-disclosures are sources of comfort and healing for the devotee or the revelations communicate surprising, disturbing, or upsetting truths. Revelation is understood by the devotee as a gift rather than an achievement, regardless of the intensity of the "sacrifice of praise" offered during the ritual performance, and the knowledge gained from such events is always fragmentary. Slaves frequently spoke of the wilderness as a place where one might meet God. "If you want to find Jesus, go in de wilderness, Go in de wilderness, go in de wilderness."[4] Theologian Delores Williams argues that during slavery, slaves had a primarily positive conception of the wilderness, seeing it as a place of freedom and transcendence.[5] Such freedom was not wrought without hard struggle. "The wilderness experience was not an easy one," says Williams, as "one struggled in the wilderness with oneself in the process of meeting Jesus."[6] Yet slaves were often persistent in their efforts to undergo wilderness experiences, as it was a place where Black men and women could meet God and be transformed by the event.

Throughout the Spirituals, the most consistent symbol used to describe the shift from ordinary time to ritual time is "crossing over," a nested symbol that can also mean existential conversion, entry into spiritual conflict, or transition

---

4. This lyric is from the Spiritual "Go in the Wilderness." This Spiritual and all others noted or discussed in this chapter can be found in *Slave Songs of the United States: 136 Songs Complete with Sheet Music and Notes on Slavery and African American History*, comp. William Francis Allen, Charles Pickard Ware, and Lucy McKim Garrison (n.p.: Pantianos Classics, 1867), unless otherwise noted.

5. Delores Williams, *Sisters in the Wilderness: The Challenge of Womanist God-Talk* (New York: Orbis Books, 1993, 2013), 100.

6. Williams, *Sisters in the Wilderness*, 100.

from this life to eternal life with God. Thus, participation in the Spirituals was potentially a crossing over of one type or another. One song, "Ship of Zion," encourages the listener to "Sail, O believer, sail, Sail over yonder . . . and view de promised land." Another, "My Army Cross Over," commands the listener to cross over, possibly into battle against the spiritual forces of evil: "My brudder, tik keer Satan, My army cross over. . . . Jordan riber rollin', Cross 'em, I tell ye, cross 'em, Cross Jordan (danger) riber." One might also cross over into a converted life of following Jesus, where the world itself takes on new meaning and significance. "I look at de worl' and de worl' look new, I look at de worl' and de worl' look new." In all cases of crossing over, one experiences a shift from one understanding of reality to another, and the Spirituals' general conception of crossing over gives rise to a distinction between "this world" and "the other side," which may also be called "the heavens." The event of crossing over may be initiated by the believer but may also be encouraged by heavenly beings, especially angels, and the theme of angels as pathways to the heavens is prevalent throughout the Spirituals. One song exclaims: "Bright angels biddy me to come; Bruddr, guide me home an' I am glad, Bright angels biddy me to come." Another song beckons: "Come down, angel, and trouble the water, Come down, angel, and trouble the water, And let God's saints come in." And yet another, "I'm gwine to my heaven, I'm gwine home, Archangel open de door." Crossing over usually occurs over the seas, but one may also enter the heavens through visions, in hearing music, or even by way of a divine chariot ride.

Crossing over from this world into the heavens is more about a religious experience of another place than it is about a direct encounter with God. Thus, one may have a vision of God, but one may also encounter any number of other beings. We have already mentioned angels, and alongside them the Spirituals are replete with stories of encounters with the ancestors of biblical faith like Moses or Daniel or some of Jesus's New Testament followers including John and Mary. These ancestors and disciples operate much like the ancestors of traditional African religion; that is, they are those who in their lives achieved some high status in the eyes of a family, clan, or nation. They are dead but continue to maintain a presence among the living, forming key strands for the fabric of moral and social life. The ancestors and disciples of the Spirituals aren't omnipotent, but they are superhuman, with the power to protect society and punish offenses, and they are regarded as the moral watchdogs of the community and the authority figures that maintain social and moral norms. In one song we hear: "I'm a huntin' for some guardian angel Gone along before, Mary and Marta, feed my lamb. . . . Simon Peter, feed my lamb, a-sittin' on de golden order." In another we are told: "If you look up de road you see fader Mosey [Moses]. Join de angel band, If you look up de road you see fader Mosey." One song commends the biblical story of Lazarus as a model to emulate in response to the problem of death: "I want to die like-a Lazarus die, Die like-a Lazarus die." In one song, a character notes, "I had a mighty battle like-a Jacob and de angel, Jacob, time of old," and in another, songwriters tell the story of meeting Hercules on the way to a meeting: "Went to de meetin'. Met brudder Hacless. Wha' d'ye tink he tell me? Tell me for to turn back."

Although the antebellum Spirituals venerate a number of saints, the figures of "Mary," Moses, and Daniel are among the most prominent, and together these create a chorus of witnesses that served as the background for African American religious and social life. The Spirituals do indeed venerate other saints, patriarchs, and disciples. For example, songs like "John of the Golden Order," "Wrestle on Jacob," and "I Want to Die like-a Lazarus Die" lifted up other nineteenth-century ancestors. Paul and Silas also make a few appearances. Yet one cannot deny the prominence of "Mary," which in fine refers to at least three different figures: Mary Magdalene, the twin figures of "Mary and Marta," and that of a fictive figure named "Sister Mary." Yet the Spirituals are constituted such that the distinction between these figures becomes blurred, thus opening up the general figure "Mary" to a range of interpretations even beyond these three. Mary Magdalene appears in songs like "Hail Mary" and "The Resurrection Morn," and both songs position Mary as the connecting link between Jesus's ministry and freedom from slavery. "Hail Mary" moves from making a general inquiry for "some valiant solder, here, To help me bear the cross," to a proclamation of the end of white governance: "Done wid massa's hollerin', Done wid missus' scoldin'." In similar fashion, the song "The Resurrection Morn" discusses how Mary Magdalene runs to tell the disciples the news of Jesus's resurrection after discovering Jesus's empty tomb. Yet one can easily hear a double meaning in the opening verse: "O run, Mary run, Hallelu, hallelu, O run, Mary, run, Hallelujah!" as well as in later verses, "But she see a man a-comin', . . . And she thought it was de gardener." Thus, the first figure of Mary, that is, Mary Magdalene, is a figure that potentially signifies not only Jesus's ministry of deliverance, but more specifically, the possibility of deliverance in both existential and political forms.

While the distinctions between the various figures of "Mary" may become blurred in their singing, a close reading or listening isolates the twin figures of "Mary and Marta" as specifically *epistemological* figures. As represented in the Spirituals, Mary and Marta are authoritative examples for how all persons should be willing to learn from God. They are also key figures that come into play in the Spirituals' consciousness on our models for the acquisition and use of knowledge. This can be seen in songs like "The Lonesome Valley," "Happy Morning," and "Religion So Sweet." "The Lonesome Valley" instructs the listener on how to "get religion," saying that one must go into the lonesome valley, and also that one might "get religion" by lifting up Mary and Marta as examples. Mary and Marta are depicted as getting religion by "read 'em" (reading) the "letter" of Jesus. The lyrics read: "want to get religion? Go down in de lonesome valley.... O feed on milk and honey. O John he write de letter. And Mary and Marta read 'em." The song "Happy Morning" encourages Mary and Marta to stop weeping, since Jesus has risen from the dead: "Weep no more, Marta, Weep no more, Mary, Jesus rise from de dead. Happy morning." It signals the epistemological significance of Mary and Marta, and it associates knowledge of God in Jesus Christ with an existential state of joy. Finally, in the song "Religion So Sweet," Mary and Marta make yet another appearance as twin figures that are yet again associated with spiritual knowledge. Here, they are lifted up as examples of "a-huntin . . . seeekin" for God even in the face of trial. Mary and Marta experienced weeping, but also "religion so sweet." Thus, the antebellum Spirituals lift up Mary and Marta as key ancestors. They are examples of the authority of women's experiences, women's wisdom, and women's ways of knowing the divine. They symbolize the spiritual quest into the wilderness, the facing of hard trials, and of finding God, drawing near to God, and of the joy unspeakable that ensues.

Finally, the antebellum Spirituals venerate Mary in the figure of "Sister Mary" alongside the previously mentioned figures of Mary Magdalene and Mary and Marta. While these two Marys refer to biblical figures, "Sister Mary" operates as more of a general fictive character that plays a variety of revelatory roles explicitly in relation to questions of collective and social morality. Sister Mary is thus a partial guide to the African American Spirituals' perspective on questions of the moral status of the state of nature, a.k.a. the natural law. For example, the song "There's a Meeting Here Tonight" seems to explicitly reject notions of a moral or natural law: "Brudder John was a writer, he write de laws of God; Sister Mary say to brudder John, 'Brudder John, don't write no more.' Dere's a meeting here to-night, Oh!" The song suggests that the law of God is somehow no longer authoritative, and it replaces the laws of God with prayer meetings. In the song "Rock O' Jubilee," Mary is a figure that stands next to God at the doors of heaven and seems to possess an authority with respect to who is allowed to enter: "Stand back, Satan, let me come by. . . . My Fader door wide open now. Mary, girl, you know my name." In the song "Join the Angel Band," Sister Mary is challenged to "stan' up for Jesus" by joining the "angel band." The angel band is an army, a musical army, that is gathering itself in the Spirit realm. It consists of a host of angels, saints, and Spirits that are united for the cause of heaven. Among them are "Daddy Peter," "fader Mosey," "Maum Nancy," and countless other "brudders an' sisters." And it calls to Sister Mary: "Sister Mary, stan' up for Jesus." Sister Mary signifies a shift in the locus of moral authority from a natural or moral law to that of the community, and more specifically, a musical community, also called a band.

Alongside the figure of "Mary," the figure of Moses is a spiritual ancestor within the corpus of the antebellum African American Spirituals. Moses is most frequently represented as acting for the deliverance of the children of Israel from Pharaoh, such that Moses comes to represent the theme of divine deliverance from oppression among the ancestors. Here, the Spirituals exhibit an exodus thrust, thus overlapping with later "exodus theologians" like Rev. Dr. Martin Luther King Jr., Gustavo Gutiérrez, and James H. Cone. Yet while these more recent theologians emphasize the narrative and theological dimensions of the exodus, the Spirituals also locate the exodus motif within the ancestral ethos. Thus, the Spirituals understand the motif of deliverance from oppression not only as God's desire but also as a central feature of the moral background and ethos of African American religion and culture. Moses is one of the key ancestral figures that represents the principle of deliverance from oppression. The songs "Let God's Saints Come In" and "Come Along Moses" do so by representing Moses as liberator: "Say, Moses go to Egypt land, And tell him to let my people go"; and again, "Come along, Moses, don't get lost. . . . Strech out your rod and come across." In yet another song, "Join the Angel Band," Moses takes on mythical status as leader of the "angel band." Here, the term "angel band" has a double meaning. On the one hand, it draws on Israel's musical celebration after they successfully crossed over the Red Sea and effectively defeated Pharaoh's army. On the other hand, the song has transformed this band into a chorus of humans, spirits, and archangels joined together for the cause of heaven: "Do, fader Mosey, gader your army. O do mo' soul gader togeder." The term "angel band" is thus a play on words that blurs the boundary between the band found in heaven and the one here on earth, and Moses becomes a cosmic figure of deliverance from oppression.

Daniel is another key ancestor that appears in the antebellum Spirituals. Like Moses, Daniel represents the motif of deliverance from oppression. Yet beyond this, Daniel also represents the principles of religious tolerance, the freedom of conscience, and prayerful resistance to tyranny. In the biblical account, Daniel, a high officer in the court of King Darius, is condemned to death and thrown into the lions' den after disobeying a royal decree that no prayers should be issued to anyone but the king. Daniel is an incredibly pious man, such that he continues to pray to the God of Israel even after the king's prohibition. After leaving Daniel in the lions' den overnight, the royal court expects to discover Daniel's remains, but when they look into the lions' den, they find that Daniel's "God sent his angel, and he shut the mouths of the lions."[7] The Spirituals take up this narrative in songs like "O Daniel" and "Lean on the Lord's Side." "Lean on the Lord's Side" uses Daniel as a model for how one should choose to prayerfully follow God even in the face of trial. It tells how Daniel survived by leaning on the Lord's side. In this way it praises the principles of religious tolerance, freedom of conscience, and also deliverance from oppression. Yet the creativity and improvisational skill used to portray Daniel's actions transform him into a mythical strongman, thus also conveying the message of resistance to tyranny and the possible destruction of oppressive institutions: "Daniel rock de lion joy . . . De golden chain to ease him down . . . De silver spade to dig his grave." The official translation of "rock de lion joy" is "racked the lion's jaw," yet the phrase may also be heard as "rocked the lion [into] joy," since the lions did not devour Daniel and were at peace. The song "O Daniel" joins the chorus of deliverance from oppression and freedom of conscience: "O my Lord delivered Daniel, O Daniel, O Daniel . . . why not deliver me too?" Thus, Daniel is also among the angelic and ancestral band.

To see the heavens, one must cross over to the other side, and this is not possible by human will alone. Although many songs referenced "going to the wilderness" as one possible pathway, this was only one, and one that could not be reproduced with any scientific predictability. It was always possible that one's journey into the wilderness remained simply that, occurring without conversion, without literal or figurative death, or without spiritual battle. Conversely, it is possible to cross over in spaces that are far removed from the wilderness and located even in the centers of concrete spaces of civilization. The Spirituals understand crossing over to be about more than simply traversing physical geographies. Crossing over is also a transcendental journey that takes one to another state of existential consciousness. To the extent that crossing over involved the spiritual experience of divine revelation, crossing over required not only the faith of the participant but also the free movement of the divine as an action of self-disclosure. Crossing over thus involved both a voluntary giving over from the devotee and a responsive taking over by God. The slaves frequently sang about this experience of crossing over as one of crossing the seas on a ship. "Don't you see that ship a sailin'?" asks the chorus

---

7. Dan. 6:21 NIV.

in the song "The Old Ship of Zion," "Gwine over to the Promised Land? ... shall I ever be the one, To go sailin'?" While these lyrics no doubt represented a literal, rather than a figurative, hope, as Liberia was being colonized during this time, for others it represented the spiritual journey into the heavens. Slaves imagined themselves being taken over to the other side on a ship, the "Old Ship of Zion." The ship of Zion isn't piloted by God herself, nor by "King Jesus [who] is the Captain," but by the Holy Ghost. The slaves spoke of the Holy Ghost quite infrequently but did testify to the belief that on the old ship of Zion, "The Holy Ghost is the Pilot."

God Got Plenty of Room: On Heaven in the Spirituals

Heaven as described in the Spirituals is marked by the three distinctive features of sacredness, spaciousness, and musical sound. Heaven has the capacity to house all of creation, including all *righteous* past, present, and future generations. Songs speak of family members and loved ones that have crossed over to the other side, now awaiting our own arrival. "When we do meet again, When we do meet again, 'Twill be no more to part," and again, "Good-bye, brother.... We part in de body but... We'll meet in de heaben in de blessed kingdom." One song implies the spaciousness of heaven with the story that "Sixteen souls set out for Heaven. O brudder an' sister, come up for Heaven. Daddy Peter set out for Jesus. Ole Maum Nancy set out for Heaven." Another song tells us that "Dere's room enough, room enough, room enough in de heaven, my Lord.... [I] Been all around de Heaven, my Lord, I've searched every room—in de Heaven, my Lord." The song title "God Got Plenty of Room" also speaks to this spacious aspect of heaven, as do the titles "In the Mansions Above" and "Build a House in Paradise." These lyrics about the spaciousness of heaven suggest a sense of another world, where the saving and electing grace of God is coextensive with the fabric of all creation, including human beings. The Spirituals use the language of election and covenant sparingly, but they frequently deploy a threefold logic of free grace, judgment, and faith. The free grace of God extends to all peoples and places, such that one song tells how someone "found free grace in the wilderness," and another, "Where to go I did not know, Ever since he freed my soul. I look at de worl' and de worl' look new." Although "Adam, you ate that apple," God's free grace offers us the possibility to "join the band" by placing our faith in God. In exchange for free grace, each of us will one day be judged by God.

De Lord Is Per-Wide, Rock O' My Soul, and Holy-Ghost the Pilot

In addition to conceiving of heaven as a spacious place, the Spirituals portray heaven as a sacred place. The strong sense of the sacredness of heaven is communicated, for example, in the song "John John, of the Holy Order," where the image of John upon a "golden order" is repeated. The lyrics describe John "Sittin' on de golden order; John, John wid de holy order, Sittin on de golden order, To view de promised land." The song "Heaven Bell a-Ring" describes how heaven functions as a proving ground for one's deeds here on earth, ensuring that heaven remains a holy and righteous place: "Say when you get to heaven say your work shall prove. Your righteous Lord shall prove 'em well. Your righteous Lord shall find you out. He cast out none dat come by faith." In heaven, one is not exposed to the harsher aspects of life as it exists on earth: "Dere's no sun to burn you.... Dere's no hard trials. Dere's no whips a-crackin', Dere's no stormy weather." Songs also express how evil institutions like slavery, corrupt religion, and forced labor have been eradicated in heaven, allowing for the reign of peace, justice, gladness, and glory. "No more hundred lash for me. No more mistress' call for me," exclaims one song. Another song, "Sabbath Has No End," serves as a collective expression of a desire for rest from hard labor: "Gwine to walk about in Zion, I really do believe; walk about Zion, ... Sabbath has no end." Throughout the Spirituals, heaven is alternately described as the "oder bright land," as the "oder bright world," and as Paradise. Heaven is a place of gladness, of joy, and of "jubilee." Finally, in heaven, one might be graced with a partial glimpse of God, Jesus, or the Holy Ghost. The Spirituals offer relatively few images of the divine Trinity, implicitly conceiving God, Jesus, and the Holy Ghost as mysteries that can never be completely comprehended, even by heavenly beings that live within the presence of God without end.

The third distinctive aspect of the Spirituals' depiction of heaven is its sonic and acoustic nature. Sound, especially musical sounds, gives aesthetic grandeur to heaven and implies that the heavens themselves are constituted and sustained through a continuous balance of musical consonance. The acoustic nature of the heavens is suggested, for example, in sonic portrayals of heavenly beings. The angel Gabriel blows on his trumpet to call the saints to heaven: "Blow your trumpet, Gabriel, Blow louder, louder, And I hope dat trump might blow me home to de new Jerusalem." In the song "Michael Row the Boat Ashore," we are told that "Michael boat a gospel boat ... Michael boat a music boat. Gabriel blow de trumpet horn ... Michael haul the boat ashore. Then you'll hear the horn they blow." Other songs with titles like "Heaven Bell a-Ring" and "Bell Da Ring" communicate how heaven uses musical sounds, especially bells, to mark significant occasions, and the lyrics of the latter go into detail: "De heaven-bell a heaven-bell. De heaven-bell I gwine home. I shout for de heaven bell. . . . You can't get to heaben, When de bell done ring." Another song asks: "O don't you hear the heaven bells a-ringing over me? It sounds like judgement day!" Again, several heavenly beings, especially angels, are portrayed as possessing musical talents that may be used for a range of purposes. In addition to figures already noted like Michael and Gabriel, one Spiritual depicts angels encircling the divine throne as also possessing musical talents. As noted in the song "I Can't Stay Behind," "I've searched every room—in de Heaven, my Lord. De angels singin'—all around de trone." In the song "King Emanuel," songwriters even cleverly convey the notion that heaven is so constituted by music that one might create musical sounds simply by touching various objects. "If you walk de golden street, and you join the golden band . . . If you touch one string, den de whole heaven ring."

The Spirituals' depiction of heaven is indeed a depiction of another world, but the Spirituals also describe heaven in ways that suggest it has certain resemblances to life here on earth. This resemblance is seen in human existential expressions of joy and relief in heaven and in mundane activities like walking, talking, and singing. Resemblances between heaven and earth can also be seen in the various names given to heaven in the Spirituals. Heaven is also interchangeably called Zion, the New Jerusalem, the Promised Land, and Home. Each of these four names as articulated in the Spirituals acknowledges a distinction between the planes of heaven and earth even as it also blurs this distinction. These names also blur distinctions between Black identity, Christian identity, and other Abrahamic faiths like Judaism and Islam. "Jesus is our Captain," sings one song. "He will lead us on to glory. We'll meet at Zion gateway. . . . We'll enter into glory." Another song reads: "Gwine to walk about in Zion, I really do believe; Walk about in Zion . . . Sabbath has no end." Heaven is also called the Promised Land, and this image is sometimes combined with that of the Jordan River as a great cosmic gateway into the afterlife. In order to get to the Promised Land, one must cross over "Jordan riber"; only then is one able to reach "Canaan's shore" on the other side. This identification of heaven with the Promised Land, Zion, and New Jerusalem can be observed in songs like "John, John, of the Holy Order," where John is "Sittin on de golden order, To view de Promised Land," and "O Brothers Don't Get Weary," where we are told that "We'll land on Canaan's shore, When we land on Canaan's shore, We'll meet forever more." It can also be observed in the songs "The Old Ship of Zion," where we are asked: "Don't you see that ship a sailin', Gwine over to the Promised Land?" and "My Father, How Long?" with its lyrics: "walk de golden streets, Of de New Jerusalem."

De Lord Is Per-Wide, Rock O' My Soul, and Holy-Ghost the Pilot

Rock O' My Soul: On Jesus in the Spirituals

In heaven, and in religious experience here on earth, the most pervasive presence is the reality of Jesus Christ. The Spirituals depict Jesus with the images of Lamb, Rock, and Judge. The Spirituals take for granted that Jesus is a living cosmic reality with a historical past in first-century Judea. While they offer little commentary on his past historical life, the Spirituals' discourse on Jesus as a cosmic reality also recognizes his humanity. That is to say that in the Spirituals, the cosmic Christ whose presence (re)frames all of reality is also the human Jesus of history, shaped by his life on earth. For example, in the song "I Hear from Heaven To-Day," Jesus's human birth is the cause of cosmic celebration, as even the angels rejoice: "And I yearde from heaven today, A baby born in Bethlehem, and I yearde from heaven today. De trumpet sound in do oder bright land." The song "Tell My Jesus 'Morning'" conveys the message that Jesus is both as mundane and as cosmic as each new day: "In de mornin' when I rise, Tell my Jesus huddy, oh; I wash my hands in de mornin' glory, Tell my Jesus huddy, oh." The link between the cosmic Christ and the historical Jesus can also be seen in Jesus's identity as Lamb, which refers to Jesus's cosmic work of atonement for the sins of humanity to the effect of the redemption of all creation. In the Spirituals, much of Jesus's atoning work is communicated through images of the cross and the crucifixion, or through Jesus portrayed as the "Lamb of God." The song "The Heaven Bells" declares: "O mother I believe That Christ was crucified!" The representation of the cosmic significance of the atoning work of Jesus may be seen in the song "The Golden Altar," which depicts Jesus as "de Lamb of God" worshiped by a "holy number" of saints upon a great golden altar in heaven. Together, Jesus and the holy number gaze upon the world and promise that it will suffer unjustly only a "little while longer."

The Lamb of God signifies the cosmic Christ, whose atonement universalizes God's free grace for a troubled and fallen world. The antebellum Spirituals portray the world as troubled primarily by sinners and Satan. Sinners are those who evade the free grace of God. They are often portrayed as running away or turning away from God, which represents either the sinner's refusal to seek God or the sinner's denial of the human capacity to search for God. In the cosmic sense, it represents "the Fall" as portrayed in the Genesis account, an existential move away from belief in God's free grace toward belief in a more limited view of the scope of Jesus's atonement. The sinner incorrectly believes that he or others are beyond the scope of God's free grace and sanctifying power. Thus, sinners act in ways that trouble the world, for example, with acts of hypocrisy, pride, and hatred. Satan also troubles the world, primarily by cheating the saints out of glory and by persuading them to avoid prayer. Yet, as one song title notes, the Lamb's sanctifying atonement has set "Satan's Camp a-Fire," reestablishing the conditions of possibility for reconciliation with God. The Spirituals' portrayal of atonement combines elements of multiple formally recognized "atonement theories" such that they can't be said to conform solely to either a ransom theory, a satisfaction theory, or a moral influence theory. The song "Sinner Won't Die No More" offers the most sustained treatment on the topic: "O de Lamb done been down here an' died, De Lamb done been down here an' died, O de Lamb done been down here an' died, Sinner won't die no mo'." These lyrics make clear that Jesus's atonement permanently interrupts both cosmic and human historical cycles of retributive violence for sin but doesn't say *how*. The Lamb's atonement was costly. Yet it is assured, as God achieves liberation and reconciliation for the world in the transformative love and power of Jesus's life, death, and resurrection.

In addition to the image of Lamb, the Spirituals also frequently depict Jesus with the image of the Rock. The Rock symbolizes Jesus's continuing presence and work in the world as sustainer and comforter. After his crucifixion, death, and resurrection, Jesus lives on as a transformative postresurrection power who vivifies, nourishes, and comforts all God's children in both heaven and earth. The song "Bound to Go" communicates the biblical message of building one's existence on firm foundations of faith in God (Matt. 7): "I build my house upon de rock. O yes, Lord! No wind, no storm can blow 'em down. . . . I am not like de foolish man, He build his house upon de sand." These lyrics imply that the person and work of Jesus provide existential foundations able to sustain one during life's journey. The same message is conveyed in songs like "Rock O'Jubilee" and "Rock O' My Soul," which offer repetitive proclamations of Jesus's existential significance as a sustainer and comforter: "O rock o' jubilee, poor fallen soul, O Lord, do rock' o' jubilee . . . and I rock 'em all about" and again, "Rock o' my soul in de bosom of Abraham, Rock o' my soul in de bosom of Abraham . . . Lord, Rock o' my soul." In many songs, including the ones just mentioned, the image of the Rock takes on the double meaning of both sustainer and comforter. The Rock is simultaneously presented as both an immovable foundation and a comforting, back-and-forth motion that soothes the existential ills of the child of God. Jesus's role as Rock is one of the primary ways that the Spirituals depict his postresurrection divine power. As Rock, Jesus has the power to restore depleted human capacities. This view is most clearly stated in the song "No Man Can Hinder Me," which also makes no distinction between the cosmic Christ and the historical Jesus: "Jesus make de dumb to speak. Jesus make de cripple walk. Jesus give de blind his sight. Jesus do most anything."

De Lord Is Per-Wide, Rock O' My Soul, and Holy-Ghost the Pilot

Although Jesus's presence is pervasive throughout heaven and earth in the form of sanctification and sustenance, Jesus is not readily available for mass consumption. The Spirituals emphasize the hidden nature of God and teach that one must hunt, seek, and wrestle in order to find Jesus here on earth. This can be heard, for example, in the song "Hunting for the Lord," which encourages persistence in the hunt for Jesus, as if it is common knowledge that he is hard to find: "Hunt till you find him, Hallelujah ... Till you find him ... And a-huntin' for the Lord." The hiddenness of Jesus is also expressed in the song title "Jesus, Won't You Come By-and-Bye," which suggests that Jesus's presence is not always easily accessible. The songwriters express a desire to see Jesus: "Jesus, won't you come bumby? De Lord knows de world's gwine to end up. Jesus, won't you come bumby?" The song "Go in the Wilderness" suggests that Jesus's presence grows stronger as one moves away from the trappings of human civilization: "If you want to find Jesus, go in de wilderness, Go in de wilderness. ... Jesus a waitin to meet you in de wilderness." Finally, the song "Wrestle On, Jacob," implies that Jesus is simultaneously present and absent, and that one must engage in some type of spiritual or existential struggle to find him or to be blessed by him: "De Lord will bless my soul. ... Wrastl' on Jacob, Oh he would not let him go. I will not let you go, my Lord." Jesus's presence is pervasive throughout the cosmos, but one must seek him in order to find him. One must be willing to struggle in and with one's soul. Yet, the Spirituals also note that if one seeks, Jesus may be found. One of the most powerful representations of finding Jesus on earth is given in the song title "Jesus on the Water-Side," whose lyrics depict Jesus reposing by the waters, which themselves bridge heaven and earth: "Heaven bell a-ring, I know de road, Jesus sittin' on de water-side. Do come along."

In addition to images of Jesus as Lamb and Rock, the Spirituals also portray Jesus as Judge. One way that Jesus's role as judge is portrayed is through the scene of the final judgment, which takes center stage in the song "The Day of Judgement." The song draws on the parable of the sheep and the goats in Matthew 25 to communicate that Jesus is the cosmic judge of the world: "And you'll see de stars a-fallin, And de world will be on fire. ... And de Lord will say to de sheep, For to go to Him right hand; But de goats must go to de left." Although the Spirituals use the scene of the final judgment to communicate the theme of Jesus as judge, the most frequent image deployed to convey this message is that of Jesus upon a milk-white horse. This image appears in the song "I an' Satan Had a Race," as well as "Meet O' Lord" and "No Man Can Hinder Me," and others. In "I an' Satan Had a Race," Jesus sits upon a milk-white horse as he judges a contest between a child of God and Satan, concluding that Satan has cheated: "Satan tell me to my face, He will break my kingdom down.... Jesus mount de milk-white horse. Say you cheat my fader children." The song "Meet O' Lord" uses the image of the milk-white horse as it expresses the desires of enslaved folk for Jesus to finally judge the children of God as victors: "Meet, O Lord, on de milk-white horse, An' de nineteen wile in his han'; Drop on, drop on de crown on my head, An rolly in my Jesus arm."[8] The image of the milk-white horse appears again in "No Man Can Hinder Me": "Satan ride an iron gray horse. King Jesus ride a milk-white horse." In the song "Jesus Won't You Come, By-and-Bye," the image of the horse is used as songwriters express confidence that Jesus has the ultimate authority to make judgments about the world: "You ride dat horse, you call him Macadoni, Jesus won't you come bumby?... De Lord knows de world's gwine to end up, Jesus won't you come bumby?"

In Jesus's role as Judge, Jesus has himself experienced a transformation of sorts, from that of Lamb, that is, as the one who has been judged, to that of Judge, the one who judges. The Spirituals make clear that Jesus is the cosmic Judge who has the final say on who will make it to the Promised Land, but also on historical matters and events as well. In the Spirituals, the authority of Jesus's judgment crosses the boundary between sacred time and ordinary time, and between salvation history and empirical history. This understanding of Jesus's judgment is communicated directly, as in songs like "Jesus Won't You Come By-and-Bye" (above), and also indirectly, as in song titles like "Lord, Remember Me" and "Who Is on the Lord's Side." The latter titles indicate an awareness that Jesus possesses the power of inclusion and exclusion in Zion. The lyrics of "Lord, Remember Me" imply that Jesus holds the authority of final judgment even over the power of Death, which "kill some souls and he wounded some.... I lay out in da grave and I stretchee out e arms, Do, Lord, remember me." In these ways, the Spirituals acknowledge Jesus as the cosmic judge who holds the final authority on the matter of our inclusion in the New Jerusalem. At least two criteria come forward in the Spirituals that Jesus uses to determine one's citizenship in Zion, namely, commitment to Christ and a willingness to feed Jesus's sheep. "Who Is on the Lord's Side" stresses the importance of commitment to Jesus: "Who is on de Lord's side, None o' God's chil'n nebber look back, Who is on de Lord's side." The commandment to feed Jesus's sheep is found in "John, John, of the Holy Order": "Mary and Marta, feed my lamb, feed my lamb, feed my lamb; Simon Peter feed my lamb, a sittin' on de golden order." The Spirituals convey that Jesus is a righteous judge, that God is not mocked, and that Jesus will come again to judge the living and the dead.

---

8. "Nineteen wile" = anointing vial.

De Lord Is Per-Wide, Rock O' My Soul, and Holy-Ghost the Pilot

De Lord Is Per-Wide: On God and Possible Futures in the Spirituals

Yet as noted, Jesus's judgment is not only a cosmic phenomenon but may also occur as a concrete historical event. Thus, the Spirituals not only discuss Jesus's universal judgment of free grace and final judgment, but also discuss God's activity of judgment in history. In this way, the inexhaustible mystery of God comes forth as revelation, providence, and possible future. One of the primary ways that God reveals God's self and exercises providence in the Spirituals is as Deliverer from oppression. The Spirituals disclose an understanding of God as a God who saves, both existentially and historico-politically. This can be seen in the song "Let God's Saints Come In," where five of the song's six verses tell the biblical story of deliverance and exodus from Egyptian captivity: "There was a wicked man, He kept them children in Egypt land. God did say to Moses one day . . . go to Egypt land, And tell him to let my people go." The song recognizes God as a God who acts in history on behalf of the freedom of his children and against tyranny and oppression. It is a testament to faith, and also a possible future for the oppressed. God's actions in the Spirituals imply that God sees bondage and oppression as evils. God desires to transform oppressive institutions toward freedom, eradicate them, and deliver his children from them. God's judgment against tyranny and oppression and the expectation of his providential acts of liberation in history are also in the song "O Daniel," which compares contemporary struggles of church members to the biblical story of the prophet Daniel's captivity and deliverance: "O my Lord delivered Daniel, O' Daniel, O' Daniel, O my Lord delivered Daniel, O why not deliver me too?" For the Spirituals, God is a God of deliverance whose divine judgment against tyranny and oppression opens possible futures of deliverance and justice.

Indeed, the theme of God as Deliverer remains a persistent and recurrent one throughout the Spirituals, such that it may be said to operate as the theological undercurrent of the corpus of songs. One way of understanding this phenomenon is that slaves intentionally hid themes of deliverance in the songs. While this likely happened, the Spirituals themselves also display two other features. First, deliverance is a theme found not only in the discussion of the Trinitarian God, but also, as we have seen, in the discussion of the ancestors. Figures like Daniel, Moses, and Paul and Silas communicate the message of God's deliverance. The Spirituals also imply that God's liberating activity may appear to be hidden in the Spirituals because God's deliverance often emerges out of activities that are not seen as efficacious for deliverance. In this way, God uses the "foolish" songs of the world to confound the wise. This phenomenon can be seen best in the biblical story of Joshua and the battle of Jericho (Josh. 5–6), which is reproduced in the

Spiritual "Pray All De Member." Joshua and the Israelites are delivered from the tyranny of the city of Jericho by playing their music rather than by wielding their swords and spears. Joshua and his band march around the city of Jericho multiple times as divinely instructed, playing music each time, and the city ultimately falls. The Spiritual begins with two verses that encourage the listener to pray: "Pray all de member, O Lord, Pray all de member, Yes, my Lord!" Yet in the third verse, the song shifts from a discussion of prayer to a discussion of Jericho, reframing the meaning of prayer in the process: "Jericho da worry me, O Lord! Jericho da worry me, Yes my Lord!" The reference to Jericho is a reference to how music enabled the Israelites' deliverance, and the Spiritual now interprets the meaning of a Jericho victory for the slaves' deliverance in the antebellum context: "I been to Jerusalem . . . Patrol aroun' me . . . Tank God he no ketch me."

In addition to depicting God as Deliverer, the Spirituals also depict God as Provider. Throughout the Spirituals, God is recognized as providing resources for the physical as well as the existential needs of humanity. The song "Jehovah, Hallelujah" offers praise to Jehovah for meeting the needs of his children: "Jehovah, Hallelujah, De Lord is per-wide. De foxes have-a hole, an' de birdies have-a nest. De Son of Man he dunno! Where to lay de weary head." On the one hand, the song acknowledges the real hardships of life. While some may have homes and the resources necessary to participate in social life, others don't, and thus occupy a position similar to one experienced by Jesus. In this sense, the song draws from Matthew 8, where Jesus suggests that his life is one of hardship and homelessness. Yet even as the song acknowledges life's hardships, it also opens up an alternative possible future with the message that the Lord is "per-wide," that is, will provide. Here, the song resonates with biblical passages that speak of God's provision like the passage found in Matthew 6, where Jesus uses the birds and flowers as examples to teach us to "not worry about tomorrow." The waters, the produce of the land, and human creativity in art and technology testify to this. Images of berries and fruit also hold a central place in the Spirituals as metaphors for God's provision of physical and existential resources, and for the possibility of a new future marked by sufficiency and even an abundance of resources. The Spiritual "Bound to Go" talks of berries: "One mornin' as I was a walkin' along, I saw de berries a-hangin down. I pick de berries and I suck de juice, He sweeter dan de honey comb." The song "Nobody Knows the Trouble I've Had" also talks of berries: "Nobody knows de trouble I've had, Glory hallelu! One morning I was a-walking down . . . I saw some berries a-hanging down. . . . I pick de berry and I suck de juice." In the Spirituals, God is a God that provides (possible futures of) physical and existential resources.

The third depiction of God in the Spirituals is one deduced from *indirect* language about God in various descriptions of heaven and of God's activity on earth. The Spirituals take for granted that God is composer, and this is depicted in primarily musical, architectural, or existential metaphors. For example, the Spirituals have countless images of heaven that depict divine acts of architectural composition. These include language of a "New Jerusalem," of a "heavenly home," of "searching the rooms" of heaven, of "building a house in paradise," and of "mansions above." Other songs also assume divine actions of architectural composition. For example, the song "God Got Plenty O' Room" begins by emphasizing heaven's spaciousness, of assuming God's capacity for composition: "God got plenty o' room, got plenty o' room, 'Way in de kingdom,' God got plenty o' room my Jesus say, 'Way in de kingdom.'" The Spirituals also depict God as a coarchitect of converted souls, as exhibited in language of "building one's house on the Rock" as opposed to "building on sinking sand" and language of "building one's house in Paradise." Although the Spirituals deploy architecture metaphors to describe heaven, they also make use of musical ones. Heaven is sometimes described as if its very fabric is constituted out of musical consonance, and in heaven one encounters singing angels, blowing trumpets, and the angel Michael's musical boats preparing to sail to the "other shore." The song "King Emanuel" also assumes such divine acts of composition. It also suggests that Jesus's status as "King" is a testament to his compositional feats rather than voluntary acts of divine will. Here, God is the composer whose art we praise but can never fully comprehend. "If you walk de golden street, and you join de golden band, Sing glory be to my King Emanuel. If you touch one string den de whole heaven ring. . . . O believer, ain't you glad dat your soul is converted?"

The Spirituals understand God as Deliverer, Provider, and Composer. This "view" must be put forth with humility, as the Spirituals speak more about Jesus than God, and as the Spirituals understand the Trinity to be as hidden as they are revealed. Yet the antebellum slaves of the United States held this to be a trustworthy understanding of God. As Deliverer, God has the power to deliver one from both existential and political tyranny and oppression. This act of deliverance shows us that God's desire is to transition oppressive institutions toward freedom, to eradicate them, or to deliver his children from them. To know God as Deliverer means to know a God opposed to sovereignty and capable of bringing alternative possible futures of freedom into historical reality. Adherents must thus be open to, and prepared for, the possibility of a future of freedom. As Provider, God is "Per-Wide," enlarging God's self into sufficiency and abundance for the world. This includes a wide range of earthly resources and goods. Although the Spirituals do not address the environment explicitly, they do so implicitly, and the following chapter takes up this discussion in detail. Yet, we may say provisionally that the antebellum Spirituals recognize

God as providing resources for the physical as well as the existential needs of all of humanity. This is evident not only in the world's natural resources, but also in its cultural gifts as well as in the free grace provided by God in Jesus and the continued presence of the Holy Ghost. As Composer, God has made not only the earth but also the heavens, which are marked by golden streets and golden altars as well as by an acoustic fabric that is portrayed as extending the entire expanse of the heavens. As with God as Deliverer, God as Provider and Composer implies the possibility of alternative futures, ones opposed to poverty and lifelessness and oriented toward provision and creativity. Freedom, provision, and creativity are reflections of God.

Conclusion

Thus, we have seen that the Spirituals hold a view of the Trinitarian God as Pilot, Rock, and Provider. Each of these signifies a person of the Trinity that can be expanded into its own threefold form. The Provider is also the Deliverer and the Composer. The Rock is also the Lamb and the Judge, and the Pilot is also the Ghost that enlivens, and the Protector that brings forth the saints and the ancestors. God acts in the world to deliver his children from oppression and thus stands in opposition to sovereignty. God also acts to provide an abundance of resources for the basic needs of humanity, and to compose an aesthetically pleasing home for humanity. This view of God is overlaid with a cosmic Christology whose body, like God's, bridges the heavens and the earth. The metaphors of Christ—Lamb, Rock, and Judge—all have connections to earthly life, and in ways that embrace life and the world inclusively rather than according to an exclusionary cultural logic of sovereignty. This is most clearly seen in Jesus's role as Judge, where he and he alone holds the power to judge and segregate the goats from the sheep, that is, life from good life. The Holy Ghost acts as Spirit, Ghost, and Pilot. As Spirit, the Holy Spirit enlivens, quickens, vivifies, and inspires. As Ghost, the Holy Spirit brings forth the spirits of the saints, ancestors, and archangels. As Pilot, the Holy Ghost makes it possible for us to cross over to the other side, in ways similar to God's crossing over to the world. The Spirit has the power to enliven but does not have the power of death nor that of judgment. Also, the Spirit's ship of Zion has room for us all, and thus the Pilot prohibits the principle of sovereignty. The Trinitarian God is God as unconditional love and transformative power, yet one that requires human response. Yet the following chapter explores more deeply how God is already present in and relating to the world according to the Spirituals.

9

Roll, Jordan, Roll

On the Theomusicological Geography of the Spirituals

IN THE LAST CHAPTER, I explored the theology of the antebellum Spirituals, concluding that the songs collectively portray God as Pilot, Rock, and Provider. God is both present on earth and absent from it, or, as theologians often say, both immanent in the world and transcendent beyond it. The theology of the antebellum Spirituals did not conflate God with the world, nature, or the environment. Nor did the Spirituals imagine God as completely absent from the world. In addition to this, we also saw that the enslaved songwriters understood God's very self as serving as an existential as well as a material bridge between this world and the heavens. Historian Lawrence W. Levine argued that in the consciousness of the slaves there was a profound connection between the other world and this world, and our analysis has confirmed Levine's.[1] The entire framework of "sacred and secular" becomes inappropriate when describing the world, since slaves believed that the supernatural world impinged on the natural world. Thus, Levine, Barbara Holmes, Cheryl Kirk-Duggan, and others have noted that a sense of sacred time operates in the Spirituals, where the present is extended backward to include characters, scenes, and events from the Bible and also forward to the consummation of creation with God. Yet these thinkers do little to extend the discussion to questions of sacred space, to theologico-geographical aspects of a sacred world, or to reflections on God's presence in the world, in nature, or environment. This chapter takes up the question of theology as sacred space. I deal with the ways that God is present in the world, in nature, environment, and history.

---

1. See "Slave Songs and Slave Consciousness," in *The Sacred and the Profane*, by Mircea Eliade (New York: Harper & Row, 1961). Also see Albert J. Raboteau, *Slave Religion: The Invisible Institution in the Antebellum South* (New York: Oxford University Press, 2004), 250.

The Spirituals

"Give Up the World": On World and Wilderness in the Spirituals

In fine, the theology of the antebellum Spirituals as explored in the previous chapter was produced in large part by slaves from the South. Slaves forged many of the songs that would come to reflect a strong sense of another world primarily in southeastern slave states like South Carolina and Georgia, as well as in the Sea Islands along the eastern coastline. This region thus produced many of the images and metaphors associated with sacred time and space in the antebellum Spirituals that were discussed in the previous chapter. Thus, the southeast region has bequeathed to us portrayals of the angel Gabriel blowing his trumpet, of the disciple John sitting upon a "golden order," and of the fantastic religious fantasy of "mansions in heaven," among others. Although many slaves interpreted and defined their faith in terms of a sense of sacred time and space in heaven, others, by way of these same Spirituals, interpreted it in terms of sacred spaces and places on earth so that the heavenly and earthly dimensions are not really separated. They are bridged by the person and actions of the Trinitarian God, so that earth is also sacred space. Here, earth is understood in an expansive sense, including naturally occurring geographical spaces, human-constituted places, and even artistic and existential spaces. I begin this chapter with a brief discussion of two primary spaces presented most directly in the Spirituals. These are the spaces of "world" and "wilderness." These spaces stand as two contrasting landscapes, and the latter is one of the primary places where God's Trinitarian presence may be found on earth. When the Spirituals imply that God is not in the world, world is to be understood primarily as either *US antebellum imperial society* or as an unconverted spiritual state. Thus, the "world" doesn't include the categories of nature, environment, or earth, and in fact the antebellum Spirituals possess a rich geography beyond these two landscapes.

In turning from heaven to earth to take account of the Spirituals' theological geography, one immediately notices that the songs portray the world as a place of trouble. It cannot be denied that the songs describe the world primarily as a place of "trouble," as noted in songs like "The Trouble of the World," "I'm a-Trouble in De Mind," and "I'm in Trouble." The troubles of the world included a life of social alienation, invisibility, and legal enslavement. Songs mention "whips a crackin," "driber's dribin," the driver's lash, forced labor, tribulations, family separation, stormy weather, and evildoers. These and other vivid descriptions tell of slaves' everyday experiences of oppression, racial discrimination, and humiliation. This is not to say that the enslaved never found joy or failed to transcend such conditions on occasion. Yet the songs testify to a world marked by trouble and hard times in US antebellum society. This consciousness is exhibited especially in songs like "Run, Nigger, Run" and "Satan and I Had a Race," each of which critically signifies on America's racist cultural practices and attitudes, and together imply that trouble may be further described as the threefold constellation of racism, race, and Satan. The Spirituals convey the message that the world that divides peoples into races pitted against one another is a world strongly influenced by Satan and evil forces, and one that exists in a state of state of sin and unrepentance. Here the world refers to the existential condition of being unconverted, of rejecting the free grace of God. Thus, songs like "Give Up the World," "You Must Be Pure and Holy," and "Turn, Sinner, Turn, O!" encourage one to forsake the world. For many, this view of the world as a place of trouble made the world appear strange, unfamiliar, and inhospitable. Thus songs like "I Want to Go Home," "Build a House in Paradise," and "I'm Going Home" express the slaves' desire for deliverance from the world.

The Spirituals depict the world as constituted primarily by trouble, but they also suggest that the earth contains places for transcendence beyond the troubles of the world. For example, slaves frequently spoke of the wilderness as a place where one might undergo spiritual conversion or development, be piloted off by the Holy Ghost, or even see Jesus. This is readily exhibited in song titles like "Go in the Wilderness," "The Lonesome Valley," and "Hunting for the Lord." In her *Sisters in the Wilderness*, theologian Delores Williams has described how African Americans have connected religious experience with the wilderness for hundreds of years and how the Spirituals depict pilgrimages into the wilderness for spiritual renewal, conversion, or transformation during the antebellum period. "For the slave, the wilderness was a positive place conducive to uplifting the Spirit and to strengthening religious life."[2] Such transformation was not romance, and the wilderness experience required intense struggle as one achieved consonance with nature. Yet slaves generally saw the wilderness as a place of healing and virtue over against US society, and thus did not seek to destroy the wilderness or transform it into civilization. It was a place where Black men and women could meet God. In fact, Williams notes that the "experience made no attempt to be gender exclusive" and that all were encouraged to participate.[3] Antebellum ethnographer William Francis Allen notes how the wilderness experience, also called the "lonesome valley,"

---

2. Delores Williams, *Sisters in the Wilderness: The Challenge of Womanist God-Talk* (New York: Orbis Books, 1993, 2013), 100.

3. Williams, *Sisters in the Wilderness*, 98.

seemed to imply entering into a new state that called gender constructions into question: "I have asked some dusky attendant its meaning, and have received the unfailing answer,—framed with their usual indifference to the genders of pronouns—'He in de lonesome vallay, sa.'"[4] Although the world was a place of trouble, slaves often found the wilderness to be an inclusive place of transformation and divine disclosure.

"Roll, Jordan, Roll": On the Theological Geography of the Spirituals

Perhaps the most well-recognized theme in reference to a naturally occurring geographic area in the antebellum Spirituals is the Jordan River. The Spirituals use the term "Jordan River" to denote a physical, existential, and cosmic entity that facilitates various transitions, including conversion, entry into spiritual warfare, deliverance from slavery to freedom, and death. The song "Roll, Jordan, Roll" offers the most immediate evidence, here denoting Jordan River as a cosmic entity. In this song, the phrase "roll, Jordan, roll" is the chorus. It indicates that Jordan River is a cosmic being whose moving waters effect transitions of equally cosmic proportions: "My brudder sittin on de tree of life, An' he yearde when Jordan roll ... O march de angel, march ... For to yearde when Jordan Roll." Jordan River is again depicted as a cosmic entity in the song "My Army Cross Over," one that reaches from the times of Moses's flight from Pharaoh to contemporary times. Here Jordan River facilitates various kinds of crossings from slavery to freedom: "O Pharaoh's army drownded, My army cross ober.... We'll cross de riber Jordan. We'll cross de danger water." The song's allusion to Pharaoh suggests that Jordan River provides not only existential freedom, but also political freedom, for the children of God. It also suggests that Jordan's river has the capacity to deny passage and to take life. In the song "Hail Mary," Jordan River facilitates a transition from slavery to freedom and may indicate a physical river rather than a cosmic entity: "Done wid driber's dribin', Roll, Jordan, roll." In the song "The Trouble of the World," Jordan possesses the ability to make one a child of God and to remove one from the troubles of the world: "I want to be my Fader's chil'en, Roll Jordan Roll. ... Say aint you done wid de trouble ob de world, Ah Roll, Jordan, roll."

---

4. William Francis Allen, Charles Pickard Ware, and Lucy McKim Garrison, comp., *Slave Songs of the United States: 136 Songs Complete with Sheet Music and Notes on Slavery and African American History* (n.p.: Pantianos Classics, 1867), 33. Unless otherwise indicated, all quotations from the Spirituals in this chapter come from this book.

Jordan River is a pervasive theme in the Spirituals, whose waters hold the powers of conversion, deliverance, and death.

In the antebellum Spirituals, the prevalence of the theme of the Jordan River is enhanced by additional aquatic images and metaphors. One of the most powerful and lasting images is implied in the song title "Michael Row the Boat Ashore." Here the waters and a boat, whether local or cosmic, are used to transport the archangel Michael from one shore to another. Another aquatic image is implied in the song "Sail O Believer," whose lyrics encourage one to "Sail over yonder And view de Promised land." Indeed, as one searches the Spirituals, a wide array of images of water and water vessels presents itself to the reader. For example: the song title "Jesus on the Waterside," which again suggests that God and water have a close association, or the lyrics in the song "I Can't Stand the Fire," which suggest the same: "I can't stan' de fire, While Jordan da roll so swif.'" The song "Praise, Member" portrays Jordan as a threshold entity, and leaves open to interpretation the type of threshold one must cross: "O Jordan's Bank is a good old bank, And I hain't but one more river to cross." In the song "Wrestle on Jacob" we find "Fisherman Peter out at sea," who "catch no fish, but he catch some soul." Here the water is the world itself, that is, the entire world of souls, in reference to the biblical passage where Jesus commands Peter to become a fisher of men. Yet the lyrics also suggest that the waters converted Peter himself, such that he was able to catch some soul by proximity. These and other images, many of which include explicit references to Jordan River, add to and enhance the prevalence of the entity in the Spirituals, such that Jordan River begins to appear to be both close in proximity to God and also endowed with certain powers of a deity. These powers present themselves to human life as both natural and existential resources for survival and quality of life. Jordan River is both passive and active, natural and moral, and earthly and divine.

"View de Land": Theological Geography on Dry Land

Although Jordan River is a prevalent reference to a naturally occurring geographic area, and while some Spirituals emphasize water, others highlight corn. The curious presence of corn is especially noticeable in the trio of songs "Shock Along, John," "Round the Corn, Sally," and "Jordan's Mills." "Shock Along, John" is constituted by the repetition of a simple chorus, whose lyrics almost directly mimic the title: "Shock along, John, shock along." In the song, the character John contributes nearly all of the effort to harvest corn and is alone as he shocks along in his seemingly endless labors. Yet the song also implies endless fields of corn that present themselves as a sea and, by extension, as a cosmos. The same overarching presence of corn is found in the song "Round the Corn, Sally," where corn exists as the center of all life and action. As with "Shock Along, John," "Round the Corn, Sally" portrays the presence of corn alongside a strong human capacity for labor, activity, production, consumption, and practice. With these terms, an agricultural theme begins to emerge, where the world is marked by the condition and produce of the land rather than the sea. The song "Jordan's Mills" also portrays a relationship between corn and deity, and even bestows the name "Jordan" on a mill, drawing a connection between Jordan River and Jordan's Mill. According to the lyrics, Jordan's Mill is "built without nail or hammer" and "runs without wind or water." Jordan's Mill grinds hay, as farmers often do for animal feed: "Jordan's mills a grinding, Jordan's a-hay." Thus, the connection between corn and deities is also present in "Jordan's Mills," as well as the strong presence of an agricultural theme that suggests a deity of resources, fertility, and produce as well as a productive and laboring human being. Jordan's Mill is earthly and divine, natural and moral.

The northeastern perspective downplays Trinitarian themes and emphasizes human agency. As previously noted, much of the Trinitarian theology in the Spirituals comes from southeastern slave states like South Carolina and Georgia, as well as the Sea Islands along the eastern coastline. Strong Trinitarian themes are also explicit and implicit in the inland states of Tennessee and Arkansas and the Mississippi River as well as the Gulf states of Florida and Louisiana. Yet the Trinitarian sensibility is downplayed in the northern seaboard states. Rather than a strong sense of an otherworldly God, the songs of the slaves made in states like Delaware, Maryland, Virginia, and North Carolina exhibit a humanistic sensibility, where man is seen as the devisor, planner, and inventor of his own fate and where human action is directed by free will. Yet this antebellum humanism is slightly different from that of the early modern Italian Renaissance. The humanism of the Renaissance, as theorized by figures like Petrarch and Erasmus of Rotterdam, was oriented primarily toward intellectual development for the preservation of the city-state. By contrast, the humanism of the antebellum Spirituals is an agrarian humanism, where human action is directed by free will *within an agrarian ecosystem*. Human action, labor, production, consumption, and development occur within the context of agricultural resources. One may shuck corn, but one also needs the productive powers of Jordan's Mill. In this sense, the antebellum Spirituals display a posthumanistic sensibility, where human agency is understood as distributed through dynamic forces of which the human participates but does not completely intend or control.[5] Furthermore, humans possess attributes that are made up of a larger, evolving ecosystem. The human is thus not autonomous from nature but is simultaneously changed by and changes the natural world.

Thus, the antebellum Spirituals recognized at least two major themes in reference to naturally occurring geographic areas, positioning them as quasi deities. While Jordan River's presence as a spiritually charged force of nature is readily evident, the presence of Jordan's Mill is less apparent and only becomes visible as one is reminded that, as recorded in the 1867 edition of *Slave Songs of the United States*, the Spirituals were collected ethnographically. In an age before the Internet, before the highway, and even before the US railroad system was completed, ethnographer William Francis Allen traveled to four major regions of the United States during the period just before the Civil War and national unification. The first region that Allen visited included the southeastern slave areas of South Carolina, Georgia, and the Sea Islands. Allen then traveled northward to the northern seaboard slave states of Delaware, Maryland, Virginia, and North Carolina. After this, Allen trekked inland to the slave states of Tennessee and Arkansas and along the Mississippi River. Moving from the inland states, Allen finally concluded his study in the Gulf states of Louisiana and Florida. Upon studying Allen's collected songbook, one finds that each region's corpus of songs presents a collective testimony to the presence of these larger, encompassing, spiritually charged earthly entities that shape both the local environment and local senses of character and identity. Thus, one may also find four quasi deities explicitly or implicitly located within the antebellum Spirituals. Despite the prevalence of the symbol of Jordan River, the river is not an all-encompassing natural force in the Spirituals, and in fact only appears to have been a major theme among the slaves in the southeastern slave states, where one also finds much of the theology presented in the previous chapter. In the northern seaboard slave states of Delaware, Maryland, Virginia, and North Carolina, the songs turn from the river to a focus on Jordan's Mill.

The trend of regional association with spiritually charged, earthly quasi deities continued as one moves from the northern seaboard to the inland states, where slaves sang of a cosmic Chariot. Among the Spirituals from the

---

5. See Diane Marie Keeling and Marguerite Nguyen Lehman, "Posthumanism," Oxford Research Encyclopedia of Communication, April 26, 2018, https://tinyurl.com/yz55k996.

inland states including Tennessee and Arkansas and along the Mississippi River, slaves did not sing at all of Jordan River. Nor did they mention corn, Jordan's Mill, or the centrality of agriculture and produce. Instead, the inland states highlight the themes of chariots and chariot wheels. These are raised to the status of a cosmic Actor. The Cosmic Chariot is especially noted in the song "Little Children, Then Won't You Be Glad?" The song begins by repeating the simple phrase of the title but, in verse 3, delves into a detailed description of the soteriological dimensions of the Cosmic Chariot: "Don't you hear what de chariot say? De fore wheels run by de grace ob God, An' de hind wheels dey run by faith." Here the chariot represents deliverance, and the song indicates that deliverance is a joint effort between God and humanity. Deliverance is both divine and human. God's grace drives the chariot's front wheels, and human faith moves the chariot's back wheels. In the most general sense, this depiction of the chariot resonates with the theological doctrines of universal election and free grace, a sensibility that was also strong among the enslaved in South Carolina, Georgia, and the Sea Islands. The chariot also represents technology, civilization, and progress and may imply the elemental power of fire. Indeed, the song "The Gold Band" also suggests a connection between divine judgment, wheels, and fire: "Sinner, what you gwine to do dat day? When de fire's a-rolling behind you, In de army, bye-and-bye." There is thus a cosmic and metaphysical dimension to the chariot as well as an earthly one, and the chariot not only represents deliverance but also grace, time, history, conversion, and divine judgment and combat or battle.

Finally, we also find a spiritually charged, earthly quasi deity in the songs of the enslaved among the Gulf states of Florida and Louisiana. Here there is talk of the Band. This talk of the Band as a quasi deity is most readily apparent in a few of the song titles of Spirituals from the Gulf states, especially "I Want to Join the Band," "The Social Band," and "Pray On," that is, keep dancin'. These titles either explicitly express or imply that membership and participation in the Band is the ultimate aim and goal of life beyond one's current state of existence. The song also implies that the body to which we are joined in Christ is a collective musical body, composed of different sections, parts, and instruments, all necessary to make sweet music. The song "I Want to Join the Band" implies that angels are included in the Band's membership: "What is that up yonder I see? Two little angel comin a'ter me; I want to join the band." The song "The Social Band" also mentions angels but includes Mary in the Band as well: "Bright angels on the water . . . I want Aunty Mary for to go with me, To join the social band." Although the social band was often sung about as an otherworldly entity, it also took on earthly form, thus bridging heaven and earth by way of communion. The best example of this may be seen in the song "My Father How Long?" which is ostensibly about the desire to join heaven's musical body: "We'll soon be free. De Lord will call us home . . . [and] My brudders do sing De praises of de Lord." Yet Allen's footnote shows how the band also took on earthly form: "For singing this the negroes had been put in jail . . . at the outbreak of the Rebellion. 'We'll soon be free' was too dangerous an assertion . . . [as was] 'De Lord will call us home' . . . for, as a little drummer boy explained it to me . . . 'Dey tink *de Lord* mean for say *de Yankees*." The Band thus represents both a cosmic and an earthly form of deliverance, grace, time, history, conversion, and judgment.

A strong existentialist sensibility comes forth in the Spirituals from the Gulf states. In labeling the Gulf states as existentialist, I draw from philosopher Lewis Gordon, who argues that philosophy of existence in African American thought is "premised upon concerns of freedom, anguish, responsibility, embodied agency, . . . and liberation."[6] These concerns are especially prevalent in the songs from the Gulf states, as opposed to, for example, the agrarian humanism that prevailed in the northeastern states. The songs convey dread, hope for deliverance, and desire for personal as well as social transformation. For example, the song "I'm in Trouble" expresses anxiety and fear about death: "I'm in trouble, Lord, trouble about my grave. . . . Sometimes I weep, sometimes I mourn . . . about my grave." The song "I Want to Die like-a Lazarus Die" also expresses anxiety about death, but does so in a way that pokes fun at death and bespeaks a hope for partial transcendence beyond the fear of death, and possibly even bodily resurrection: "I want to die like-a Lazarus die, Die like-a Lazarus die; I want to die like-a Lazarus die." The song "O Daniel" exhibits hope for deliverance from oppression, tyranny, and religious persecution, in drawing on the story of Daniel and the lions' den (see previous chapter): "O Daniel, O my Lord delivered Daniel, O why not deliver me too?" If there is a distinctive element that the Spirituals bring to the philosophy of existence, it is an existence recognized as occurring within the context of the Band rather than a radically individualized one. In the Gulf states, the enslaved do not appear to have understood existence as a solely individual question. While songs certainly acknowledge the personal dimensions of the self, the moral background and goal of the Band frame existence. Many songs venerate ancestors like Moses and Daniel, and songs like "I Want to Join the Band" and "The Social Band" position the ancestral community as goal.

6. Lewis R. Gordon, ed., *Existence in Black: An Anthology of Black Existential Philosophy* (New York: Routledge, 1997), 3.

The Spirituals

Swing Low and Mother in Heaven: On the Eclipse of the North American Orisha

A geographic analysis of the antebellum Spirituals discloses the presence of cosmic quasi deities that are difficult to distinguish from the world's natural and cultural formations. Jordan River, the Chariot, Jordan's Mill, and the Social Band—perhaps it is too much to call these figures orisha, as they might be identified from the perspective of West African traditional religion.[7] Yet, like the orisha, they operate as sources of and powers over vast aspect of natural life. Jordan River signifies many things, including Joshua's march of musical deliverance against the city of Jericho, the baptism of Jesus, the waters of the Atlantic Ocean, and conversion or death. Beyond this, Jordan River also signifies fertility, thresholds, rites of passage, and, ultimately, the possibility of the rebirth and renewal of the world. The Chariot signifies divine deliverance, judgment, and battle. Its wheels of grace might "swing low" to redeem the converted even as its wheels of fire might roll after the unrepentant sinner. The Chariot also represents technology, progress, and elemental power of fire. Jordan's Mill signifies the force of agricultural produce, and the wealth and abundance of the land are also represented in Spirituals as endless fields of golden corn. The Band signifies the chorus of witnesses that constitute the communion of the saints. This musical communion extends from hush harbors on earth to the golden streets of heaven. It also encompasses all ancestors of the faith and thus includes not only Mary and Moses and angels and archangels but also singing prisoners like Paul and Silas or those enslaved in nineteenth-century South Carolina. The child of God desires to join the band and considers it a communion of joy. As the song "King Emanuel" says: "If you walk de golden street, and you join de golden band, Sing glory be to my King Emanuel." Thus in the Spirituals, we discover traces of the River Jordan, the Chariot Wheel, the golden fields of Jordan's Mill, and the sweet sounds of the Golden Band.

Today, it is highly likely that one may hear the Spirituals without hearing any mention of the orisha hidden within. Indeed, one finds that as the Spirituals continued to be recorded by various researchers, Allen's ethnographic method was left behind, resulting in a loss of regional geographic consciousness in the Spirituals, and thus a loss of the awareness of the North Ameri-

---

7. Dorcas Akintunde, "Women as Healers," in *African Women, Religion, and Health: Essays in Honor of Mercy Amba Ewudziwa Oduyoye*, ed. Isabel Apawo Phiri and Sarojini Nadar (Maryknoll, NY: Orbis Books, 2006), 165.

can orisha as well. Other researchers who would go on to compile their own books of Negro Spirituals, including ethnomusicologist Natalie Curtis Burlin in 1918, poet and civil rights activist James Weldon Johnson in 1925, musicologist John W. Work in 1940, and historian Miles Mark Fisher in 1953, would attend to important matters but would abandon the geographic consciousness of the antebellum Spirituals. This practice seems to have begun sometime within the span of the late nineteenth and early twentieth centuries and can be witnessed as early as 1909 in a volume of the Spirituals published by military commandant Robert R. Morton at the Hampton Institute. In this volume, attention to geography is less of a focus, resulting in the effective eclipse of the symbols of Jordan River and Jordan's Mill. Jordan River and Jordan's Mill are mentioned far less frequently, relative to content, in Morton's 1909 edition than in Allen's 1867 volume. Furthermore, in Morton's 1909 volume, the symbol of the Chariot becomes an almost totalizing metaphysic, and the emphasis on the symbol of the Band as representing heavenly communion is exchanged for the symbol of "mother in heaven." The Chariot comes to be a dominant motif, occupying roughly eight times as many songs as it did in the antebellum volume (i.e., eight to one). Many of today's recognizable songs like "Good News, de Chariot's a-Comin," "Ezekiel Saw de Wheel," and "Swing Low" first appear in the 1909 volume, while almost no new songs appear there about Jordan River or Jordan's Mill.

Again, with the loss of geographic consciousness in the published volumes of the Spirituals, the antebellum emphasis on the Golden Band was exchanged for that of Mother. In the previous chapter, we observed how the antebellum Spirituals used the symbol of the "golden band" to denote the community's locus of moral authority. The golden band is constituted by a host of ancestors, former saints, and spirits in such a way that the distinction between heaven and earth is blurred as a communal web of life is created. Key figures in the heavenly Band were Mary Magdalene, Mary and Marta, "Sister Mary," Moses, Daniel, and archangels like Gabriel and Michael. Yet by 1909, the nature of the heavenly Band has shifted, such that the central figure in heaven becomes "Mother." For example, the song "Some o' dese Mornin's" presents a direct correlation between the symbol of Mother and the Band, suggesting that the Band is now constituted around the central figure of Mother: "Gwine to see my mother some o' deese mornin's. . . . Look away in de heaven. . . . Hope I'll jine de band." The song "The Danville Chariot" associates the symbol of Mother with that of the heavenly Chariot. Furthermore, it places the symbol of Mother in the place traditionally given to the disciple Peter, whom Jesus commanded to feed his sheep: "Oh I got a mother in de promised land, I hope my mother will feed dem lambs; . . . Oh swing low sweet chariot." In the song "Bright Sparkles in de Churchyard," Mother is depicted as rocking her children in a heavenly cradle: "My mother once, my mother twice . . . In de heaven she'll rejoice. Mother, rock me in de cradle all de day." In these and other songs, Mother becomes the central figure in the heavenly Band, such that the song "I've Got a Mother in de Heaven" near the end of the volume signals the effective eclipse of the Golden Band. Thus today, talk of the Golden Band has ceased along with that of the River Jordan and Jordan's Mill.

"Wrestle On, Jacob": The Music of Life and the Golden Band

In the Spirituals, one may observe the outlines of a new collective theological understanding of certain aspects of nature, earth, and environment. While this chapter attends largely to questions of space, one may also infer key features of theological time. These features of theological time in the environment find consonance with the idea of God as composer, whose musical orderings of the world give rise to the fundamental rhythms and harmonies of nature. This can be seen most clearly in the Spirituals' interpretations of the days, seasons, and other natural rhythms. Song titles like "Happy Morning," "Tell My Jesus Morning," "The Resurrection Morn," and "There's a Meeting Here Tonight" collectively give the impression that Jesus's presence and providence may be witnessed with the beginning of each new day and each evening's setting sun. This repeating pattern of each new day, also called diurnal rhythms, operates much like the ostinato in African American music. Both diurnal and ostinato patterns keep time and organize events, thus providing a foundational pulse. What is said of the days can also be said of other times and seasons noted in the Spirituals, so that nature's circadian, circalunar, and circannual rhythms resound as a rich polyrhythmic environment sustained by the musical timing of the Trinitarian God. The Spirituals acknowledge not only morning and evening as times when God's work is evident, but also summer and winter and the agricultural seasons of planting and harvesting. These rhythms constitute nature as eternally recurring polyrhythmic cycles, yet like the repetitions and ostinatos in the Spirituals, these cycles are not simply blind rotations or absolutely identical repetitions. While time cycles are fixed, they are also composed through the interplay of regular rhythms, syncopation, and polyrhythms. This large-scale, multilayered pattern, also called "the groove," gives rise to novelty, creativity, and improvisation, so that each new day, season, year, or harvest brings both a sameness and its own particular newness.

The ostinato pattern in the Spirituals is applicable not only to the various cycles of nature, but also to human ontological, existential, and historical events and affairs. Here the person and work of the cosmic Christ as recognized in the Spirituals operates as a cosmic ostinato. Musicologist János Maróthy explains that when rhythm achieves the status of ostinato, it then possesses the power to make and keep time and to serve as a constant point of reference for all musical events.[8] The ostinato organizes the phrase structure of a song's events as well as its linear metrics. It serves as the tonal center of the music and gives temporal framing to the song's meters, thus providing a resolution point in the music and guidelines for keeping the song's phrases on time and on key. Musicians call this "the groove." The person and work of Christ as Lamb, Rock, and Judge operate much like an ontological ostinato for human history. Like the ostinato, Christ serves as a constant point of reference for historical events. Christ organizes the structure of historical events and serves as the tonal center even as human actions also work to effect movements of progression. Christ provides a resolution point in history and a guideline for keeping our actions on time and on key. As Lamb, Christ extends the gift of free grace to all peoples and his sanctifying power reaches throughout the cosmos. The Lamb's atonement and liberation of humanity signal the end of human sacrifice and the end of scapegoating as requirements for atonement, communion, and exchange with the gods. As Rock, Jesus continues to work in the world as sustainer and comforter, setting the tone for an ethos of sustainability and of ecological orientation to the world. Finally, as Judge, Christ sets the tone for communities with a reminder that he alone has the final say on matters of membership in heaven. Jesus is also the Judge whose roles as liberator and sustainer offer critical values for communal evaluation.

In addition to allowing for a musical interpretation of various natural rhythms as a polyrhythmic texture, the Spirituals allow one to interpret God's acts of deliverance from historical oppression as an occasion of blues-style harmony. We recall that the blues scale is a distinctive harmonic arrangement where notes are ordered such that a dissonance or tension is created within harmonic arrangements. This dissonance functions to challenge the constancy of the arrangement, or it may also open the possibility for the musician to

---

8. János Maróthy, "Rite and Rhythm: From Behaviour Patterns to Musical Structures," *Studia Musicologica Academiae Scientiarum Hungaricae*, T. 35, Fasc. 4 (1993–1994): 421–33, https://tinyurl.com/yc78bbn4. Also see Robert Walser, "Rhythm, Rhyme, and Rhetoric in the Music of Public Enemy," *Ethnomusicology* 39, no. 2 (1995): 209, https://tinyurl.com/2489y599.

create harmony by way of a different progression. It allows for flexibility and freedom, even against the backdrop of tones that must remain at measured distance from one another. The divine acts of deliverance that are acknowledged in the Spirituals operate much like blues-style harmony. These divine acts of deliverance do not reject the idea of order itself, but they effectively challenge the constancy of seemingly harmonious social and political orders. As exhibited through the lives of ancestors like Moses, Daniel, and Mary Magdalene, God worked to challenge the authority of the "central tone" of the order. Furthermore, divine acts of deliverance as recorded in the Spirituals are also like blues harmonies in that they often give rise to different orderings, and also in that they allow for flexibility and freedom even within orderings. Thus, reading divine acts of deliverance as blues-style harmonies allows for the possibility of the coexistence of both freedom and order, rather than pitting these two concepts against one another. Finally, what is said of the blue note can also be said of the "grace note," a short ornamental note performed as an embellishment before the principal pitch. If the blue note challenges the constancy of the harmonic order, the grace note challenges the *priority* of the order. Theologically, this means that the grace note reframes all events and orders within the cosmic actions of free grace and final judgment.

For the antebellum slaves, these various formations in the natural world operated as a divine call. In the songs produced in the southeast, this call took form as the Jordan River. In the inland states, it took shape as the Chariot. Jordan's Mill emerged in the northeast, and in the Gulf states the call came in the form of the Golden Band. In these ways, heaven's call echoed throughout the antebellum worlds of the slaves, even as they struggled within and against US slaveocracy. Heaven's call could also be heard in natural rhythms like the rising and the setting of the sun or of the planting and harvesting of crops. The call was heard yet again in the Spirit's call into the wilderness to pray, in Christ's cosmic act of atonement and free grace for the world, and in God's continuing historical acts of deliverance from oppression and of sustenance for the needy. Though the call may come in many forms in the Spirituals, it always takes a form that calls for a response. In the ostinato rhythms forged by the dancers, in the balanced blues harmonies of those gathered to pray, and in the percussive melodies of the lead worshipers in the golden band, antebellum African Americans responded to the call of heaven. This dialectical struggle of call and response between human and the divine functioned like the aesthetic dynamism of the Spirituals, giving rise to a range of progressions in nature and history. Sometimes progress was successive, day to day, or from moment to moment, giving rise to sustaining repetitions, which may in turn give rise to novelty and which may also play out as revolution. At other times progress happens as something builds up over time, gradually flowering from a single idea into a continuous movement, and that, like blues-style harmony, occurs as normally silenced notes begin to sound dissonance into a chord. Progress may also take the form of a melody, where one moves forward by playing on, into, or around the established patterns in such a way that a clustering effect occurs in a particular direction.

In the early to mid-nineteenth century, slaves would gather for prayer meetings constituted by dancing, singing, and music making. The dances of the slaves were not merely dances of joy. They also incorporated other foundational cultural institutions like social exchange, war, and sacrifice. The songs that grew out of these prayer meetings were composed by a rich aesthetic texture of asymmetry, dynamism, rhythmic tension, and antiphony as well as a balanced blend of pulsating rhythms, blues harmonies, and percussive melodies. Slaves would start the call and response and enter into musical rounds of resonating praise. Lyrically, the songs spoke of enchanting visions of the heavens and of a captivating Trinitarian theological vision. As the Spirituals imagine it, the Holy Ghost piloted the worshiper to the heavens, where one encountered a grand vision of golden streets, golden altars, and angelic trumpets of war and praise. The songs tell of the reality of the cosmic Christ, the Lamb of God that was crucified. The Lamb is also the Rock, that is, the world itself as well as the anchor of the soul, and the Rock is also the Judge, whose task will be to separate the sheep from the goats at the final judgment. The songs also testify to the reality of a living God whose providence may be seen in the world's natural resources and abundant provisions, in the compositional beauty of the heavens and the earth, and in deliverance from oppression, tyranny, and slavery, even in spite of the troubles of the world. The slaves did not have a romantic or idealistic understating of life. They often came into the presence of God with beaten backs, scarred hands, worn-out shoes, tattered clothing, even broken bodies, and in the most intense climates of heat and cold. Yet in their journey into the wilderness of the hush arbors, the slaves found that their spirits could be renewed. In part, this renewal of hope, joy, and African American style *ubuntu* was facilitated by visions of the Trinitarian God. Yet the slaves also came into the presence of the Golden Band, that legendary ancestral constitution of saints, heroes, and even archangels that constituted the social fabric and moral background of slaves' collective life together. This legend, rather than a natural law or even primarily a divine covenant, the slaves bequeathed to us. Upon reflection, the Golden Band is a nested symbol, containing at least three meanings. Most immediately, the Golden Band refers to the very slaves whose musical practices produced the Spirituals. These slaves crafted songs rich in rhythm, harmony, and aesthetic textures, producing the golden sounds of the Spirituals. Beyond this, the Golden Band also signifies the moral background of saints and spirits that offers the slave community a social fabric and a constellation of moral exemplars, the band that "outshine de sun."[9] Here, "band" suggests a circle, or curvilinear shape, as the community is bound together with one another. Yet this binding remains a musical one, which allows space for freedom of expression and even improvisation. Finally, the Golden Band suggests that the ratios of musical consonance in the Spirituals might serve as a guide in matters of justice, even for those that remain less persuaded by their theological claims. Ultimately, the Spirituals are clear that there is only one final Judge. He will come again to judge the living and the dead. On that day, the moon will turn to blood, the stars will fall, and the world will be on fire.

> Then you'll hear the trumpet sound.
> Trumpet sound the world around.
> Trumpet sound for rich and poor.
> Trumpet sound the jubilee.
> Trumpet sound for you and me.[10]

---

9. "These Are All My Father's Children," in Allen, Ware, and Garrison, *Slave Songs of the United States*, 117.

10. "Michael Row the Boat Ashore," in Allen, Ware, and Garrison, *Slave Songs of the United States*, 50–51.

Index of Names and Subjects

abolitionism, 116
Abraham and Isaac, story of, 138
Abu Ghraib, 28–29
Acosta, José de, 106
Adorno, Theodor, 24, 50, 123–24
aesthetic experience (*Erfahrung*), 19
aesthetics, 113–14, 120, 140–44, 149, 186–87
African culture. *See* religion and culture, traditional African
"after-service," 119
Agamben, Giorgio, xi–xii, 9, 35
agency, human, 178–79
Agostinone-Wilson, Faith, 41–42
Akan people, 71, 87
Akintunde, Dorcas Olubanke, 70–71, 73, 75–76
Akoto, Dorothy, 75–76
Alberti, Leon, 141n20
Allen, William Francis, 18, 114, 175–76, 179, 181, 182, 183
Alperson, Philip, 127
American Evasion of Philosophy, The (West), 9n8
American exceptionalism, 99

American expansionism, 28
American Prophecy (Shulman), ix
ancestral spirituality: biblical stories and, 157–61, 169–70; practices of, 70, 71–72, 74–75, 86, 87; Spirituals' metaphors for, viii, 157–61, 181, 182, 183, 187
Anderson, Victor: critical perspective of, 10, 29–30, 46–47, 53, 54; on variety within Black experience, 12, 13–14
angel band, 159–60, 180
angels, 157, 163, 164, 174, 180, 182, 183
animism, 72, 73
antidemocratic dogmas, 28
antiphony. *See* call and response
antisemitism, 101
Aristotle, 132
Asante, Molefi Kete, 71
asymmetry, 141–43, 148, 151
atonement, 137, 165–66, 185
Austin, Stephen F., 5
authoritarianism, 28
Autobiography of Malcolm X (Malcolm X), 6

Index of Names and Subjects

Bacon, Francis, 21, 54
Baldwin, James, ix
"band, the," 148–49. *See also* Golden Band
Bannon, Steve, 42
"bare life," xi, 9, 35
Bartelson, Jens, 27–28, 39, 40
Barth, Karl, 8–9
Bataille, Georges, 137–38
Beaumanoir, Philippe de, 30
Benjamin, Walter, 50, 123
Berger, Peter, 121
Bergmann, Gustav, 52
berries, 170
Bible, 17–18, 122–23
binary form, 141, 147, 148
Black church: concepts in, 5–6, 84, 85; defined, 4; features and practices of, 4, 7–8, 83, 84, 89; suffering of, 93, 94
Black Elk, x
Black experience: blues themes describing, 94; categories determining, 28; centered in Black theology, 92–93, 96; of environmental connection, 87; Jesus's experience and, 81–82, 93, 94; postmodern approach to, 12–14; signification of, 15–16, 17–18, 20, 100, 158; of social exclusion, xi, 34, 35–37, 46, 76, 92; state of nature and, 17–18; suffering and power in, 93, 94; unity and variety within, 12, 13–16. *See also* religious experience
Black natural law, 97–100, 108, 109
blackness, ontological, 13
Black power, 93
Black theology of liberation, 91–97
blue notes, 146, 147, 148, 186
blues music: harmonic features of, 146, 148, 151, 185–86; as "secular spiritual,"
93, 126; themes expressed in, 94, 185, 186
blues scale, 147, 185
Boas, Franz, 125
Bodin, Jean, 31–32, 39
body, 62, 81–82, 89
body of God, 64
body politic, 32n11
Bolshevik Revolution, 37
Bonald, Louis de, 38
Bouleau, Charles, 141n20
Bourdieu, Pierre, 125, 132–33
Bradley, W. James, 50, 51n6
brain, 127–28
Broadie, Alexander, 45
Brown, John, 116
Brown, Wendy, 27, 33, 41
Bryant, William Cullen, 119
Burlin, Natalie Curtis, 183

call, divine, 186
call and response: in African American religious and cultural practices, 7–8, 129; asymmetrical design in, 141–43; back-and-forth movement in, 129, 130; defined, 128; as divine and human interaction, 186; harmony and, 147, 151; in invisible institution, 130; musical form of, 130–31, 141, 147, 148; musical influence of, 114–15, 129; self-consciousness in, 130–31; social nature of, 130, 136–37, 139, 152; themes expressed in, 130–31; ubiquity of, 128
call-response-reciprocate ethos, 136, 139
capitalism, 42–46, 76–77
Carmichael, Stokely, 93
Carnap, Rudolf, 52

Index of Names and Subjects

Carter, J. Kameron, 90, 100–103, 108–9
Cartwright, John, 78, 80–81
Caspers, William, 116
catallaxy, 43
Certeau, Michel de, 132
Chariot, the, 179–80, 182, 183, 186
Chernoff, John Miller, 145–46
children's rights, 75
chorus, 115, 140, 148
Christian Imagination, The (Jennings), 104
Christology, 101–3, 104, 106, 108–9
church, 63, 81
Church for the Fellowship of All Peoples, 78, 79, 80
church proper, 81
Civil Rights Act (1964), 14
civil rights movement, ix, 14
Clarke, D. S., 55
classical approach to sovereignty, 27–33, 39
classic theism, 60, 64
Cobb, John B., Jr., 61–63, 64
Collins, Patricia Hills, 14
colonialism, 17, 46, 106, 109
"color line" theory, 14
communicative action, 25
communicative freedom, 25
community organizing, 44
Comte, Auguste, 51–52
Cone, James, vii, 8, 90–97, 121, 160
conflict, 24–25
consanguinity, 75
consciousness, 10, 12, 127, 128, 130–31, 161
contemplative spirituality, 70, 83–85, 89
Cooper, Anna Julia, 97
Copernicus, Nicolaus, 57, 58

corn, 177–78
corporation sole, 32n11
corpus mysticum, 32
Cortés, Juan Donoso, 38
cosmology: in African American spirituality, 83–84, 86; medieval, 53; modern, 39, 52; Renaissance, 39; sovereignty and, 5–6, 39; Spirituals and, 133–34; in traditional African religion, 72, 73, 86. *See also* state of nature doctrine
Coutumes de Beauvaisis (Beaumanoir), 30
covenant, 103n23
covenant theology, 101–2, 103, 108–9
Crawford, Evans, 129
creation, theology and doctrine of, xi, 64–65, 103
critical realism, 54
critical theory, 24–25
Cross and the Lynching Tree, The (Cone), 93
crossing over, 155, 156–62
cultural criticism, 20, 21, 25. *See also* religious and cultural criticism, African American
cultural logic of sovereignty: African American spirituality and, 70, 84, 85, 88; Black natural law and, 97–98, 99, 108, 109; Black theology of liberation and, 96–97; covenantal theology and, 103, 108–9; defined, xi, 35; in modern societies, xi–xii, 40, 41–43; new cultural politics of intimacy and, 106–7, 108, 109; politics of whiteness as, 100, 102, 109; in rational approaches, 35, 41–45, 49, 50, 102, 103; in religious ideology, 105, 106, 107, 109; state actions

Index of Names and Subjects

justified by, 34, 35–37, 46; state of nature doctrine and, xi, xv, 35–37, 46; state sovereignty and, 39; supersessionism as, 103, 108–9; theology of liberation and, 96–97; in traditional African religion, 74–76; in Western political theory texts, xi, 35, 38, 40; white supremacy and, 85–86. *See also* supersessionism

cultural politics of intimacy, new, 105, 106–8, 109

cultural politics of respectability, 14, 15

culture: critique of, ix, 76–77; defined, 22; diseased social imagination in, 105, 106–8, 109; hermeneutics of dialogue and, 22–23; signification by, 15, 16, 17–18, 20, 100; Spirituals and, xii–xiii, 126; three deities of, 47. *See also* religion and culture, traditional African

dance, x, 18, 118, 125–26, 154, 187
Daniel, 158, 160–61, 183
Davaney, Sheila, 53
Dean, Mitchell, 43, 50
Dean, William, 53
death, 138, 139, 181
De Caro, Mario, 52–53
Declaration of Independence (1776), 33
Declaration of the Rights of Man and Citizen (1789), 33
Deep River (Thurman), x
deity, 47
deliverance, 158, 160, 169–70, 175, 180, 185
Dem Dry Bones (Powery), vii
Department of Justice, 28n2
Derrida, Jacques, 137–38, 139

Detroit riot (1965), 91
Dett, R. Nathaniel, 119
Dewey, John, 53
dialectic, 24–25
dialectical theism, 64
dialogue, hermeneutics of, xiv, 18–20, 22–23
dipolar theism, 64
Discipline and Punish (Foucault), 9
diseased social imagination, 105, 106–8, 109
dissociation, 105n26
dissonance, 142, 185–86
diurnal rhythms, 184
diversity, 79
divine disruption, narrative of, 106–8
divine economy, 65
divine election, 94–95, 96
Dogon people, 71, 72
domination, logic of, 85–86, 87
dominium, 104
"double death," 138, 139
Douglas, Kelly Brown, 95
Douglass, Frederick, 97
drums, banned, 118, 151
Dube, Muse, 83–84
Du Bois, W. E. B., vii, xii–xiii, 4, 14, 97
dynamism, 142, 143, 186–87

earth, 85, 86–87, 89, 174, 183
ecomemory, 70
economy: of nature, 65; political, 45; slavery and, 115–16, 136; theology and, 65, 100–103, 107, 109. *See also* social exchange
ecowomanism, 70, 85–88, 89
election, divine, 94–95, 96
eloquence tradition, 98–99
emanation, 64

Index of Names and Subjects

emancipation, 36, 118, 146–47
empathy, 127
empirical method, 10, 20–21, 49–52, 51n6, 57
empirical theology, 23–24
end times, 6
enlightened approach to sovereignty, 27, 34, 35–37, 39–40
environment: in African American spirituality, 77, 82, 85, 86–88, 89; nature as, 57–58; Spirituals shaped by, 124; theoretical approaches to, 57–58, 59, 63; in traditional African religion, 86–87. *See also* nature; state of nature doctrine
Epstein, Dena, 12, 119
Erfahrung, 19
ethnography, 23
EU (European Union), 41
Evans, David, 148
exclusion, xi, 34, 35–37, 46, 76, 92
existential sovereignty, 27–28, 37–38, 40
ex nihilo theology, 105–6
exodus narrative, 95, 96, 160, 169. *See also* deliverance
Exorcising Evil (Kirk-Duggan), vii, viii–ix
expansionism, 28

faith, 30, 93, 162, 180
family, viii
Farr, James, 34n16
Fisher, Miles Mark, 183
Fisk, Alfred, 78
Floyd, Samuel, 128–29
form and formal structure. *See* call and response; musical form
Foucault, Michel, 9, 39, 105n26

Fraser, Nancy, 25
Frazier, E. Franklin, 69
Frederick, Marla, 116–17
freedom: in African American spirituality, 5, 77, 82, 84, 87, 88; communicative, 25; Spirituals' expression of, viii, 152, 156, 185
free-market fundamentalism, 28
fruit, 170
Fundamental Constitutions of Carolina, 34
futures, possible, 155, 169–72

Gadamer, Hans-Georg: hermeneutics of dialogue, xiv, 18–19, 22; hermeneutics of horizons, 29; hermeneutics of world, xv, 48, 49, 57–59, 63; on play, 114; on state of nature discourse, 57–59
Garrison, Lucy McKim, 114
Garrison, William Lloyd, 116
Gates, Henry Louis, Jr., 122
Geertz, Clifford, 21, 22–24, 49
gender constructions, 175–76
genealogy, 100–103, 104–5, 108–9
Genealogy of Sovereignty, A (Bartelson), 27–28
generation, 64
Geneva Conventions, 28n2
geography. *See* theological geography
Gerhardt, Uta, 24
gift exchange, 134–36, 137, 139–40, 152–53
"gift of death," 138, 139
Girard, René, 137–40
God, traditional African conceptions of, 70–71, 87
God, Trinitarian: alternative futures possible with, 155, 169–72; back-and-

193

Index of Names and Subjects

forth motion of, 64, 166; body of, 64; compassion of, ix; as Composer, 170–71, 172, 184; creative activity of, 64–65, 78; as Deliverer, 94–95, 169–70, 171, 172; geographical emphasis on, 178, 187; hunger for, 77, 81; intimacy of, xv, 65, 107; musical timing of, 184; mystery of, 156, 163, 171; mystical conception of, 81; as Pilot, Rock, and Provider, 162; play as reflection of, 64–65; as Provider, 170, 171–72; sovereignty of, 5–6; Spirituals' approach to, 155, 170–71, 173; theological and pragmatic conceptions of, 8–9, 49, 60, 64

God of the Oppressed (Cone), 121

Golden Band, 133, 180–81, 183, 184, 186, 187–88

"good life," xi

Gordon, Lewis, 181

government, neo-liberal, 42

governmentality, 37

grace: Spirituals' conceptions of, 162, 165, 180; supersessionist logic and, 97, 98, 99, 109

grace notes, 147, 186

Griffin, David, 61

Grondin, Jean, 114

groove, 144–45, 184, 185. *See also* ostinato (aka standard pattern); rhythm

Guantanamo Bay, 28, 29

Gutiérrez, Gustavo, 160

Habermas, Jürgen, 25

habitus, 125

Hahn-Neurath, Olga, 52

Hall, Stuart, 24

harmonic scales, 146, 150, 151

harmony: dissonance and, 185–86; musical motion through, 150–51; musical order and, 145, 146, 147–49, 151, 152; in postbellum Spirituals, 146–47; themes expressed by, 148–49, 152; vertical and rectilinear aspects of, 147, 152

Harris, Melanie, 70, 85–88, 89

Harvey, David, 42

Hauerwas, Stanley, 95

Hayek, Friedrich, 44–46

Hayes, Diana, 116–17

healers, 73

heaven, 156, 157, 162–64, 171, 183

Hegel, G. W. F., 40

Heidegger, Martin, 12, 19, 50

hermeneutic of divine disruption, 106–8

hermeneutics, narrative, 95–96, 106–8

hermeneutics of dialogue, xiv, 18–20, 22–23

hermeneutics of world: in African American spirituality, 77–80, 81–82, 87–88, 89; naturalism and, 48, 49; pragmatic naturalism and, 53–60; public theology implications of, 48, 49, 63–65; term usage, xiv–xv

Herskovits, Melville, 70, 125

High God, 70–71, 87

hip-hop generation, 14–15

hip-hop music, 129

history, modalities of, 105n26

Hobbes, Thomas, 17, 46

Hogue, David, 127

Holmes, Barbara: contemplative spirituality of, 70, 83–85, 89; on worship practices of slaves, 116–17, 124–25, 173

Holy Ghost, 162, 172, 187

Homo Sacer (Agamben), 9

Honneth, Axel, 25

Index of Names and Subjects

hooks, bell, 12–13
Hopkins, Dwight, 91
Horkheimer, Max, 24, 50
"hum, the," 129
human agency, 178–79
humanism, 178
Hume, David, 21, 53
hunger, spirituality of, 70, 76, 77, 81
Hunsinger, George, 95
Hurston, Zora Neale, 126
Husserl, Edmund, 19

identity, 26–27, 47, 105n26, 106, 108, 164
imitatio Christi, 104, 106
immigration and migration, 28, 29, 44
Inbody, Tyron, 10, 54
incarceration. *See* mass incarceration
instrumental rationality, 52
International Monetary Fund (IMF), 42
Interpretation of Cultures, The (Geertz), 22
intimacy, new cultural politics of, 105, 106–8, 109
invisible institution, 116–17, 120–21, 128, 130
Israel, 8, 101–2, 106–7, 108–9. *See also* supersessionism
Iyanaga, Michael, 125, 128

Jackson, Robert, 27, 30, 31
James, William, 53
Jefferson, Thomas, 35–37
Jennings, Willie James, 103–8, 109
Jesus and the Disinherited (Thurman), 76
Jesus Christ: Black experience and, 81–82, 93, 94; as cosmic and mundane, 165; Israelite narrative disrupted by, 106–7; Jewish genealogy of, 101–2, 108–9; as Judge, 165, 167–68, 185, 187, 188; as King, 171; as Lamb, 165–66, 185, 187; as ontological ostinato, 185; as Rock, 165, 166, 185, 187; seeking and wrestling with, 167; Spirituals' indirect treatment of, 155
Jewish culture and thought, 108
Johnson, Elizabeth, 60
Johnson, James Weldon, 183
Jones, Arthur, 126
Jones, Charles Colock, 116
Jordan River, 176–77, 178, 179, 182, 183, 184, 186
Jordan's Mill, 178, 179, 182, 183, 184, 186
Joshua, 169–70
Judge, Jesus as, 165, 167–68, 185, 187, 188
judgment, 162, 165, 167–68, 185, 187, 188
justice, xv, 25, 91, 93, 95, 188

Kant, Immanuel, xi, 33, 100, 102, 108
Kantorowicz, Ernst, 32
Kaufman, Walter, 29n3
Kee, Alisdair, 46–47
Kennedy, Robert F., 91
Kersten, Jens, 153
King, Martin Luther, Jr., ix, 91, 97, 160
King's Two Bodies, The (Kantorowicz), 32
Kirk-Duggan, Cheryl, vii, viii–ix, 173
Kolinski, Mieczyslaw, 125
kosmos, 134
Kraft, Victor, 52
Krasner, Stephen, 40

Lamb, Jesus as, 165–66, 185, 187
Langer, Suzanne, 143
language, 22–23, 54–55, 56, 57–59

Index of Names and Subjects

Lee, Jarena, 102
legendary constitution, 74, 75
Leopold, David, 94
Leviathan (Hobbes), 17
Levine, Lawrence, 173
liberal naturalism, 56
Lincoln, C. Eric, 4, 5, 116–17
Little, Malcolm (aka Malcolm X), 6
liturgies, 124, 154
Lloyd, Vincent, 90, 97–100, 108, 109
Locke, Alain, vii, 113, 115, 140, 146
Locke, John, xi, 33–34, 35, 40
logical positivism, 20–21, 22–23, 51–53
logic of domination, 85–86, 87
logos, 134
Lomazzo, Gian Paolo, 141n20
Long, Charles, xv, 15–16, 29–30
love, ethic of, 103
Luckmann, Thomas, 121
Luhmann, Niklas, 24
Lyell, Charles, 118

maafa, 113
Macarthur, David, 52–53
MacIntyre, Alasdair, 95, 132
Magesa, Laurenti, 70–71
Maistre, Joseph de, 38
Malcolm X, 6
Malthus, Thomas, 45
Mamiya, Lawrence H., 4, 5
Marable, Manning, 45
Marcuse, Herbert, 50
market rationality (neoliberal rationality), 42–46
Maróthy, János, 142–43, 144, 185
Marx, Karl, 25, 121
Marxism, 94
"Mary," 158–60, 180, 183
"Mary and Marta," 158–59, 183

Mary Magdalene, 158, 183
mass incarceration, 4–5, 28
materialism, 52, 76–77, 82
Maultsby, Portia, 128
Mauss, Marcel, 134–35, 137, 152–53
Mbiti, John, 83–84
McDaniel, Charles, 43
McIntosh, D. C., 11
melody, 151–53
Mendoza, Eugene, 70–71, 74
mentality, 55
Merlau-Ponty, Maurice, 12
methodological individualism, 52
Migliore, Daniel, 64, 156
militarism, 28
Mill, John Stuart, 45
mimesis, 123–24, 138–39
mimetic rivalry, 138–39
modern scientific naturalism, 50–52
monarchial sovereignty, 31–33
monotheism, radical, 47
Morrison, Toni, ix
Morton, Robert, 183
Moses, 158, 160, 183
"Mother," 183–84
music, cosmology and, 134
music, in Black church, 7–8
musical consciousness, 127
musical form: asymmetry in, 141–43, 148, 151; binary, 141, 147, 148; dynamism in, 143, 186; experience of, 150–51; orchestral, 140; repetition in, 143, 148, 150; structure and spontaneity in, 143–44; tension and dissonance in, 142, 185–86; time and, 149. *See also* call and response; ostinato (aka standard pattern)
musical motion, 130, 149–52
musical progression, 149–52

196

Index of Names and Subjects

musical systems, 127, 145–46
mysticism, 70, 76–82, 89
Myth of the Negro Past, The (Herskovits), 70

Nankani women, 86–87
narrative hermeneutics, 95–96, 106–8
National Committee of Negro Churchmen, 91
nationalism, 40
Native Americans, x, 118
"natural," 48
natural inequality, doctrine of, 33–34, 35, 40
naturalism: defined, 48; liberal, 56; pragmatic, 53–60; scientific, 49–53; theological, xv; theological and philosophical implications of, 49
natural law: Black, 97–100, 108, 109; instrumental rationality as, 52; Jefferson's logic of sovereignty rooted in, 36–37; state of nature as, 159
natural theology, xi, xv. *See also* state of nature doctrine
nature, 57–58, 65, 148–49, 184, 186. *See also* environment; state of nature doctrine; wilderness
Negro Church in America, The (Frazier), 69
Negro Family in the United States, The (Frazier), 69
neo-fascism, 41–42
neoliberal rationality, 42–46
neoliberal state, 42–44
neo-Spirituals, 126
Newton, Isaac, 50
Niebuhr, H. Richard, 47
nihilism, 29
Njoroge, Nyambura, 75

Notes on the State of Virginia (Jefferson), 35–36
Nwadiora, Emeka, 71

Oduyoye, Mercy Amba, 83–84
OEEC (Organization for European Economic Cooperation), 41
Ogden, Schubert, 11
Olodumare, 71, 72, 73
Olson, Carl, 135
ontological blackness, 13
orchestral chorus, 115, 140, 148
orisha, 73, 182–83
ostinato (aka standard pattern): asymmetry and, 142; function of, 143, 144, 145, 184, 185; natural and human cycles as, 184–85; themes expressed by, 152, 153; theological parallels, 185. *See also* call and response

"parergonality," 40–41
parody, 105n26
Parsons, Talcott, 24
participatio Christi, 104, 106
PATRIOT Act, 41
Patterson, Orlando, 121–22
Payne, Daniel Alexander, 18, 118
Peace of Westphalia (1648), 33, 46
Peirce, Charles Sanders, 53
pentatonic scale, 147
perception, 12
percussion, 115, 128, 151
Perkinson, Robert, 4
Peter, 157–58, 162, 177, 183
phenomenological hermeneutics, 10–12
Philosophia Naturalis Principia Mathematica (Newton), 50
plantation economies, 116
Plato, 134

Index of Names and Subjects

play, 114
pluralism, 79
"political, the," 38, 63
political economy, 45
political theology, 38, 39, 46–47, 98, 106–7, 108
politics, Western, xi, 17
politics of respectability, 14, 15
polyrhythms, 143, 184
polytheism, 47
positivism, 20–21, 22–23, 49, 51–52, 53
possible futures, 155, 169–72
potlach, 135–36
poverty, 15
power, sovereign, 17
Power of Black Music, The (Floyd), 129
Powery, Luke, vii
practice, theory of, 132–33
pragmatic method, 53
pragmatic naturalism, 53–60
pragmatism, 53, 59, 60, 63
prayer, x, 72, 73, 77
prayer meetings, 123, 133, 187
Price, Huw, 56
Price, Tanya, 118
process metaphysics, 61–63
prophetic voice, ix–x, 33–34, 153
proprietary sovereignty, 33–35, 40
providence, 170, 171–72
PTARE (Popular Traditional African Religion Everywhere), 72
publicity, 63
public life, American, 63
public theology, African American: apolitical character of, 63; Black natural law and, 90, 97–100, 108, 109; covenantal theology and, 90, 100–103, 108–9; defined, 29; everyday life and, 29, 30; functions of, 25–26; global scope of, 47; hermeneutics of world and, 48, 49, 63–65; new cultural politics of intimacy and, 103–8, 109; pragmatic naturalism and, 55–63; sovereignty in, 47; theology of liberation and, 91–97

quartet, 146, 147, 148

Raboteau, Albert, xii, 18, 69, 116–17, 118, 122, 154
race: exclusion and, xi, 34, 35–37, 46, 76, 92; modern discourse on, 28, 100, 105, 107; signification of, 15–16, 17–18, 20, 100; as socially constructed, 13, 15–16, 17–18, 101–2. *See also* Black experience
Race: A Theological Account (Carter), 100
racism, silence on, 91–93
Radical Monotheism and Western Culture (Niebuhr), 47
rap music, 129, 144
rational choice theory, 52
Reclaiming the Spirituals (Smith), vii
reconciled community of racial difference, 77–80, 81, 82
redemption, covenantal economy of, 101–2, 103, 108–9
religion, modern American, 43–44, 101–2
religion and culture, traditional African: ancestral spirituality in, 70, 71–72, 74–75, 87; cultural logic of sovereignty in, 74–76; environmental care in, 86–87; eradication of, 69; High God in, 70–71, 87; moral fabric of, 75; prayer in, 72, 73; retention of, 69–70, 113, 117, 127, 182–83; Spirits in, 70, 71–73, 86, 87, 89; state of nature

and, 72; syncretism in, 73; world in, 73–74

religion and spirituality, African American: African culture and, 69–70; call-and-response logic in, 129; contemplative spirituality, 70, 83–85; contemporary state of, 88–89; as cultural-critical countervoice, ix; cultural logic of sovereignty in, 70, 84, 85, 88; deliverance motif in, 160; ecowomanism, 70, 85–88; integration and syncretism in, 71; as invisible institution, 116–17; mysticism, 70, 76–82, 89. See also Black church; religious experience; state of nature doctrine

religious and cultural criticism, African American, 10–16, 20, 21, 23–26

religious experience: approaches to studying, xiv, 10–16; of author, 3–9, 20; critical realist view of, 54; mystical nature of, 80, 81; neurological processes in, 127–28. See also Black church; religion and spirituality, African American

Renaissance period, 30–31, 39

repetition, 143, 150. See also ostinato (aka standard pattern)

respublica Christiana, 32

revelation, 156

rhetoric of contrast, 98–99

rhetoric of tradition, 98–99

rhythm: in creation of Spirituals, 118, 151; cyclical path of, 145, 150, 152, 184; musical motion and, 149, 150; musical order and, 144, 145–46, 147–49, 151, 152; in nature, 184, 186; of prophecy, x; spirituality and, 87–88; tension in, 142, 143, 151; themes expressed in, 148–49, 152. See also ostinato (aka standard pattern); polyrhythms; syncopation

rhythmic spirituality, 87–88

Ricks, Willie, 93

Ricoeur, Paul, 95

rights, 33, 36

ring shouts, x, 117–19, 125–26, 128

Rise and Demise of Black Theology, The (Kee), 46–47

risk rationality, 42–46

Rock, Jesus as, 165, 166, 185, 187

Rosenberg, Alexander, 53

Rousseau, Jean-Jacques, xi, 33

Rush, Fred, 123

Sacred Earth, 85, 86–87, 89

sacred space, 174

sacred time, 87, 124–25, 154, 156, 168, 173, 174

sacrifice, religious, 105n26, 137, 138, 139

Sale, Maggie, 129–30

Sands, Rosita, 119

Satan, 165–66, 167–68, 175

scapegoat mechanism, 138–40, 185

"scape-*logos*," 139–40, 151

Schaefer, Kurt C., 50, 51n6

Schmitt, Carl, xi, 37–38, 63

scientific age (aka technological age), 49–53, 103, 105–6

scientific method, 10, 20–21, 49–52, 51n6, 57

scientific naturalism, 49–53

Scripture, 17–18, 122–23

"Search for Identity, The" (Thurman), 80

sects, 81

self-consciousness, 130–31

self-determination, 80

Index of Names and Subjects

self-sovereignty, 80
sexuality, Black, 126
Shaw, Rosalind, 125
Shelby, Tommie, 12
shouts, 125. *See also* ring shouts
Shulman, George, ix–x
signification, 15–16, 17–18, 20, 114, 122, 158. *See also* signifyin' practices
Significations (Long), xv, 15–16
signifyin' practices, 95–96, 122
silence, 91–93
sin, 165–66
"Sister Mary," 158, 159–60, 183
Sisters in the Wilderness (Williams), 175
Slave Religion (Raboteau), 18
slavery: cultural logic of sovereignty and, 34, 35–37; cultural retention during, 69–70; experience of suffering in, 93; plantation economies and, 115–16, 136
slaves, antebellum: biblical hermeneutic of, 123; consciousness of, 120–22, 127, 173; as economic commodities, 115–16, 136; evangelization of, 116; in Golden Band, 187–88; legal status of, 36; sacrifice and atonement for, 137; scapegoating of, 139–40; social exchange among, 136, 137; wilderness experience for, 156, 175; worship of, 18, 116–17, 123, 133, 187
Slave Songs of the United States, 179
Slessarev-Jamir, Helene, 43–44
Smith, Adam, 45
Smith, Yolanda, vii
social brain, 127
social construction, 25–26
social exchange, 134–36, 139–40, 152–53

social imaginary, 101, 120
social imagination, diseased, 105, 106–8, 109
social integration, 24
social sciences, methodology of, 21, 50–51, 52
social theory, xi, 20–25
society, American, 63, 76–80, 81, 82
Souls of Black Folk (Du Bois), xii, xiii, 14n20
sovereignty: African cultural conceptions of, 74–75; Black church's conceptions of, 5–6, 84, 85; classical approach to, 27–33, 39; contemporary trends in, 40–46; cultural significance of, 28–29; defined, 5–6, 27; discourse on, xv, xvii, xviii, 32, 37, 38–39, 40–41; enlightened approach to, 27, 33–37, 39–40; existential approach to, 27–28, 37–38, 40; religious significance of, 47; self-sovereignty, 80; in social exchange, 153; term, origin of, 30. *See also* cultural logic of sovereignty
Sovereignty (Jackson), 27
space, musical, 126, 144–49, 152
space, sacred, 174
Spirit(s): in African American spirituality, 81, 82, 85–86, 87, 88, 89; embodied participation with, 62; hermeneutics of world and, 65; public theology and, 30; rationality and, 65; Spirituals' depiction of, 162, 172, 187; theological conceptions of, 65, 107, 172; in traditional African religion and culture, 70, 71–73, 75, 86, 87, 89. *See also* Holy Ghost
spirituality of hunger, 70, 76, 77
Spirituals, antebellum: aesthetic

200

dimensions of, 113–14, 120, 126, 140–44, 186–87; atonement in, 137, 165–66, 185; commodification of, 126, 146–47; as cosmological art, 134; creation of, 118–19, 121, 122–24, 127, 146–47; "crossing over" theme in, 155, 156–62; dance and, x, 18, 118, 125–26, 154, 187; disapproval of, 118, 119; divine call in, 186; erotic content of, 126; experience of suffering in, 93; in factories, 119–20; features of, 115, 119, 128, 151; God depicted in, 155, 169–72, 173; grace conveyed in, 162, 165, 180; heaven depicted in, 156, 157, 162–64, 171, 183; historical context of, 113; historic importance of, xii–xiii; invisible institution and, 120–21, 128, 130; Jesus depicted in, 155, 165–68; as meaningful collection of songs, 117; melody in, 151–52; musical influence of, 114–15; musical progression in, 149–52; nature in, 93–94; orchestral chorus in, 115, 140, 148; percussive dominance in, 115, 128, 151; prophetic voice of, ix–x; published volumes of, 114, 182–83; as religious practice, 113, 117–19, 124–25, 156; secularization of, 126; as social practice, 132–40; space and, 126, 144–49, 152; term, meaning of, 126; theological geography of, 174, 177–84; theological signification in, 114, 158; theology and aesthetics in, 113–14; types of, 114; wilderness depicted in, 161, 174, 175–76. *See also* call and response; God, Trinitarian; harmony; musical form; rhythm; time; world, Spirituals' depiction of
Spirituals and the Blues, The (Cone), 93

standard pattern. *See* ostinato (aka standard pattern)
state of nature doctrine: Black experience framed by, 17–18; contemplative spirituality and, 83–84; covenantal theology approach to, 100–103, 108–9; cultural logic of sovereignty expressed through, xi, xv, 35–37, 46; cultural politics of intimacy approach to, 103–8, 109; defined, xi, 17; discourse on, xv, xvii, xviii, 57–59; ecowomanism and, 85–86, 87, 88, 89; as hermeneutic, 57–59; in late medieval Catholicism, 104; in Marxism, 94; mysticism and, 81–82, 89; natural law approach to, 97–100, 108, 109; scientific approaches to, 57–58, 59, 61, 64–65, 104; in slave religion, 124; Spirituals' perspective on, 159; theology of liberation and, 93–94, 96–97; in traditional African religion, 72; in Western political canon, 17, 36–37; in white American theology, 94
state sovereignty: during classical age, 30–33, 38–39; modern waning of, 39, 40–42, 46; Thurman's critique of, 79–80
Stewart, Earl, 141, 142
Stone, Deborah, 43, 50
suffering, 82, 93, 94
supernaturalism, 60, 64
supersessionism: Black natural law and, 97–98, 99, 108, 109; Christology and, 101–3, 108–9; as cultural logic of sovereignty, 103; cultural politics of intimacy and, 106–7, 108, 109; in political theology discourse, 98. *See also* cultural logic of sovereignty
Supreme Creator. *See* High God

Index of Names and Subjects

symbols, 21–22
symmetry, 141–42, 148, 151
syncopation, 142–43
syncretism, 71, 73
systems theory, 24

tactic, 133
Tanner, Kathryn, 23
technological age, 49–53, 103, 105–6
technological rationality, 50–53, 56–57
Texas, 3–5, 28, 29
Texas Tough (Perkinson), 4
theism, 60, 64
theological discourse, xv, 63, 97, 102, 103–4, 105–6
theological geography, 174, 177–84
theological isolationism, 105
theological naturalism, xv
theology: aesthetics and, 113–14; covenantal, 101–2, 103, 108–9; of creation, xi, 64–65, 101–3, 105–6; economy and, 65, 100–103, 107, 109; empirical, 23–24; of liberation, 91–97; race and, 101–2; social influence on, 92, 121; supersessionism in, 101; Western, 102, 103–4, 105–6; white American, 91–93, 94, 96, 121
theomusicology, viii–ix, 174, 177–84
theory of practice, 132–33
thick description, 23, 24
Thomas of Aquino (Thomas Aquinas), 104
Thurman, Howard, 70, 76–82, 89
time: musical, 127, 140, 142, 144–49, 152; path of, 50, 61–62, 88, 142; practice of Spirituals and, 133; sacred, 87, 124–25, 154, 156, 168, 173, 174; theological, 184
Todd, Asante, 3–9, 20

tonal languages, xiv, 127
tones, musical, 127, 140, 145–46
Tracy, David, 63
transcendence, 60, 83, 156–57, 161–62, 175
Transformation of Black Music, The (Floyd), 129
Trinity. *See* God, Trinitarian
Tutu, Desmond, 74

ubuntu, 74, 75
United States, 29, 79
universitas, 32n11

Valignano, Alessandro, 105
Van Bergen, Jennifer, 41
verifiability, 49–50, 52, 53, 93
violence, mimetic, 138, 139
volunteerism, 44
Voting Rights Act (1965), 14

Walker, Alice, 86
Walker, Tamara, 136
Walled States (Brown), 27
"walling," 41
Walser, Robert, 144
Walton, Jonathan, 4
Ware, Charles P., 114
Ware, Frederick, 91
Watch This (Walton), 4
Watson, John, 18, 118
West, Cornel, vii, 7, 9, 12, 28, 53
West Texas, 3–4
"white," 100, 102
Whitehead, Alfred, 61
white supremacy, 85–86, 100, 101, 102
Wieman, Henry Nelson, 11
wilderness, 156, 161, 174, 175–76
Williams, Delores, 156, 175
Wilmore, Gayraud, 116–17

Index of Names and Subjects

Wimbush, Vincent, 123
women's health and rights, 75–76, 85
Work, John, 183
world: in Black theology of liberation, 93; contemplative view of, 84; ecowomanist view of, 87–88; human agency and, 179; linguistic communication and, xiv; Marxist conception of, 94; mystical view of, 76, 77–80, 81–82, 89; pragmatic naturalist view of, 55–59; process theological view of, 64–65; scientific naturalist conception of, 48, 51–54; symbolism and term usage, xiv–xv; in traditional African religion, 73–74. *See also* hermeneutics of world
world, Spirituals' depiction of: crossing over, 156–57; geographical conceptions, 174–76; God-world relationship in, 165, 166, 167–68, 169, 171–72, 175; heaven in, 163, 164; as place of trouble, 93, 165–66, 174–75; transcendent places in, 175
World Bank, 42
World Trade Organization (WTO), 42
worldview, 58–59
worship, 18, 81, 116–17, 123, 133, 187

Yemoja, 73
Yoruba people, 71, 72, 73

Zbikowski, Lawrence, 144–45
Zinn, Howard, 116
Zurara, Gomes Eanes de, 105

Index of Spirituals

"Bell Da Ring," 163–64
"Bound to Go," 166, 170
"Bright Sparkles in de Churchyard," 184
"Build a House in Paradise," 162, 175
"Come Along Moses," 160
"Ezekiel Saw de Wheel," 183
"Give Up the World," 175
"Give Way, Jordan," 155
"God Got Plenty O' Room," 162, 171
"Go in the Wilderness," 156, 167, 175
"Good News, de Chariot's a-Comin'," 183
"Hail Mary," 158, 176
"Happy Morning," 159, 184
"Heaven Bell a-Ring," 163
"Hunting for the Lord," 167, 175
"I an' Satan Had a Race," 167–68, 175
"I Can't Stand the Fire," 177
"I Can't Stay Behind," 164
"If Ye Want to See Jesus," 141
"I Hear from Heaven To-Day," 165
"I'm a-Trouble in De Mind," 174

"I'm Going Home," 175
"I'm in Trouble," 174, 181
"In the Mansions Above," 162
"I've Got a Mother in de Heaven," 184
"I Want to Die like-a Lazarus Die," 158, 181
"I Want to Go Home," 175
"I Want to Join the Band," 180, 181
"Jehovah, Hallelujah," 170
"Jesus on the Water-Side," 167, 175
"Jesus, Won't You Come By-and-Bye," 167, 168
"John John, of the Holy Order," 163, 164, 168
"John John of the Golden Order," 158
"Join the Angel Band," 159–60
"Jordan's Mills," 177, 178
"King Emmanuel," 164, 171, 182
"Lean on the Lord's Side," 161
"Let God's Saints Come In," 160, 169
"Little Children, Then Won't You Be Glad?," 180
"Lord, Remember Me," 168

Index of Spirituals

"Meet O' Lord," 167, 168
"Michael Row the Boat Ashore," 163, 177
"My Army Cross Over," 157, 176
"My Father, How Long?," 164, 181
"Nobody Knows the Trouble I've Had," 170
"No Man Can Hinder Me," 166, 167, 168
"O Brothers Don't Get Weary," 164
"O Daniel," 161, 169, 181
"Praise, Member," 177
"Pray All De Member," 169–70
"Pray On," 180
"Religion So Sweet," 159
"Rock O' Jubilee," 159, 166
"Rock O' My Soul," 166
"Roll, Jordan, Roll," 176
"Round the Corn, Sally," 177, 178
"Run, Nigger, Run," 175
"Sabbath Has No End," 163
"Sail O Believer," 177
"Satan and I Had a Race," 167–68, 175

"Satan's Camp a-Fire," 166
"Ship of Zion," 157
"Shock Along, John," 177–78
"Sinner Won't Die No More," 166
"Some o' dese Mornin's," 183
"Swing Low, Sweet Chariot," 128, 141, 183
"Tell My Jesus 'Morning,'" 165, 184
"The Danville Chariot," 183
"The Day of Judgement," 167
"The Gold Band," 180
"The Golden Altar," 137, 165
"The Heaven Bells," 165
"The Lonesome Valley," 159, 175
"The Old Ship of Zion," 27, 161–62, 164
"The Resurrection Morn," 158, 184
"There's a Meeting Here Tonight," 159, 184
"The Social Band," 180, 181
"The Trouble of the World," 174, 176
"Turn, Sinner, Turn, O!," 175
"Who Is on the Lord's Side," 168
"Wrestle on Jacob," 158, 167
"You Must Be Pure and Holy," 175